IN · DEO · SPERAMUS

Halman

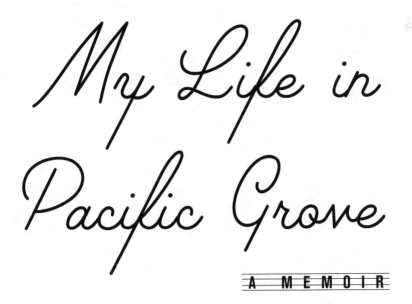

My Life in Pacific Grove

A MEMOIR

Wilford Rensselaer Holman

ORIGINALLY TRANSCRIBED BY LOUISE V. JAQUES

Annotated and Edited by Heather Lazare

 PACIFIC GROVE BOOKS | Pacific Grove, California

LCCN 2021943287

ISBN 978-1-953120-15-1 paperback
ISBN 978-1-953120-35-9 hardcover
ISBN 978-1-953120-36-6 eBook

Cover and interior design by Elina Cohen

Printed in the United States of America

www.pacificgrovebooks.com

Each golden moment lost,
Is lost forever,
Never to return again!

—W. R. Holman

Holman Family Tree

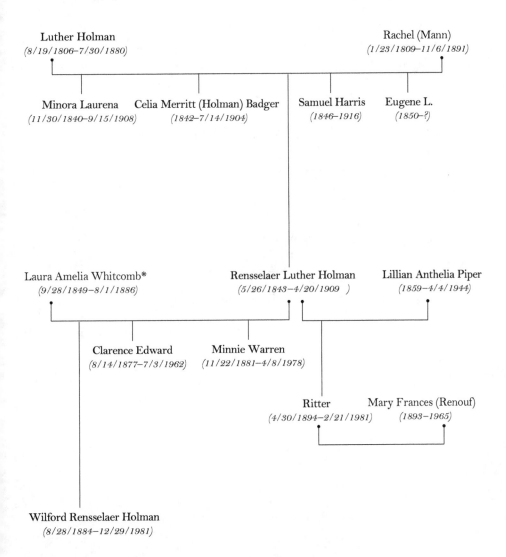

Luther Holman
(8/19/1806–7/30/1880)

Rachel (Mann)
(1/23/1809–11/6/1891)

Minora Laurena
(11/30/1840–9/15/1908)

Celia Merritt (Holman) Badger
(1842–7/14/1904)

Samuel Harris
(1846–1916)

Eugene L.
(1850–?)

Laura Amelia Whitcomb*
(9/28/1849–8/1/1886)

Rensselaer Luther Holman
(5/26/1843–4/20/1909)

Lillian Anthelia Piper
(1859–4/4/1944)

Clarence Edward
(8/14/1877–7/3/1962)

Minnie Warren
(11/22/1881–4/8/1978)

Ritter
(4/30/1894–2/21/1981)

Mary Frances (Renouf)
(1893–1965)

Wilford Rensselaer Holman
(8/28/1884–12/29/1981)

* Laura's relatives can be traced back to John Alden, a crew member on the 1620 voyage of the Mayflower, meaning her children, Clarence, Minnie, and W.R. Holman, and their ancestors, all have a relative who came over on the Mayflower.

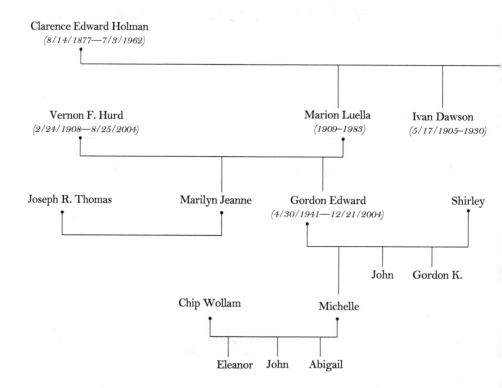

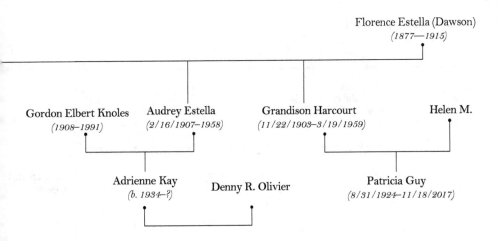

Florence Estella (Dawson)
(1877—1915)

Gordon Elbert Knoles
(1908–1991)

Audrey Estella
(2/16/1907–1958)

Grandison Harcourt
(11/22/1903–3/19/1959)

Helen M.

Adrienne Kay
(b. 1934–?)

Denny R. Olivier

Patricia Guy
(8/31/1924–11/18/2017)

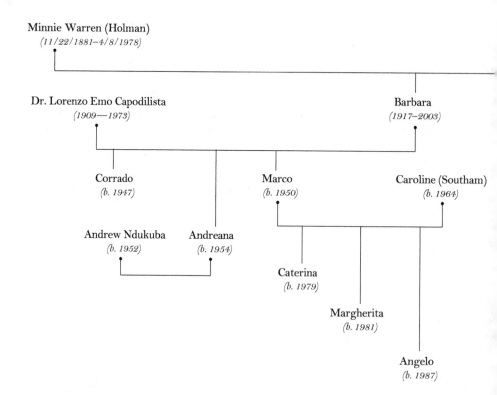

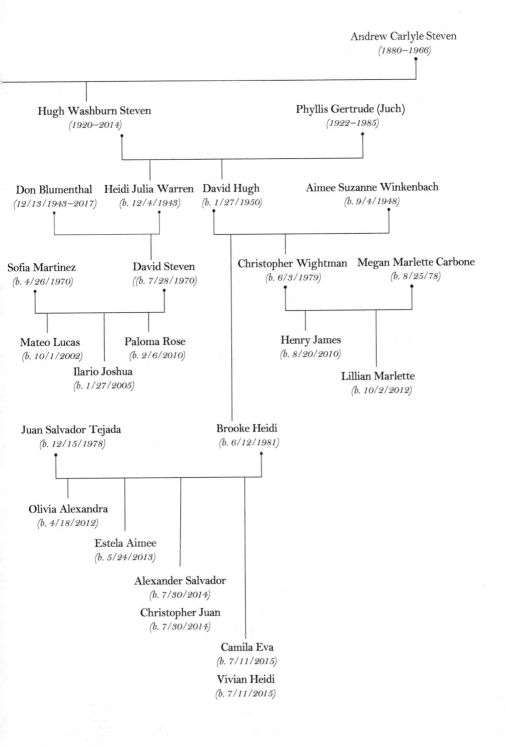

Andrew Carlyle Steven
(1880–1966)

Hugh Washburn Steven
(1920–2014)

Phyllis Gertrude (Juch)
(1922–1985)

Don Blumenthal
(12/13/1943–2017)

Heidi Julia Warren
(b. 12/4/1943)

David Hugh
(b. 1/27/1950)

Aimee Suzanne Winkenbach
(b. 9/4/1948)

Sofia Martinez
(b. 4/26/1970)

David Steven
((b. 7/28/1970)

Christopher Wightman
(b. 6/3/1979)

Megan Marlette Carbone
(b. 8/25/78)

Mateo Lucas
(b. 10/1/2002)

Paloma Rose
(b. 2/6/2010)

Henry James
(b. 8/20/2010)

Ilario Joshua
(b. 1/27/2005)

Lillian Marlette
(b. 10/2/2012)

Juan Salvador Tejada
(b. 12/15/1978)

Brooke Heidi
(b. 6/12/1981)

Olivia Alexandra
(b. 4/18/2012)

Estela Aimee
(b. 5/24/2013)

Alexander Salvador
(b. 7/30/2014)

Christopher Juan
(b. 7/30/2014)

Camila Eva
(b. 7/11/2015)

Vivian Heidi
(b. 7/11/2015)

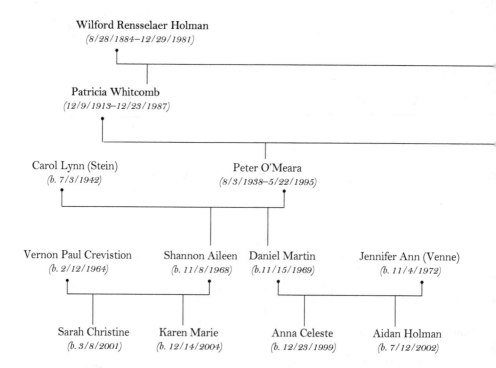

Wilford Rensselaer Holman
(8/28/1884–12/29/1981)

Patricia Whitcomb
(12/9/1913–12/23/1987)

Carol Lynn (Stein)
(b. 7/3/1942)

Peter O'Meara
(8/3/1938–5/22/1995)

Vernon Paul Crevistion
(b. 2/12/1964)

Shannon Aileen
(b. 11/8/1968)

Daniel Martin
(b.11/15/1969)

Jennifer Ann (Venne)
(b. 11/4/1972)

Sarah Christine
(b. 3/8/2001)

Karen Marie
(b. 12/14/2004)

Anna Celeste
(b. 12/23/1999)

Aidan Holman
(b. 7/12/2002)

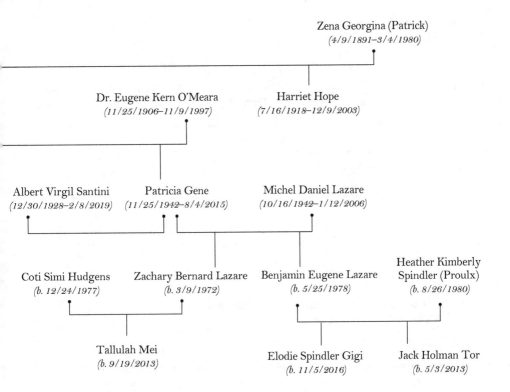

Zena Georgina (Patrick)
(4/9/1891–3/4/1980)

Dr. Eugene Kern O'Meara
(11/25/1906–11/9/1997)

Harriet Hope
(7/16/1918–12/9/2003)

Albert Virgil Santini
(12/30/1928–2/8/2019)

Patricia Gene
(11/25/1942–8/4/2015)

Michel Daniel Lazare
(10/16/1942–1/12/2006)

Heather Kimberly
Spindler (Proulx)
(b. 8/26/1980)

Coti Simi Hudgens
(b. 12/24/1977)

Zachary Bernard Lazare
(b. 3/9/1972)

Benjamin Eugene Lazare
(b. 5/25/1978)

Tallulah Mei
(b. 9/19/2013)

Elodie Spindler Gigi
(b. 11/5/2016)

Jack Holman Tor
(b. 5/3/2013)

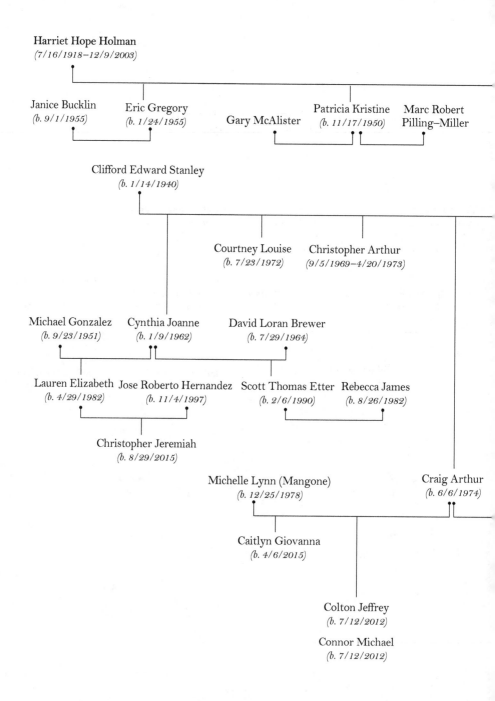

Harriet Hope Holman
(7/16/1918–12/9/2003)

Janice Bucklin
(b. 9/1/1955)

Eric Gregory
(b. 1/24/1955)

Gary McAlister

Patricia Kristine
(b. 11/17/1950)

Marc Robert
Pilling–Miller

Clifford Edward Stanley
(b. 1/14/1940)

Courtney Louise
(b. 7/23/1972)

Christopher Arthur
(9/5/1969–4/20/1973)

Michael Gonzalez
(b. 9/23/1951)

Cynthia Joanne
(b. 1/9/1962)

David Loran Brewer
(b. 7/29/1964)

Lauren Elizabeth
(b. 4/29/1982)

Jose Roberto Hernandez
(b. 11/4/1997)

Scott Thomas Etter
(b. 2/6/1990)

Rebecca James
(b. 8/26/1982)

Christopher Jeremiah
(b. 8/29/2015)

Michelle Lynn (Mangone)
(b. 12/25/1978)

Craig Arthur
(b. 6/6/1974)

Caitlyn Giovanna
(b. 4/6/2015)

Colton Jeffrey
(b. 7/12/2012)

Connor Michael
(b. 7/12/2012)

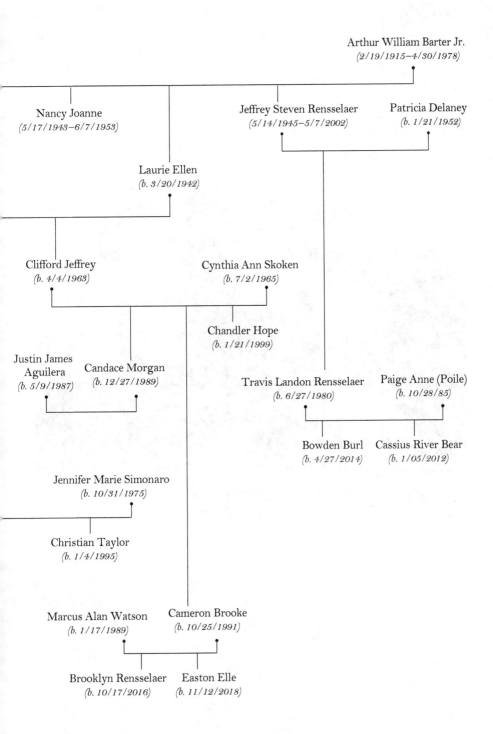

Arthur William Barter Jr.
(2/19/1915–4/30/1978)

Nancy Joanne
(5/17/1943–6/7/1953)

Jeffrey Steven Rensselaer
(5/14/1945–5/7/2002)

Patricia Delaney
(b. 1/21/1952)

Laurie Ellen
(b. 3/20/1942)

Clifford Jeffrey
(b. 4/4/1963)

Cynthia Ann Skoken
(b. 7/2/1965)

Chandler Hope
(b. 1/21/1999)

Justin James
Aguilera
(b. 5/9/1987)

Candace Morgan
(b. 12/27/1989)

Travis Landon Rensselaer
(b. 6/27/1980)

Paige Anne (Poile)
(b. 10/28/85)

Bowden Burl
(b. 4/27/2014)

Cassius River Bear
(b. 1/05/2012)

Jennifer Marie Simonaro
(b. 10/31/1975)

Christian Taylor
(b. 1/4/1995)

Marcus Alan Watson
(b. 1/17/1989)

Cameron Brooke
(b. 10/25/1991)

Brooklyn Rensselaer
(b. 10/17/2016)

Easton Elle
(b. 11/12/2018)

The Holman family home, built in 1888 at
769 Lighthouse Avenue, Pacific Grove, California

Table of Contents

PART II

Newspaper and Magazine Articles, and the Steinbeck Letters

PART III

The Pacific Grove Charter

Introduction

SOME OF THE BEST CONVERSATIONS HAPPEN AFTER DINNER, WHEN EVeryone is sated and we linger over dessert. In the years of family dinners and those conversations around the table, Patricia "Genie" (O'Meara) (Lazare) Santini, my mother-in-law, would talk about her family. Genie's grandparents were Wilford Rensselaer and Zena (Patrick) Holman; her mother was Patricia Whitcomb (Holman) O'Meara. Genie's Grandpa Holman stories were some of my favorites; he was a jokester, a lover of nature, a frugal businessman, and a civic leader. She remembered Grandma Holman as extremely well-read and a fastidious dresser who was rarely without her gloves and hat, and looking the part of the women's fashion buyer well into her eighties.

Sometimes I would pull out my phone to jot down notes, but mostly I would sit, our baby on my lap, and listen. I remember thinking that I would have to ask her to repeat these stories sometime, that we should be recording her, but somehow the effort in these effortless moments was too much. When Genie died in August 2015 we were all heartbroken. There are so many things I wish I would have asked her, so many stories I didn't hear, so much clarification I'll never get.

But she had given me a volume by her grandfather, W.R. Holman, something he had started working on in his ninety-fifth year, a present he had given to his close relatives and friends.

W.R. Holman and his wife Zena were the proprietors of Holman's Department Store in Pacific Grove, California. What started in 1891 as Towle & Holman, owned by W.R.'s father, Rensselaer Luther Holman, and his business partner, G.W. Towle, Jr., would become The Popular Dry Goods Store, then R.L. Holman, then, eventually, Holman's Department Store: the biggest store between San Francisco and Los Angeles for decades—under the guidance of Mr. and Mrs. Holman. W.R. was named store manager in 1905, and while he stepped away from the day-to-day workings of the store in 1947, he remained the president until 1981. Holman's boasted forty-six departments at one point; it was a place where you could buy anything (except alcohol): shoes, dresses, sweaters, books, toys, tomatoes, milk, carrots, washing machines, cars, shovels, gasoline—Holman's had the first service station on the Peninsula—and of course, lunch. The Solarium on the top floor provided a panoramic view of Monterey Bay and was the favorite eating destination of many locals and tourists. (My mom's childhood order: a tuna sandwich and a vanilla milkshake.) While the business sold to Ford's in 1985, today you can still find Holman's at 542 Lighthouse Avenue, with retail on the first floor and condos above; the Holman name still graces the front of the building.

Mr. and Mrs. Holman also owned Holly Hills Farm in Watsonville—one of the biggest holly farms in the country in its time. They would harvest the holly in November and December and ship elaborate wreaths around the country (and also sell them at Holman's). If you live in Pacific Grove and have a holly tree in your yard, it was likely planted from a seedling purchased from Holman's. W.R. donated thirty trees to the El Carmelo Cemetery and you can still see a few along the cemetery's border with Lighthouse Avenue. In the late 1950s, Genie's family moved from Pasadena to Watsonville and her father, Eugene Kern O'Meara, ran the farm, which was eventually sold.

Both Mr. and Mrs. Holman were advocates of preservation and conservation. Among his many campaigns, W.R. fought against the overfishing of abalone, while Mrs. Holman worked to preserve the Asilomar Conference Grounds, as well as the adobe buildings of Monterey. Her collection of rare and first-edition books can be viewed at the Zena Holman Research Library at Asilomar Conference Grounds. Her Jack London collection was donated to the State of California and is now housed at the Jack London State Historic Park in Glen Ellen, California. The Holmans collected Native American artifacts, and their vast collection was donated to the state parks of Monterey; pieces from the donation are on rotation at the Pacific House in Monterey.

It wasn't until my husband, Benjamin Eugene Lazare, great-grandson of Mr. and Mrs. Holman, and I read W.R. Holman's mimeographed, self-published memoir, which he had dictated to his caretaker, Louise V. Jaques in 1979, that I truly came to understand the contributions Mr. and Mrs. Holman made to the community of Pacific Grove. Our lives were full—our son, Jack Holman Tor Lazare, was about eight months old the first time we read through W.R.'s memoir, and we were living in a home the Holman's have owned for generations, at 752 Lighthouse Ave., Pacific Grove. It is particularly noticeable because the garden is lined with holly, W.R. Holman's plant-passion. We knew there was something important and worth sharing in those pages, but between work and family, our time was incredibly limited.

Today—it's 2022—this memoir remains important, even more so with another great-great grandchild for W. R. and Zena, our daughter, Elodie Spindler Gigi Lazare. Quarantine has proven to be the time to tackle the Holman boxes Genie left to us. This project unfolded over our years at home as I worked through every one of the boxes Genie had stored: boxes full of family photos, copies of *Game & Gossip* and *The Board and Batten*, newspaper articles, personal correspondence, postcards, unlabeled daguerreotypes, large-format negatives, and property deeds.

You're holding this book because of the dedication of Patricia Hamilton of Park Place Publications, and because my neighbor, Donald Livermore, loaned Patricia his copy of this memoir (gifted to him by W.R.). Patricia and I met years ago and shared an office in downtown Pacific Grove for a while—I took the morning shift at the desk with my laptop, and she would come in to work later in the day after I'd left for preschool pick-up. An office filled with plants and elaborate crown molding and lavender walls was the perfect place to edit. I am a book editor. Having worked for Random House and Simon & Schuster, and now running my own independent book editing business, it seemed I was the right person to help bring W.R. Holman's words into the twenty-first century. Patricia is an advocate of local history and through her urging, I reserved a few week's time in my schedule so I could work on turning W.R. Holman's dictated memoir into this book. Of course, what I thought would be a few weeks turned into two years of organizing, scanning, collating, and clarifying—a pile of old newspapers or box of family photographs never far from my reach. I spent many nights hovered over a lightbox (thank you, Bill and Kirsten Janes!), trying to determine if we needed to scan one more photo of endless rows of the Holly Hills Farm (we did). Monterey Bay Photo Lab was an excellent resource for digitizing the large format negatives.

Joyce Krieg worked diligently to transcribe the mimeographed book into a Word document, which I then edited. Without Joyce's careful copying and proofreading, and the encouragement from the ever-positive Patricia, this reprint of Holman's memoir would not exist. Thank you to Sarah Sarai for a thorough copyedit, and to Elina Cohen for the beautiful typesetting and book jacket.

My husband and children and my stepdad, Ross Allen, have patiently supported me as I spent many nights and weekends going through boxes that took over much of our living room. Whether I was trying to decipher John Steinbeck's difficult scrawl, or attempting to figure out which "Pat" I was looking at (Mrs. Holman was called "Pat;" their daughter was Patricia, and their granddaughter was also Patricia . . .), my family encouraged me to keep going. While getting his master's and teaching credential, Ben found time to retouch, examine, and color balance each of the nearly 150 photos in these pages. He is an incredible person and I'm so lucky to be married to him. This book, ultimately, is for our children, our niece Tallulah Lazare, and for the many others on our family tree, so that W.R. and Zena Holman can, in a way, be a part of their lives. And speaking of the family tree, many cheers to the relatives I contacted out of the blue, who told me delightful stories and gathered birthdates for me; to Carol O'Meara, Laurie Stanley, David Steven, and Andreana Emo Capodilista, I am especially grateful.

I have tried to keep my editorial comments to a minimum and intrude only when I can offer clarification—you'll see me pop into the footnotes throughout. There were so many places where I wanted to ask "Why?" and say "Tell me more about that," but in many cases we'll just have to imagine the answers. The book was originally organized a bit differently. I've shifted sections so that W.R. Holman's story is up front. It's important to remember that the words are as he wrote them, so while we might cringe at using "Indian" rather than "Native American," I didn't want to inject anachronisms. I agonized about not changing his words because I wanted him to be seen in the best light possible. His anti-Japanese sentiment is evident when he speaks of abalone fishing, but I have included his words as written/said, as they are a part of who he was. I can't insert cultural sensitivity into history when it didn't exist.

The latter half of the book contains newspaper articles, personal letters from John Steinbeck to Mrs. Holman, as well as the Pacific Grove City Charter, and all that W.R. Holman did in order to support it.

In reading W.R. Holman's words, I am reminded how important family history is, and hope his efforts inspire you to write down some of your favorite memories so the generations after you will be able to know you—without ever actually knowing you.

Thank you for your interest in Pacific Grove and in the memoir of W.R. Holman.

I hope you enjoy these pages.

—Heather Kimberly Spindler Proulx Lazare
Pacific Grove, California, April 2022

Zena and W.R. Holman with their granddaughter Patricia "Genie"
O'Meara [later Santini] on her wedding day to Michel Lazare.

A Note on the Text

THE FIRST CHAPTER OF PART I CONSISTS OF W.R. HOLMAN'S DICTATION to Louise Jaques. While it was not always entirely clear where W.R. was speaking and where Jaques was left to interpret his thoughts and her notes, his quotes are as accurate as possible. His energy and knowledge are evident and true to his spirit.

Chapters 2 through 9 of Part I are all W.R. Holman's words.

Part II includes newspaper and magazine articles, as well as the Steinbeck letters. Part III documents Holman's efforts to make Pacific Grove's town charter equitable for all.

I've inserted my voice in the footnotes and in brackets throughout as an [Editor's note] when more context is useful. In Parts II and III, it's my voice introducing new chapters. I have done my best to differentiate between direct quotes and transcript.

—*Heather Lazare*

PART I

Wilford Rensselaer Holman,

in His Own Words

W.R. Holman in his twenties.

1

How My Father Came to California

RENSSELAER LUTHER HOLMAN IS PART OF THE SIXTH GENERATION OF Holmans in America. Rensselaer was the son of Luther and Rachel (Mann) Holman and was born May 26, 1843, in Underhill, Vermont. He married Laura Amelia Whitcomb in 1871 in Underhill. Then he planned to leave for California.

About that time, many families on the Atlantic Coast were pinched for the ordinary comforts of life. Young men seeing no satisfactory future before them were dazzled by the account of the marvelous production of the Comstock Lode, and the rapid growth and accumulation of wealth at San Francisco, California. The recent extension of the railroad into places previously inaccessible, and California's newly booming industry and mild climate, resulted in one hundred and seven thousand people coming to California in 1875. This year was eventful for San Francisco—new stock excitement, completion of the Palace Hotel, a theater, establishment of the Bank of Nevada, opening of Montgomery Avenue, advancement of Market Street near Third to rival with Kearny

Street as a fashionable promenade—the city had not seen such a large immigration since 1850!

There were three routes from the Atlantic seaboard: overland by train, or by boat to the Isthmus of Panama, or to "Round Cape Horn" at the southern tip of South America. The trip took over four months to complete.

Rensselaer Holman boarded a schooner to sail "Round the Horn" to San Francisco. Two hours after the ship pulled out of Boston, she hit rough sea; it was rougher when she came to the Gulf Stream. In the waters off South America, it was rougher still, but when she reached Cape Horn, the waters were the roughest in the world.

The schooner rode the swells, lashed by cold winds of a snowstorm, bucking a choppy sea—passengers stayed sick and scared in wet cabins behind barred doors to prevent them from being washed overboard. Passengers were so seasick, some lost twenty pounds from this experience.

Then there was a wild ride in a hollow of a wave and the schooner hit the Pacific, and she sailed on waters like a lake in summertime. Passengers ate and gained their weight back. There were more episodes like the one described before the schooner reached Panama. As Rensselaer planned to return to his wife in Vermont, he talked to a travel agent in Panama City about the Isthmus of Panama route. He was told that this whole neck of land between North and South America was the narrow crossing between Panama City at the Pacific end and the City of Colon at the Caribbean end. The Isthmus includes the Isthmus of San Blas and Isthmus of Darien with the Mosquito Gulf northwest of the Gulf of Darien. The drainage area reaching from the Caribbean to the Pacific is navigable by small boats—the mean temperature being 80 degrees Fahrenheit.

Rensselaer spoke to the travel agent about returning to Vermont by the Isthmus when the time came. The agent warned him of the danger of malaria mosquitoes, but Rensselaer felt it could not be as bad as the heavy seas and winds he experienced "Round the Horn," a trip he never forgot.

San Francisco at last! W.R. Holman describes the city as follows: "They have the best weather in the world . . . there are not days but weeks when the skies are indescribably glorious . . . the air has an undeniable softness and sweetness—a tonic that braces the nerves to a joyous tension, making the very sense of existence a delight . . . San Francisco is probably the most cosmopolitan city of its size in the world. Nowhere else are witnessed the fusing of so many races, the juxtaposition of so many nationalities, the babel of so many tongues . . . "

In his book, *City of the Golden Gate: A Description of San Francisco in 1875*, Samuel Williams[1] described the people of the city: "San Francisco has rather more than her share of eccentric characters. Foremost among these is 'Emperor Norton,' a harmless creature, who firmly believes he is the legitimate sovereign of the United States and Mexico; issues frequent pronunciamentos; exacts tribute from such citizens as humor his delusion; spends his days walking around the streets, his evenings at the theater, and his nights at a cheap lodging house."

W.R. Holman continues to describe the city: "There are eight joss houses (Chinese Temples) . . . Chinatown is a system of alleys and passages . . . into which sunshine never enters—with dirty rivulets flowing into the great stream of life in this human hive . . . never at rest.

"San Francisco yesterday a desert of sand dunes, today a city of a quarter million people, with an aggregate wealth of five hundred million dollars, with more than sixty millionaires there . . . and California

---

1 Williams, Samuel. *City of the Golden Gate: A Description of San Francisco in 1875.* Published in 1921 by the Book Club of California.

Street is a speculator's paradise . . . fortunes are made or lost in a day!"

Rensselaer found his first job in San Francisco kneading bread dough in huge vats with his bare feet! Then he sold peaches on the streets.

In his late twenties, Rensselaer was a strong, handsome man. His life's interest was for the welfare of his young wife, his parents, relatives, and his friends, all living in Vermont, a state with half of its 300,000 population owning or working on farms; 100,000 gainfully employed in the lumber market. (Vermont at that time being the third largest lumber-center in the United States with 80% of its export in lumber, produced from forests of white pine, spruce and hemlock, and hard woods. Vermont had a sawmill run by a waterwheel!)

Rensselaer's father, Luther, had an acre of maple trees, which he inherited.

Many people worked in the wood pulp and paper factories, others in marble and granite quarries, foundries and machine shop products, scales and balances manufactured at St. Johnsburg, roofing and building material, cotton and woolen goods, furniture, medicines and compounds and general merchandise.

Rensselaer Holman, an enterprising man, was familiar with farm equipment, hardware and the building supply business. There was a great need of these items out West, but first he would introduce the grain harvesting machinery. There was a need for cheaper bread in California.

Sacramento, capital of California, ninety-one miles by rail northeast of San Francisco, is where R.L. made his new home. He went back to Vermont by way of the Isthmus of Panama as arranged on his journey north. Soon after he returned with his wife by train, to settle in Sacramento.

In the next decade, he prospered in his business and his wife gave him three children, Clarence Edward Holman, Minnie Warren Holman, and Wilford Rensselaer Holman. In 1886, when Wilford was a year and a half, his mother, Laura Amelia Whitcomb Holman, died.

Luther Holman, son of Solomon and Sally Holman, married Rachel Mann in Vermont on March 23rd, 1837.

Rachel (Mann) Holman, daughter of Samuel Mann of Randolph, VT.

Left: *R.L. Holman as a young man.* Right: *Laura Amelia Whitcomb Holman as a young woman.*

R.L. and Laura Holman.

R.L. and Laura Holman with their eldest son, Clarence.

2

Moving to Pacific Grove

IN THE MONTHS THAT FOLLOWED MY MOTHER'S PASSING, MY FATHER became ill. He also severely hurt himself while lifting a keg of nails from a wagon.

My crib was placed on a stairway landing in my father's house in Sacramento, at 16th and Pine Streets, where my brother, sister, and I were born. Minora Laurena Holman, my father's eldest sister, came from Vermont to care for us. From that time on, my Aunt Minora devoted her whole life to us.

As I grew older, she promised me a penny if I took my afternoon nap. With this penny held tightly in my hand, I'd run across the street to a store to buy candy.

There was a little girl, Roxy Thompson, who lived close by. One day we were playing in the street. I swore aloud. Her mother angrily shook a feather duster at me from her second-story window, saying "Go home!"

When my Aunt Minora and my father took a walk on the streets, I hopped the curb to the gutter ahead of them to listen to what they said.

My father now had a large wholesale hardware store in the business section of Sacramento. He had the two Thompson brothers from Vermont run the store for him. One was a bookkeeper and the other a salesman.

My father had bought two sections of acreage in Stockton. He grew hay on this land. His harvester machine's blade caught our dog that ran into the hay to catch rabbits. It cut off his legs.

Grapes were grown also. When the price was low, the grape vines were pulled out. Later, when my father had passed the prime of life, the price of grapes was good, and he tried to grow grapes again, but it was too late for him.

He was a wonderful father, a well-loved man. We children spent two unforgettable weeks with him in a rented cottage on the ocean front of Pacific Grove, swimming, gathering shells and starfish on the beach. The climate was delightful. He decided to make Pacific Grove his home. He ordered a house to be built on Lobos Street. Upon its completion, he sold his business in Sacramento to the two Thompson brothers.

I was four years old when we left Sacramento in a two-horse open shay (surrey) with a top on. My father drove the horses; Aunt Minora sat on the seat beside him with me on her lap. My sister, brother, and Lee Chong, our Chinese cook-housekeeper, sat in the back. He was with us for many years. Aunt Minora taught him English every day.

Twenty miles out of Stockton we stopped overnight at the Mountain House. The lady caretaker picked me off Aunt Minora's lap, and she did something to me I did not like. She hugged and kissed me!

We continued our trip the next day. We had to go over the mountains down into the green valley into the Pacheco Pass to enter beautiful Pacific Grove—wildflowers blooming everywhere, fields of golden poppies too!

Father had definite reasons for making our home in Pacific Grove.

The climate there was wonderful! No mosquitoes. He suffered severely from malaria in Sacramento. He said, "Pacific Grove will one day be a prosperous city."

Minora Laurena Holman, W.R.'s aunt, R.L.'s eldest sister.

W.R. Holman with his siblings (from left-to-right) Clarence Edward Holman, W.R. Holman, and Minnie Warren Holman.

W.R. Holman, four years old.

R.L. Holman's ranch in Linden, outside of Stockton, California.

R.L. Holman and his family at their home in Sacramento. In the wagon: Clarence Holman, W. R. Holman stands on the steps, R.L. Holman leans on the staircase railing. Women on the porch from left to right: Celia (Holman) Badger (R.L.'s sister) is in all black and her daughter, Nina Badger (later Moore), is to her right. Rachel (Mann) Holman is seated; Minnie, in a white dress, is in front of her grandmother. Minora is at the far right. [Editor's note: In W.R. Holman's recollection, his family traveled to Pacific Grove from Sacramento with Aunt Minora and no one else, but this shows that his aunts, grandmother, and cousin were in Sacramento as well. They may not have journeyed together, but we can see that his Vermont relatives came to Sacramento first. Later they ventured down to Pacific Grove, most likely waiting for the larger house at 769 Lighthouse to be ready.]

3

My Early Years in Pacific Grove

FATHER INVESTED HIS MONEY FROM THE SALE OF HIS BUSINESS IN SAC-ramento into land in Pacific Grove, from Lighthouse Avenue to Short Street, between Wood and Granite Streets, buying an extra small house on Lobos Street, with its backyard running through to Wood Street, for us to live in. Number 218 Lobos Street is a two-story, well-built red-wood building with an outhouse. The land then extended from Lobos to Wood Street. House still stands. Outhouse is a tool shed.

When we arrived, we found no bathroom there. My father was told that when people came to Pacific Grove, a resort town, to live, they were not to put in a bathroom, but to use the bathtubs at the bathhouse on the beach, with running salt water, hot or cold. That night, Aunt Minora sat me down on a wooden board across the washtub to bathe me. The others took sponge baths. In the summertime we went to the bathhouse on the beach. After, we sat on the porch of the outhouse to listen to the band concert playing on the bandstand on the beach. We looked at the rocks on the coastline, the water in the bay, the waves splashing, and the hundreds of tourists on the beach.

Our first summertime in Pacific Grove was over. I was enrolled at Miss Frisbee's kindergarten at 228 18th Street, walking distance for a little boy from Lobos Street.

===

I had a wonderful collection of over one thousand eggs, each carefully blown from one hole. These eggs came from wild sparrows, beautiful white topknots, so plentiful then, wild canaries, singing as they nest, wild wrens, blue jays, pygmy owls, hoot owls, robins, meadowlarks, wild pigeons, cliff swallows, tree swallows, ground swallows, woodpeckers, sandpipers, nuthatch, and hummingbirds' eggs were the smallest in my collection—the size of a white bean.

The other day I went to 16th and Central in Pacific Grove to see again the high-peaked gable roof of the old Chautauqua Assembly building. It is now practically hidden from view by treetops. It brings to mind my boyish pastime to look for birds' nests in high places in buildings and trees in Pacific Grove, Carmel Valley, Salinas, and as far as Watsonville.

It was a late, damp afternoon. I was playing with other boys in the Chautauqua yard when I saw a sparrow's nest under the eaves at the very center of the gable roof. I hoisted myself onto a spreading oak tree, climbed the limb that put me on the Chautauqua roof's edge, balanced my way up to the top and straddled the gable, bent over, took the eggs out of the nest, and put all four of them in my mouth for safe keeping. I then cautiously balanced myself for the descent. Suddenly, I lost my footing, slid all the way down to the edge of the roof, missed catching the oak's limb, falling twenty feet to the earth, landing on my behind. I got up, brushed myself off, looked about me. Silently I thanked God that I missed a plank with a rusty nail in it as I landed. What happened to the eggs? Well, I don't know.

=

Soon after our arrival in Pacific Grove, my father's friend, Mr. Justin, a splendid architect-carpenter from Vermont, came to build a ten-room, one modern bathroom, three-story house with four gable roofs on my father's land. The front faced Lighthouse Avenue, bordered on the east by Wood Street, the west by Granite Street, and the north by lots up to Short Street owned by neighbors.

The land on Lighthouse Avenue had to be cleared of trees. Father hired a strong Indian, who came daily to chop the trees down, roots and all. With him he brought his tools and his squaw. She sat under a shady tree while he worked. When he finished, father hired a giant of a Manchurian gardener to cultivate the land before Mr. Justin arrived.

Mr. Justin, with the help of Mr. Buffen, a local carpenter, took three years to construct 769 Lighthouse Avenue, the cook's cottage on Wood Street, and a barn with a hayloft on Granite Street behind our house.

I remember toddling over there from Lobos Street through our backyard to watch them build our new home from the start of excavation. I went there every day until the house was built.

At the time, tireless father, not as well as he should have been, brought from Sacramento his two-horse farm wagon loaded with hardware, building material, lime, plaster, cement, lathe, shake and shingles, nails, and bolts. He planned to have his own business here. However, after he was prepared to do business, he was notified by the Pacific Improvement Company that in his deed he had no rights to operate such a business. He must stop his activities or forfeit his land here. I noticed from that time, he worried a lot.

As Mr. Justin and Mr. Buffen worked on the house for the next three years, I watched them make ready for the foundation. They took from a two-horse drawn farm wagon many loads of bricks carried from three railroad cars at the tracks from San Jose. Then they connected pipes to the cesspool, cut up redwood for the building, set up the windows and doors, until, little by little, the house took shape. I watched them all the time even when they placed tall ladders against the house and I climbed them; they never once said, "Go away. Go home!"

The local painter took over when Mr. Justin and Mr. Buffen left. He asked father for two-and-a-half barrels of good linseed paint mix. I saw the painter take away a gallon of paint with him every time he went home.

Finally, 769 Lighthouse was ready to move into—and timely too! 218 Lobos was getting too crowded. Father, Clarence, and I slept in a three-story bunk bed in the small back room. I was put in the top bunk!

This bed was made of half-inch galvanized pipe, with mattresses over coil springs made at father's coil spring factory, which was a back-room in the Sacramento store. There a man operated a foot-propelled machine that turned straight steel wire into coil springs.

=

Lee Chong, our Chinese cook-housekeeper, moved into the "Cook's House" on Wood Street. He was a small man, with long black hair in a plait; he was a high-born Chinese from China. He was the finest-dressed Chinaman in all of California. The tassel of his handsome silk hat stemmed from an Imperial Yellow braided button. He rose early in the mornings to sweep the garden paths, then he did everything else in the house to make us comfortable. Every afternoon he sat by Aunt Minora to learn to read, a talent, I fear, he never mastered.

Lee Chong always had a special treat for me. He made especially large pancakes at breakfast, and deep-fried bowls of crispy golden potato chips for us to munch on. "Wiff, I cook large pancake for you!" he'd say.

Dressed in his elegant, embroidered silk gown, shoes and cap, he visited his friends in Chinatown. He was the most admired man in Chinatown. He sometimes took me to enjoy the sweetmeats his friends gave to me. I learned to mimic their quick way of talking. I still do this. People think I speak Chinese.

In the afternoons he cycled in the woods, wearing soft shoes. One day he lost control of his bike. It crashed into the lighthouse gatepost at the end of the bicycle path. The handlebar went into him, exposing his gut. A pharmacist and a nose, ear, and throat doctor attended to him, who left Clarence, sixteen, and I, "Wiff," twelve, to nurse him with hot towels. He suffered a lot for three days, then died in the house father especially built for him to live in.

His friends prepared him for his funeral. They also took away all his fine silk embroidered clothes, shoes and belongings. He was the only man from China here to ever be taken to his burial place at China Point in a horse-drawn hearse father ordered for him. All his friends followed it on foot as it wound its way through Chinatown.

I will always remember Lee Chong.

===

While still in kindergarten, I took my last penny from father. Father took me to the corner grocery. I stood by the candy jar and put an open palm behind my back. Father dropped a penny in it for the candy I wanted. It was the last penny he ever gave me. After that, I enjoyed earning my own money.

I never missed a chance to make my own keep. For twenty-five cents for hours of work, I cleaned neighbors' sidewalks, and paths, weeded gardens, and patiently gathered pine cones that had been laying for years and years on the forest grounds. I sold them in hundred-pound barley sacks for ten cents, or three sacks for two-bits (25¢). My chums,

George and Bill Ingram, were partners in this. We had a lot of fun going from door to door selling sacks of pine cones. When Bill was a man, he had the largest contracting business in Monterey. He built the Monterey Theater. His brother drowned.

==

A dozen chickens from the Carmel Valley cost four dollars. After I dressed them for sale, they sold for 65¢ each. Again I went door to door to take orders for "fresh dressed chicken" for Sunday dinner. One man said to me, "I bought a chicken from you last week. I cooked and cooked it, took an ax to chop it up, it was still tough!"

==

In Carmel Valley I bought live ducks and geese, put them in my spring wagon, drove to Chinatown, and picked a good street corner to wait for customers. One by one they came, took their choice of fowl and went away. Before sunset they returned to pay me. I never lost a penny there.

Chinatown was settled in 1880 near Cabrillo Point, and remained there for many years. Now it is occupied by the boatworks and Stanford Marine Station. In my opinion the Chinese were the rightful owners of this property.

==

I rode bareback on Maud S., our buggy horse, clear around the barbed fenced fields, through the woods or on the sand dunes.

==

From age six to sixteen, I attended the grammar school on Forest Avenue. Every day there was so much to do. One spring day when bands of wild pigeons were flying in to feed on the new-grown barley fields towards the lighthouse (now the La Porte's house)[2], the boys fell on top of me while playing ball at school. This put my foot out of joint. I started to hop on one foot to go home. On the way, the Wells Fargo delivery rig passed by, stopped, and the two drivers helped me onto the rig and brought me home.

Father sent for Dr. Trimmer to attend to me. He gave me a pair of crutches and ordered me to stay on the couch by the bay window for a week.

When school was out, I saw my friend Dayton Dawson run by the window with his shotgun. "Wait for me," I called. He waited while I hopped to the front door to pick up my shotgun, then hopped down the garden steps to go with him and the other boys to shoot the wild pigeons feeding on the new-grown barley. The boys clambered over the white picket fence to go into the field. I crawled under the fence, and lay on the ground to wait for my first shot. Ahead of me was a bare tree. Suddenly, a band of pigeons, chased by the boys from the barley field, began to roost on this tree. I shot down as many as I could from where I lay, as the boys came from the barley field with none.

=

When Dayton Dawson and I were fourteen, we made a huge firecracker out of a long, four-inch diameter cardboard tube used to roll linoleum carpets for shipment to my father's store. Into it we put strings of small firecrackers attached to a long black fuse that hung out from one end of the tube. We carried this contraption, wrapped in red, white, and blue tissue paper, on our shoulders and marched with it into a Fourth of July

---

2 The Victorian mansion at 1030 Lighthouse Avenue, on the corner of Lighthouse and Seventeen Mile Drive.

crowd on the beach, laid it down on the sands, lit the fuse and when the firecrackers crackled, the crowd scattered in all directions.

As the years went by, the bathhouse was torn down, and glass bottom boats were the tourist attractions.

==

I will always remember Pacific Grove street sounds with a smile. There was the rattle of wagon wheels, horses' hoofs, and the sound of the tin horns peddlers used to attract people, "Rags, bottles, sacks!"

==

"Flesh fishees—samon, rok-cod, founder," (salmon, rock cod, flounder) Chinese fish peddlers on the street called out.

With his two baskets swinging on a bamboo pole over his shoulder, one stopped near the house, laid his burden down, and picked out a good fish to take across the street to a customer. I looked into the basket, saw a strange fish and dangled it between two fingers.

The peddler gave one yell, and leapt across the street waving his sharp fish knife. I ran into our barn. He followed me, yelling all the way up the ladder to the hayloft. I leapt through the open shaft twenty feet to the hay pile on the ground and quickly ran away.

==

Then there was the singing laundryman. He washed and ironed all day long. At night he made his deliveries in his spring wagon, singing loudly in Chinese.

==

The first silent film was shown in the hall of the Methodist Church. Everybody in Pacific Grove was there, including one member of

Chinatown. When it was over, his voice came over the crowd as he loudly uttered in Chinese his amazement of what he had seen. The following night the picture was shown again. Our Chinese was there with as many friends as he could bring. They were as surprised as he was, and their loud and excited Chinese was heard throughout the hall.

=

Then there was the Postmaster, Robert Mitchell, known as "Whistling Bob" because he always blew a merry tune while on the street to his job at the post office, located on Fountain Avenue, the building that I now own.[3]

=

One day at the big railroad engine house, I had a terrible experience at the train turntable, where I played hopping trains from San Francisco and elsewhere being turned around to go back from where they came. I missed as I grabbed the railing, and the wheels scraped my leg! I can't understand to this day how I did not lose it! I never went there to play again, even to see Mr. Sutton go around the incoming trains to strike all their wheels with a ball-peen hammer to look for cracks or a broken wheel by the sound of the stroke. If the wheel was all right, the stroke from the hammer would ring like a bell.

---

3 He did, in fact, own property on Fountain Avenue (everything between Lighthouse Avenue and Central), but I believe he meant the 216 Grand Avenue. building he also owned. It was the first post office in Pacific Grove; later it was a telegraph office. The building remains in the Holman family. W.R. Holman later repeats "Fountain Avenue" to reporter Neill Gardner, but in a tape-recorded interview in October 1976, says, "First Post Office of Pacific Grove, right up there off Lighthouse on this side, just back of the bank—the first two-story building at the corner there, Grand Avenue, first house beyond the bank from Lighthouse. There was an art dealer downstairs."

==

There were many grammar school friends, Dayton Dawson, as I mentioned, for one, Clell Trine another. One summer day we went to find work in San Jose, rented an apartment by the tracks and found jobs with a tomato cannery. We worked at unloading empty gallon cans from the train to be taken to the tomato cannery to be filled with tomato juice or catsup. Trine worked inside the plant, and since he had no change of clothing, he smelt of sour tomato day and night. We ate at a slop house for 15¢ a meal. I became so sick, I thought I'd die. Finally we left and got home somehow.

==

Bill Noyes was another chum. We made a two-seat bootblack stand with a chrome railing. Opposite father's store was the cigar store where I worked mopping floors, and in the back room where men played cards at nights, I cleaned out the spittoons. The owner let us put our bootblack stand at his doorway. My father was ashamed of me. To avoid me, he went to the far end of the sidewalk to cross the street.

One day Bill Noyes said he was going to take a six-months' course at Pacific Coast Business College in San Jose, where college graduates studied. We were only grammar school graduates. I said I'd go with him. We shared an apartment for four-and-a-half months when I set a record for the school by graduating before six months, on July 10, 1903!

==

I remember when Pacific Grove was a large forest of high trees such as the pine, cypress, and oak. The air was filled with the fluttering, twittering and singing of wild canaries, the singing linnets, the white breasted and top knot blue jays and wild pigeons. Flowers of every hue carpeted the forest floor, and golden poppies were everywhere. Spring was indeed here.

I loved the winding trails leading to here and there—excepting for a narrow dirt road leading to Point Pinos Lighthouse—a road built by the U.S. Government, or the Coast Guard, and never deeded to the City of Pacific Grove, as far as I know.

218 Lobos Street, the Holmans' first home in Pacific Grove.

Lee Chong, the Holman family's cook and housekeeper.

Lee Chong as a young boy.

Lee Chong's house at 208 Wood Street.

"Happy School Days 1892." W.R. Holman and his elementary school classmates. W.R. is standing in the back row, the second child from the left.

Young W.R. on his horse.

Above: *Lovers Point Beach, late 1800s.*

Right: *W.R. Holman with his classmates. He is standing, second from the left. His friend Dayton Dawson is also standing, fourth from the left.*

*First Post Office in Pacific Grove;
216 Grand Avenue.*

*Lovers Point Beach: [Editor's note: I believe
this is Clarence Holman and that this photo was
taken during a visit to Pacific Grove, before
R.L. Holman and his family moved there.]*

*Forest Avenue, taken from just
below Lighthouse Avenue looking
toward Monterey Bay, late 1880s.*

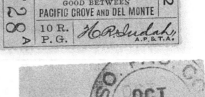

Top: *Southern Pacific Railroad Commuter ticket,
good between Pacific Grove and Del Monte (front).*
Bottom: *Back of the Southern Pacific Railroad
Commuter ticket, stamped October 6, 1890.*

Original tent city in Pacific Grove located between 17th and 18th Street. Taken from Lighthouse Avenue, looking toward Monterey Bay.

The Holman family at their finished home, 769 Lighthouse Avenue, Pacific Grove. From left to right: Vermont relative (unidentified), Rachel (Mann) Holman (seated), R.L. Holman (standing), Minnie Holman, Clarence Holman, Vermont relative (unidentified), Aunt Minora Holman, W.R. Holman (seated), Vermont relative (unidentified), Aunt Celia (Holman) Badger, cousin Nina Badger.

4

My Father as I Remember Him

HE WAS A GOOD LOOKING AND A GENEROUS MAN. HE HAD MANY friends. 769 Lighthouse overflowed with relatives from Vermont. In some cases he paid their railroad fare to and from Pacific Grove. He loved this town as I do.

He invited his widowed mother [Rachel (Mann) Holman], in her seventies or eighties, to live with us. I was eight when she became ill in the parlor. I ran to tell father, who was in the garden. He rushed in, carried her upstairs to her room, which was opposite the corridor to his own room. Grandmother never walked down again. She died and was laid in state in the parlor. Father sent Clarence, a growing boy, to take her back to Vermont to be buried by her husband, my grandfather Luther, who died in 1880.

=

Father occupied the master bedroom on the second floor. Aunt Minora, Minnie, and the guests shared the floor with him. Clarence and I slept on the third floor under the gables. We faced a wonderful view of Monterey Bay.

Every morning we were up early, dressed and noisily ran down the back stairs. Father scolded, "You sound like Norman horses!"

But we had chores to do before going to school. My job was to look after our productive cow, to clean out her stall, feed, and milk her. Then I'd deliver the milk in pints, half quarts, and quarts in an open-mouth pitcher to my father's customers, and take the cow out to pasture in the field. When school was over, I brought the cow back to her stall for the night.

——

Father was a member of a whist club. They gathered at 769 Lighthouse once a month for a "whist-feed." There were four tables in the parlor for the players. They stayed until late at night playing whist and eating the good food prepared by my Aunt Minora under the hanging gas lights with bright glass bowls on them.

——

Aunt Minora Holman was born in 1840, in Randolph, Vermont. She reached womanhood during the Civil War, when men were at war. Her young life was spent caring for her parents and their other four small children: Celia Merritt, Rensselaer Luther, Samuel Harris, and Eugene. She was forty-four when mother died. She came to care for us in Sacramento. I was two. She devoted her life to bringing me up to manhood, then cared for my sick father in Stockton [at his ranch in Linden]. She died there in 1908.

My Aunt Minora! She was always at home for me to run to. Always had time to rub my head as I rested by her knee as she sat in the parlor reading her Bible. I would sit at her feet with my head on her lap for her to rub and scratch, then put her hand down my back and do the same thing. She kept me quiet by the hour. For years she kept accounts for her church at the Methodist Assembly Hall, where I went to Sunday School. She saw to it that I said my prayers at night. On the evenings she went to church, she carried a "Bull's Eye Lantern" to light her way on the dark streets of Pacific Grove.

Aunt Minora and Lee Chong: these two wonderful people raised me.

==

A Mr. Towle and my father ventured into a business on Lighthouse Avenue. They were the proprietors of a store, "The Popular," dealers in dry goods, boots, shoes, clothing, hats, caps, notions, etc. Their slogan was, "Best Goods Always on Hand at Lowest Prices."

In Alaska, gold was found in the Klondike. One night, without telling Father, Towle emptied the store's till of all the cash. He left with his father and brother to find gold.[4]

Clarence, at that time, was still a growing boy, too young to help father. Today, I wonder how he managed to run his store, which he renamed the "R.L. Holman."

On each side of the small store was a counter, one for ladies' merchandise, the other for men's goods. Above them was a line to hang the merchandise for display, ladies' underwear to the left of the store, and men's ties to the right. Eighteen-inch-deep shelves against all three walls held yardage and other merchandise. In the middle of the floor space was a display table.

In the basement, father stocked rolls of linoleum, sewing machines, baby buggies, cots, mattresses, window shades, rolls of 220 warp (very fine) Japanese matting, and coarser matting from China. All these items were sold or rented to the summer tourists and local trade.

---

4 This is refuted by Towle's relatives and the narrative changes later according to Holman, who said that his father bought out Towle.

Besides this merchandise, he carried a heavy stock of wallpaper. People from all over the county and countryside came to buy fifty to a hundred bundles of wallpaper at a time.

On slow days, he taught me to reroll yardage to fit the shelves against the walls. He tore off a large amount of brown wrapping paper from a roll, put it on the floor, unwound a whole yard-wide bolt of calico or other yardage onto the paper, handed me a plyboard cut to the size of the shelves, saying, "Wiff, now you take and roll that up, square to the front, so it can go in the shelves even."

Each of the bolts was from twenty-five to thirty yards long. I rolled it up with one hand.

=

We were busy. I delivered sewing machines on my shoulders, put up shades, put down mattings and delivered all merchandise my father sold or rented. I mopped the floors, cleaned the shelves, displayed the merchandise, and once a week I washed the front windows. Everything was always spick and span.

=

On quiet winter days the neighborhood tradespeople visited round the warm, iron pot-bellied stove in father's store.

In Monterey were three general merchandise stores owned by old, old settlers, way back in the Spanish/Mexican days. The owners were at one time peddlers, selling pins, needles, and such. Their stores were in operation when father opened The Popular.

Mr. Gunderscoferd owned the White House; Mr. Harris owned the Red House. Mr. Goldstein opened his Long Shore doors at the corner of Alvarado and Franklin, where there once was a saloon where many a cowboy rode his horse through the swinging doors to the bar. And for years and years where an Indian stood at the entrance, ringing a bell and calling out, "Keeno tonight—Keeno tonight!" This old building was moved to New Monterey. It is still in use as a retail place.

One day a small delegation of Monterey shop owners: Mr. Gunderscoferd, Mr. Harrison[5], Mr. Goldstein, and the owner of The People's Store, opened later, visited father to ask if he would mark his merchandise the same price as they were selling it for. At that time, I, a boy of fourteen or so, stood up and said, "No, you sell at your price, and we'll sell at our price." Father said, "The boy is right." And so, that is how it was.

=

A competitor came to town. He invested in a few cottages to live in and to rent. He opened a similar business as father's right across Lighthouse Avenue from him. Much time was spent trying to "freeze" one another out of business by keeping open days and nights. One night, my father said to Pacific Grove night watchman, Mr. Wolfcoxson, "I want to lay down to sleep on the counter with the lights on. You watch the store for me."

Father wore the competitor out. He locked up his store, burnt his cottages to collect his insurance and left town.

=

R. L. Holman Store moved a few times on Lighthouse Avenue. During one of the moves, my father left me in charge of the old one while he prepared his new store. He had an older man, Mr. Andrew W. Anderson, help me for a ten-dollar gold piece every week. My father gave me the money to pay him and since it was the size of a two-cent piece, I

---

5 While there was a Mr. Harris in the previous paragraph, it is unclear if he means Harris here.

gave him the two-cent piece. He got awful mad with me when he could not pay for his groceries on pay night. "Don't you do that to me again— that's enough."

Mr. Anderson was our loyal, faithful, and reliable employee. He worked close to me at the store. He lived in his own home on Lighthouse Avenue with his wife, whose brother, a retired banker from Fresno living on Central Avenue, helped look after Andrew in his old age. Father used to send me to take him for a ride in the surrey. I had a hard time getting him in and out of it, but I did. Today I think of him often as I, at ninety-five, have a hard time getting in and out of an automobile when I am taken out for a ride.

==

Before reaching fifty years old, father married. [In 1893 he married Lillian Anthelia Piper.] I thought it was nice. However, on her return from their honeymoon, she said to me, "You are not to leave the yard without first asking me."

The land around us was open fields and forests. I stared at her, turned and walked out of the house. I never once asked her permission to go out of the yard.

==

For years I was a volunteer of the Pacific Grove Fire Department. It took a good twenty strong men to pull the water hose cart. We marched in all the parades with it. We went as far as Salinas and Watsonville for firemen's drill or competed in the "Hose Race." There were few fires, but I was there. After I left the brigade, I still went to the fires when I heard the alarm.

There was a paper drive to save the trees. Folks collected newspapers and packed them down in the basement of the Congregational

Church. One day the paper caught fire and burned the church to the ground.

Another fire broke out in the closet of the second or third floor of Hotel El Carmelo. We soon put that out.

The loft of the Mammoth Stables where hay and feed was kept burst into flames. The horses were led to the corral in the back of the building. The fire was put out before it did any great damage. When the automobile era began, the stables were dismantled.

All Pacific Grove turned out when there was a fire on 19th and Lighthouse. My father stood there with other fathers of boys my age running in and out of the burning house, to save the owner's furniture and things. When the fire was under control, my father said to me, "I am very proud of you for the way you handled the furniture and the way you put it down outside. Very proud of you."

What Father said made me feel good.

Later, fire hydrants were supplied for by the City. At citizens' request, some were placed close to their homes. City-supplied water was used to put out a fire no matter how much water was used.

=

On April 18, 1906, the earthquake struck San Francisco. We felt it in Pacific Grove. However, the fire that burnt Chinatown here occurred on May 15, 1906.

During spring and summer, the Chinese went out with lit boats into the sea to attract squid. Tons of squid were brought to shore, and spread out on land to dry out. The stench was terrible. It drove the tourists away. Property owners in Pacific Grove and Monterey wanted the city to do something about this.

Chinatown was built in four sections of two-room cottages backed up to a narrow alley to the beach. Pacific Improvement Company supplied Chinatown with water, and a fire hydrant in the center of town, with a four-inch wide fire hose within reach of all the houses.

A fire started that spread to three sections of Chinatown. Every Chinaman deserted his home and belongings and went to China Point. Not one of them fought the fire. I tried to save some of the things for them. I ran into the biggest store there, jumped on the counter to save the merchandise, handing it to the folks there, telling them to save it for the Chinese. Instead, they just looted Chinatown. When the blaze was over, I was on the railway track by the section of Chinatown that did not burn down. There I saw a young man throwing a lit torch into a building, then threw a can of fuel after it. It went off with a bang. With an ax in his hand, he ran to the fire hose to cut it. I recognized him as a city employee. Soon after, he left town with his wife and two children.

That was the end of old Chinatown.

=

Everyone had to keep their shades up at nighttime, as playing cards, dancing and drinking were not allowed in Pacific Grove. Father, Mr. Jubb, a retired man from England, and Mr. Noyes, Bill's father, who went to Central America once a year to look after his sheep business there, invested in building the Mariposa Building on Lighthouse Avenue in New Monterey, for people to go to dance and have fun. Father gave me a new pair of dancing shoes. I took them with me to the Mariposa Building, hung around with other boys at the front door, even went inside to look, but was too shy to learn to dance. I never did learn to dance. Mariposa Building became a white elephant.[6]

---

6 Mariposa Hall still stands at 801 Lighthouse Avenue in New Monterey, just over the Pacific Grove city line. In an advertisement in the *Monterey Peninsula Herald*, September 28, 1956, Rudolph's, the store that took over Mariposa Hall in 1906, commemorated fifty years

=

Father made his final move. He opened his store on Lighthouse Avenue and 17th Street, Pacific Grove, about 1897. The back of the building faced the Chautauqua Hall on Central and 17th Street. He placed a large sign above the front of the store, clear across, covering the full front from end-to-end, R.L. HOLMAN. Inside, the area was large. There were the two counters, one for ladies' wear and general merchandise, the other for menswear with men's suits in the rear. Shelves lined the three walls. In the center of the store, the length of the counters was a shoe section for men, women and children. I sold many a pair of shoes.

An entrance on 17th Street led into the furniture section. Father stored hundreds of bundles of wallpaper at a time, floor linoleum, straw mattings, window shades, baby buggies and new mattresses laid six to eight feet high. The flooring was of wood, with a few holes in them. Rats lived under the flooring. They never bothered us until one day

---

in business in that location and took out a four-page advertisement detailing more about the origins of the Hall: "The original owners, R.L. Holman, W. J. Judd, and Phillip Oyer, planned the building as the first step in an ambitious enterprise which was to centralize a Peninsula recreation area around Mariposa Hall. As stated in an issue of the *Monterey Cypress* at the time, Mariposa Hall was to serve as a combination community center-social hall for the Peninsula area and the many tourists who flocked to this area during the summers. In addition to the dance floor and reception rooms, the new hall contained a ladies billiard room and one for the men, a cigar stand and even a bowling alley. When the enterprise had proved itself, the plans called for development of a family hotel, a bathhouse at the beach and a system of hot salt water baths. It is interesting to note that the beach in question is now covered by Monterey's famous old Cannery Row. This area was once an excellent bathing area known as McAbee beach. For unknown reasons, Mariposa Hall did not fulfill the owners' dreams, and after a time the building was used for a dancing school. Later, it was considered as a car barn for the horse-drawn trolley cars which once ran between Monterey and Pacific Grove. This did not prove feasible after Lighthouse Avenue was graded and electric cars came into use."

I put traps over the floor holes. The next day we found the new mattresses torn to threads.

Father's office was in the back. Clarence, Stella Dayton, Mr. Ellis, his daughter, two menswear salesmen, the salesman in charge of shoes, and I, worked for Father. When there was a parade in Pacific Grove or Monterey, Clarence rented a four-horse bus, with Holman's banner draped over it; I sat by Clarence as he drove all Father's employees in the bus, down Lighthouse to Lighthouse Avenue in New Monterey to Alvarado Street in Monterey. We waved and smiled at the crowd. In later years we drove in a motor bus, followed by our truck and an automobile in parades.

====

Father's wife had a baby [Ritter Holman] at home. He cried a lot.

Clarence married Estella "Stella" Dawson. Father's wedding present to them was 213 Granite Street. Sister Minnie moved into the Wood Street cottage. Shortly after my return from San Jose, I moved into a rented cottage with another fellow. Aunt Minora went to live with her relatives, the Moores[7], in Monterey.

Father said to me, "Come home. There are so many rooms there. It is so empty now." I said, "No." However, I was there with him at the store daily, except when it was closed on Sundays. On weekends I tidied his desk, usually piled high with paperwork. On Mondays, he'd say, "Now I can't find a thing!"

---

7 Aunt Minora lived with her niece, Nina (Badger) Moore. Nina's mother was Celia (Holman) Badger, R.L. and Minora's sister, who moved from Vermont to California with Nina and her mother Rachel (Mann) Holman in 1886.

My sister Minnie was an intelligent young lady. She firmly believed a lady should not work at a store, but should marry. She graduated from high school, but since she did not want to work at the store, she went back to school for three more years and graduated for the second time.

After Father died, she and I moved into the Lobos Avenue house. She made a comfortable home life for us, and became engaged to a banker [Andrew Steven] who gave her a diamond ring, which she lost, so he gave her another. Theirs was a good marriage; they had a girl [Barbara (Steven) Emo Capodilista] and a boy [Hugh Washburn Steven]. Minnie lived to be ninety-five years old.

=

Work at the store grew heavy. I worked there days into the small hours in the morning dusting shelves, straightening merchandise, marking them with both cost and retail prices for inventory purposes, cleaning floors, washing windows, etc., as I had done since I was a boy.

There was a big trade for floor mattings. All sizing of mattings had to be done on the sidewalk after store hours. I'd do that. Then the employees came back at eight at night to sew them together—in-out and under.

Indeed, we were fortunate to have such loyal employees. Some stayed with me for over thirty years. Some visit us now!

=

Rodmere was my faithful German police dog for sixteen years. He was a pup from the first litter of the first pair of German police dogs brought to the United States after they were smuggled out of Germany.

══

I went to visit my brother Clarence at his ranch in Aromas. He raised apricots, apples, and sheep. He said to me, "Wiff, get out of the store into the fresh air." Unexpectedly, his ram butted me ten feet from where I stood. I decided then and there that I preferred to work for Father.[8]

══

Father's health failed. About 1904, he left his wife to go to his ranch in Linden, twenty miles from Stockton. Aunt Minora went along to look after him. They lived like old-time settlers with the barest of necessities. Father tried to raise grapes, but it was too late for him to profit by it. He and Aunt Minora were happy with their chickens and visits from Father's children[9].

A gain, he let me "loose" at the store.

══

One cold winter's day, a creditor of Father's arrived. He said he had come from San Francisco to padlock the store, "and I've come for my money. I am not going to leave without it!" He banged the table as he said this. I explained our store depended on the summer trade. He would get his money after summer. He said, "I've come for my money and I'm not going to leave without it. I'm going out now, you be here when I get back."

---

8 Clarence later purchased a 600-acre ranch in Carmel Valley, calling it Holman Ranch. He " . . . transformed the property into a guest ranch with the only rodeo arena in town. The Holmans . . . built guest bungalows and stables, along with the first inground pool in Carmel Valley." Via the Holman Ranch website, https://www.holmanranch.com/our-story.

9 Minnie stayed with R.L. Holman in Linden for extended periods, corresponding with W.R. Holman.

He returned in fifteen minutes. He ordered me to, "Get your check-book out." I said, "You'd get me in trouble, the account is overdrawn now." He banged the desk.

"Get your checkbook out," commanded a man from the bankruptcy court who came to padlock the store. I took out the checkbook. He stood over me. "Now write."

I wrote twelve checks dated on the first of the month for a year. He took the checks, saying, "The money must be in the bank on the due dates."

Later I learned that in the fifteen minutes he was gone from my of-fice, he went to see Mr. Eckhart, cashier for years and years with the Pacific Grove Bank, who said to him, "If you close him out, you'd get fifteen cents to the dollar. If you leave the boy alone, you may get more or you will get all of it."

That was the last time anyone called me "Boy." I was twenty, five foot eleven and a half, one hundred thirty-five to one hundred fifty pounds, depending on how hard I worked.

The amount owing was forty thousand dollars. It was difficult, yet all the checks I signed were paid on the due dates.

I slept in the room under father's office. My working hours were now longer than before. All night I marked merchandise and cleaned the store. I finished working at seven, unlocked the front door so the employees could come in at eight to work, then went to bed. At eight, my senior clerk kicked at my door, "Get out of that bed and get to work." From that time on, no matter how tired I was, I opened the door at eight to welcome my faithful employees.

I did what I had to do. Sweep the floors, wash the windows, straighten out the shelves, attend to customers, deliver orders, receive shipments of merchandise, mark them for sale, and so on, and so on. I dreamed then of having the finest department store in Pacific Grove, just like the Emporium building in San Francisco. This dream, after many years of hard work, became a reality.

═══

In 1907 my Aunt Minora died, and Father passed away in Linden in 1909. They are buried in Sacramento by my mother's grave.

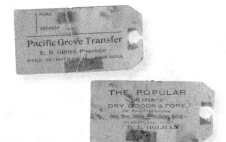

Top: *Hang tag for E.B. Gross, which would be fixed to the luggage of new arrivals in town (front).* Bottom: *E.B. Gross hang tag (back), advertising The Popular.*

A receipt from Towle & Holman.

Left: *Cover of* Good Dress *by Towle & Holman, Fall and Winter catalog from 1897-1898.*
Right: *A page from* Good Dress *by Towle & Holman.*

Pacific Grove business license issued to G. W. Towle for a Dry Goods store in 1891. This is the business license that would be used for The Popular.

The signage in front of The Popular.

Charlie Clup of Clup Bros. standing in front of The Popular.

Interior of R.L. Holman's. R.L. Holman is second from the left.

Interior of Holman's, 1898. Left to right: Andrew W. Anderson (of Mr. Holman's gold piece/two-cent piece trick), F.W. Ellis, R.L. Holman, and Miss Ellis.

Holman's Department Store participating in a parade in Pacific Grove, 1907.

The fire brigade, July 4, 1904, at 9th Street and Lighthouse in Pacific Grove. W.R. Holman is second from the right, standing.

Business card for W.R. Holman when representing his father.

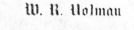

W.R. Holman and Rodmere.

The Holman siblings, early 1900s, from left to right: W.R., Minnie, and Clarence.

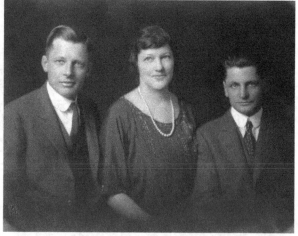

5

My Career in Pacific Grove

TO REMINISCE ABOUT MY CAREER AT AGE NINETY-FIVE, AND ADD eight months to that, I find myself timewise going backwards and forwards, forwards and backwards to tell it.

After Father's death, there was the matter of probate. For seven years it lasted. On the first of the month, Silas Mack, my father's attorney, went with me to the Superior Court in Salinas to settle the matter. Every month the judge said, "Holman's case postponed to 10:30 o'clock on the first of next month."

Silas Mack was a fine man. He, his family, and my Aunt Minora were members of the Congregational Church. At the end of seven years, he called upon the estate for his fee: "For seven years service my charge is $3,000 to be credited to Silas Mack's account at Holman's Department Store. My family will draw on my account for their merchandise at Holman's."

Mr. Mack died before his wife did. She visited their two missionary sons in South America. She died there about 1978.

==

Holman's closed on Sundays. I went to Lovers Point. I love the Pacific Ocean and the bay. Never, never get tired of it. I stopped to talk to the folks there, especially the Donkey Man. His name was Mr. Alison. He rented out donkeys for rides and to be hitched to surreys for tourists by the day in the summertime ever since the early days of the Del Monte Hotel in Monterey and the El Carmelo Hotel in Pacific Grove. He owned twenty donkeys, saddles and surreys. He was getting on in years. He said to me, "I'll tell you what I'll do for you. You give me $25 a month as long as I live and I'll give you my property in Pacific Grove." I took him up on that, though it was hard for me to raise $25 a month for him and fix up his old buildings. He sold out his business. A few years later he went to his brother down south and died.

When the time came, I donated most of his property to be used for city parking in Pacific Grove. I retained an old building for myself.

==

The population in Pacific Grove doubled since I was a boy. The census reported in 1910 that there were about 1,000 people in Pacific Grove and 2,500 in Monterey. In 1920 the population doubled. The tourists as usual flocked in by the thousands.

A bookkeeper was hired to look after the cash and thirty-day credit accounts at Holman's. I saw to it that our shelves were well stocked with merchandise at competitive prices, because I worked through the Board of Trade in San Francisco. They sent me the list of bankrupt stores in Northern California, giving me the dates of inspection and the time sealed bids must be in their office. Bidders must attend the auction on the day these bids were opened. I became quite knowledgeable as to the value of all kinds of merchandise, and my sealed bids were always a little higher than a group known as the "forty thieves."

A day came when they approached me not to bid. They will do the bidding and give me the stock for less than they paid for it.

The finest shoe store in Monterey, "Bertold," folded. Their three attorneys held the auction there. The "forty thieves" were at this auction. They saw me and made me the offer not to bid. However, I did bid. Again I was the successful bidder. What a rumpus there was!

Once or twice locally, I bought out a whole store; the sale at the hat store was so successful, I had to close the door on one group of women in there, then let them out before allowing the women waiting on the sidewalk in to buy hats.

Our nearby farmlands grow an abundance of fresh produce. An extension was built at the back of the store for our deliveryman to bring the truckloads of fresh vegetables and fruit for our customers to buy.

A "WANT BOOK" was placed in each department to put requests for items we did not carry. These customer requests were ordered for the store to carry on its shelves. The store's reputation was: "If you can't get it anywhere else, get it at Holman's."

Holman's is a family store. We served thousands of people with thousands of needs. It has been my life's work to serve my loyal customers.

WILFORD R. HOLMAN

PRESIDENT
HOLMAN'S DEPARTMENT STORE

W.R. Holman's business card.

6

My Wife, Zena Georgina Patrick

A TRAVELING SALESMAN CALLED ON ME AT THE STORE. I TOLD HIM I needed a good salesgirl in the Ladies' Ready-to-Wear Department. He said, "I have just the girl for you." He gave me the phone number of the store Zena Patrick was working for in Salinas. She answered. I told her who I was, then asked, "Can you talk?"

"Of course I can talk," she answered.

When she came to apply for the job, I was returning from home, and I met her on the sidewalk in front of the store. She was a slim, beautiful girl with lovely brown hair on which she wore a big hat with a large ostrich plume. I took to her right away.

I had with me a little brown dog; its fur matched my brown suit, brown hat, and shoes. Later she told me she liked me at first sight.

Father had bought a quantity of handsome ladies' suits that became out of style. Zena looked them over in a most professional way. "I can sell this stock only for the yardage in them at $2.50 a suit." I gave her the job right away, then I proudly walked with her up Lighthouse Avenue to a rooming house on Pacific Avenue (a few blocks from Lobos where Minnie and I lived) so Zena Patrick could arrange for her room. Next day she returned with her belongings and started to work at the store. Right away we enlarged the Ready-to-Wear Department to sell the old, expensive ladies' suits for $2.50 each.

In no time the old stock was sold. Zena bought new stock to take its place. Shortly after that, I started calling her "Pat." She was very popular with customers, and soon established an excellent following. She worked at the store for some time before we became engaged. One day we took the Southern Pacific passenger train to San Francisco with the alteration lady and my good friend and store assistant, Walter Whitney, to witness our marriage there. When we arrived, we learned all the ministers were attending a convention in Pacific Grove. Finally we found a parson who was in his work clothes doing his gardening. I asked him to marry us. He said, "Not in these clothes." We waited for him to change. He married Pat and me in the parlor with all due formality.

The two-story house on Lobos was our first home. Minnie moved in with Minnie Johnston, the sister of the Johnston brothers on Cedar Street I'll tell you about later. She became my children's "Aunt Donnie." Pat had her first baby at the Lobos house. I was the first to lay eyes on our daughter Patricia Whitcomb Holman when she was born. Five years later we moved to 213 Granite Street, the house Father gave to Clarence when he married. Clarence sold it to me, and our daughter Harriet Hope Holman was born there.

With all her house chores, Pat soon worked right along by my side at the store. Now we worked days and way into the nights, but we were happy because, as Pat said, "We were young, healthy, ambitious and very much in love."

Seven years after father died, the Superior Court in Salinas granted the settlement of his will. The attorney there congratulated me on the management of Holman's Store. He said, "I never thought you'd make it."

That afternoon when I returned to Pacific Grove, I was told the judge cancelled his order to settle the will at the request of the two lawyers representing father's widow. I immediately called for a meeting. Pat went with me to 769 Lighthouse where Mrs. Lillian Holman lived since her marriage to my father. Her two lawyers were there too.

I offered my resignation at the store. I was tired of working so hard and having this bickering. I would leave the store. They cried out, "Oh, don't do that! No one but you can run the store!" His widow and her son got the cash from the sale of the ranch in Linden after that mortgage was paid off.

In this way I inherited father's mortgaged property in Pacific Grove and we became more frugal than ever. Every spare nickel we saved went right back into the store, and to pay the mortgages. We had no car. We had no washing machine. Pat hand-washed our laundry. I repaired our old houses. Our tenants were poor. One burned the front steps for firewood. Once while fixing a roof, I fell off it to the sidewalk.

Pat and I worked as one. Our success was a joint endeavor. Our marriage was a lovely life. My dear Pat. I miss her.

On leaving 769 Lighthouse, Mrs. Lillian Holman sold father's Vermont furniture to a dealer. I rented out the house as is until Pat made it ready for us to move into it. We loved it. Our front garden was covered with clover leaves. Pat saved a few with a note attached: HANDLE WITH CARE PLEASE.

Soon after the will was settled, I incorporated Holman's Department Store. Equal amounts of stock were issued to my brother, sister, and myself. I was its President, and Pat the Secretary, both lifetime assignments. My brother and sister were not interested in working at the store.[10]

———————

10 However, their children's spouses would prove instrumental to running the store later.

Zena Patrick Holman as a young woman (note the plume!).

Storefront of T.C. Reavis and Company in Salinas, where Zena Patrick worked before Holman's.

Zena (front) and W.R. (back left, laughing), with a friend out for a ride in their spring wagon. The Carmel Mission is behind them.

Employee card for Zena Patrick at Holman's.

W.R. Holman and Zena eating watermelon.

W.R. Holman holding Patricia Holman outside their home on Lobos Street.

The Patrick siblings at 213 Granite Street: (left to right) Veda Patrick, Patricia Holman (little girl in front), George Patrick in back, Gladys Patrick, Zena Patrick Holman, and Victor Patrick.

Zena Holman with her daughters Patricia (left) and Harriet (right).

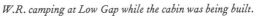

W.R. camping at Low Gap while the cabin was being built.

Low Gap cabin.

Mr. and Mrs. Holman on the deck of their log cabin in Low Gap, Ukiah, California. *"A thousand logs it took to build this cabin,"* said W.R. The fireplace, built by Mrs. Holman's brother Victor Patrick, was big enough for a person to stand inside. Jeffrey Steven Rensselaer Barter (Harriet (Holman) Barter's son) lived here in the late 1970s. From 1981-1983, Genie (O'Meara) Lazare (at the time) lived here with her husband Michel Daniel Lazare and their two children, Zachary Bernard Lazare and Benjamin Eugene Lazare.

W.R. Holman on his 84th birthday, August 28, 1968, with his daughter Patricia (Holman) O'Meara at the cabin in Low Gap.

7

Holman's Department Store

LIFE IN PACIFIC GROVE BEFORE WORLD WAR I HAD A PIONEER QUALITY. Not half the homes had indoor plumbing. Houses were heated by pot-bellied stoves, fireplaces, or kitchen range. To clean a rug, it was hung on a line in the backyard and beaten. Grass was cut with a sickle.

I slept, ate, and worked at R. L. Holman, then situated in a building on 17th and Lighthouse which father leased for twenty years before retiring to Linden. At the time the store was incorporated, two painters from an outdoor advertising company, each starting from opposite ends of the store sign, worked towards the center of it, changing the name of the store from R. L. Holman, to read:

HOLMAN'S DEPARTMENT STORE (1914)

When the entire population of Monterey County, including the coast and Carmel Valley, was less than 15,000, I had for years more than thirty billboards throughout the county. The signs drew business to Holman's as well as to the entire Peninsula when, as a whole, the

Peninsula was not known to the thousands of tourists passing from north to south and south to north. Thus Monterey and Holman's grew and prospered from this additional business.

Most of the signs were ten-feet tall and fifty-feet long; one was only thirty-feet long. The one in downtown Monterey was sixty-feet long. It could be seen all over town.

Valley & Green painted billboards to advertise the advance coming of circuses throughout the world. When they were in Monterey, I went to them and hired their rapid painters to paint the billboards I had put up to advertise R. L. Holman. These same men worked on our store sign to read Holman's Department Store.

Every week I sent out printed circulars advertising Holman's merchandise. Frank Mendoza was my distributor. He walked from house to house, putting a circular on the porch and weighing it down with a rock. It took him a week to cover Pacific Grove, Carmel, Monterey, Oak Grove, and Seaside. He did this for me for fourteen or fifteen years. For seven years before, he drove a wagon always loaded with fresh produce for Mr. King, the grocer in Monterey. He did things slowly. I never once saw him trot or gallop his horse; he walked his horse as it pulled the wagon to and from Seaside. Much of Holman's success is due to the long walks Frank Mendoza made for me.

Frank married one of the King girls and he finally became a director of Tom Work's Pacific Grove Bank. Tom owned nearly everything on the Peninsula and abouts.

Each year for about forty years, Holman's Department Store contracted for billboard space to advertise its merchandise. These signs extended beyond Watsonville almost to Santa Cruz and beyond King City. They have been the means of bringing hundreds of thousands of dollars of business to the Peninsula, especially at Christmastime. The money otherwise would never have been spent here.

We stopped using billboard signs when Monterey County issued a zoning ordinance to do away with advertising on billboards. Yes, it was time to stop. By then Holman's was well-known. Some people called Pacific Grove City, the Holman City.

MY FRIENDS THE JOHNSTONS

Mr. and Mrs. Johnston, with their grown children, Ed Johnston, a well-built man, and Charlie Johnston and Minnie Johnston, came from San Jose. They settled on nearly a block of land on Cedar Street, between Laurel and Short Streets, a few blocks from us.

Ten days before they arrived in Pacific Grove, there was a big wind-storm that blew down a pine tree on the land they bought. I chopped it free from the ground and into four-foot lengths, tied a rope around them to drag them to our barn.

I saw the Johnstons for the first time on the day they came to town from San Jose. Mr. & Mrs. Johnston, their two husky sons, and three equally husky helpers, and their daughter Minnie, drove up in a heavy truck drawn by two horses. They had followed my tracks down the street, saw the four-foot lengths of pine in our barn. They did not say a word to me, nor did I speak to them when the men leapt out of the truck, loaded the pine into it, and drove off.

This incident was never once mentioned by my father or any of us. But they took to me and I took to them. They invited me to special meals and I went with them in their boat to gather abalone near the 17 Mile Drive. For vacation I went with them to the back hills near King City.

The Johnston brothers took special care to build their storage house on Cedar Street according to the permit issued by the Pacific Improvement Company.

The foundation is one-foot deep, lined with bricks. On this they put up four strong walls of redwood and redwood shakes dipped in linseed oil for the roof. The wood came from Santa Cruz mills.

Windows and two side entrances were installed. A heavy sliding door covered the whole front entrance. Above it, the loft door opened outwards. The storage house looked like a huge, beautiful country barn.

Of very special note is the spacious loft, supported by sturdy posts set firmly on a heavy brick foundation. Ladders placed against them led to the loft.

This 30-ft x 60-ft x 20-ft building is well built. It has withstood eight decades of heavy winds and rain. It has housed thousands of tons of storage such as household furniture, crates, pianos, trunks, suitcases, hand grips, horses, hay, feed, rocks, cement, lumber, odds and ends, transfer trucks, diesel trucks—you name it—was stored there.

The Johnston brothers serviced thousands of tourists. They met all the trains. 25¢ to transfer a trunk. 15¢ for suitcase or hand grip. They moved furniture for every household in Pacific Grove. Not once, but many times. The Johnstons were highly respected citizens. The storage house was a center of activity. When there was an overflow of unpaid storage, I was asked to hold an auction to sell closed boxes, crates, things. Built around it were cottages with gardens and shrubs—all this on the Johnston's land. Ed, Charles, and Minnie never married. The brothers built a cottage on the storage house grounds to sleep in and ate at Minnie's when Mr. and Mrs. Johnston died.

One day, Ed ruptured himself. Minnie made him give up on the transfer business. Charles operated it until he died. Ed joined the trustee-governed City of Pacific Grove as City Clerk. He came to see me when I worked on the Pacific Grove Charter. Ed threatened to sue me. When the Charter was voted in, Ed joined the Pacific Grove Bank as its bank clerk. On weekends and holidays he was usually seen at the cemetery helping the families clean up the graveyard.

Ed died. Minnie rented the storage house to a riding school. They put in stalls for horses and stored feed, hay, and saddles. The building was vacated and Minnie sold me the storage house and the land on which it stands.

My wife's brother, Victor, who worked for me, cemented the floor of the building. For years we kept all kinds of things there. I became quite ill for years and left the well-built storage house to look after itself, and the oaks on the lots.

In 1978, my wife Zena and I deeded the storage house and lots on Cedar Street to Louise V. Jaques, who, for nearly a decade, has faithfully served us in all the necessary capacities to keep us comfortable.

It is my earnest wish she will enjoy this gift to her of this storage house erected so carefully by two great citizens of Pacific Grove, Ed Johnston and his brother Charles Johnston. [Louise Jaques sold this property in the early 1980s. The barn was torn down and a new home was built in its place; 240 Cedar Street.]

Holman's Department Store receipt.

Holman's exterior, 1924.

Billboard for Holman's and the Santa Claus Special.

Right: *Hang tag from the Johnston's Bros. Transfer and Storage Co. (front).* Bottom: *The reverse side of this hang tag is an advertisement for Holman's. W.R. Holman used these tags to strike up business as soon as people arrived in Pacific Grove, as his father had done with The Popular.*

The Johnston's barn on Cedar Street.

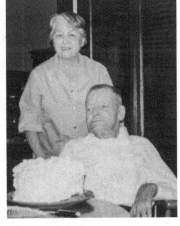

W.R. Holman and Louise V. Jaques, 1975.

8

The New Holman's Department Store

THE PACIFIC IMPROVEMENT COMPANY OWNED THE EL CARMELO HOTEL on Lighthouse Avenue. It was built before father arrived here. The hotel was renamed Pacific Grove Hotel because its mail was sent to Carmel in error.

After World War I, due to high taxation, the hotel was being dismantled. I watched it torn down board by board and carried away. Charlie Omstead, the hotel manager, stood outside his office on the other side of Lighthouse. I walked over to him and said, "Charlie, I'll give you $10,000 for that block of land the hotel is on." (I did not have $10,000.)

Charlie shook his head. "Don't think P. I. will consider it." I started up the street back to the Store when I heard Charlie holler, "Holman come back. The P. I. attorney wants to talk to you." I went back and we talked. The attorney said, "I'd take your offer to the P. I. Company in San Francisco tonight, but I know they will say no. I'll phone you tomorrow."

Next day he phoned to say I could have the land and to take all the time I needed to pay for it on a six-percent basis. I took him up on this.

I told my board of directors I had bought the El Carmelo block for $10,000. They said, "It isn't worth it, but we'll take it."

The lovely garden in front of the El Carmelo was left as it was. I put in swings and a slide so children could play there, and closed the garden when a child hurt himself. The Pacific Grove Chautauqua of 1922 erected a tent there for their meetings. The Durant car agency was housed in a building at the back of the block. It became a 24-hour Square to the Cent garage, servicing hundreds of cars. To advertise it there was a large carpenter's square with an emblem of a penny on the roof.

The last year of father's twenty-year lease at 17th and Lighthouse Avenue for Holman's store was now upon us. The property was sold. We had nowhere to go. I had to build on the Carmelo block.

The bank loaned me the money and excavation of the grounds began. Every foot of the foundation had to be blasted. In doing this I nearly lost the whole of Lighthouse Avenue. One Pacific Grove Supervisor said he wished I would do just that! To build Holman's, 12'x12' posts had to be set properly and fastened with cables to the property across the street! Rock and gravel, scooped up from the excavation, piled up as high as the Holman building. It was called Holman Mountain. Children played on top of it. When Pacific Grove High School was being built, I gave the mountain to a contractor for the School Board to fill in the large hole on their land for a playground. With Holman's Mountain gone, I built the much needed parking lot and bought more land in that area to build the present Holman Appliance building and parking space.

In this Depression period, people said, "Holman is building his monument. Where is he going to get the business?" In six months we had our basement, first, and second floor built. The whole town danced on each floor as it was completed!

All merchandise in the old store were packed and boxed. Showcases, shelves, and tables were brought to the new building and put in the places I marked off for each department. We had no money to build new shelves and things then. Little by little Holman's was beautified. It was written up in publications on the Peninsula. In a year's time, I repaid the loan. The Manager said, "Holman's is not a department store, it is a gold mine!"

=

Joe Cramer from San Jose introduced me to buying small shops and stores through the Board of Trade. They sent lists of foreclosures from San Francisco and Los Angeles bankruptcy courts. From this I found merchandise I needed for Holman's. I, sometimes with Pat, went far and wide in the state to see these stores. In the San Francisco court area, I submitted closed bids. In the Los Angeles court area, I made open bids. Fortunately, my early training in merchandising made my bids highly competitive with those of the old-timers in the field of bidding. This profited me greatly.

I acquired a small five-and-ten-cent store south of San Francisco. I drove up there in my pickup with a trailer attached to it. I packed and boxed all the inventory, loaded them into the pickup and put all the showcases, shelves, and things that came with the bid into the trailer. It was 3:00 a.m. before I started for Pacific Grove. A few miles out of Salinas, the police stopped me because there was no back light on my trailer. Another delay was in Salinas to get the light put on. I got home a very, very tired man!

When I bought more than one store in an area, two Holman's clerks helped me pack, box, and load merchandise into huge trucks. Once Pacific Railroads let me have two boxcars to transport my goods to Pacific Grove.

==

The new Holman's, built in 1924, had four floors, 100,000 square feet, 46 departments and 200 employees. Pat became the main buyer in charge of eight or ten buyers to keep Holman's up-to-date in merchandise. Holman's became the finest mercantile establishment on the Monterey Peninsula. Our Slogan—"We sell everything that men, women and children use, wear or eat!"

Holman's employees were our family. For years they shared our hard work, our joys and prosperity as Holman's grew. Yet our relationship towards one another was formal. We addressed one another as Mr., Mrs., or Miss.

The El Carmelo Hotel, which would become the site of Holman's Department Store.

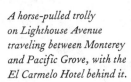

A horse-pulled trolly on Lighthouse Avenue traveling between Monterey and Pacific Grove, with the El Carmelo Hotel behind it.

Looking from the El Carmelo Hotel toward Lighthouse Avenue.

W.R. Holman standing over the excavation of Lighthouse Avenue between Grand and Fountain Avenues.

Jim Grenier at the plow excavating for Holman's. Credit: Kimball Burton Studio.

Hundreds gathered at the 1924 opening of Holman's, where a town dance took place.

Holman's employees from their Christmas ad.

9

Memories of Monterey and Pacific Grove

EACH YEAR, DURING CONVENTION[11] TIME, WEALTHY TOURISTS FROM all over the world came to see the gardens with the beautiful floral effects in every section of the grounds of Monterey's luxurious Del Monte Hotel and its country club, kept so lovely by the hundred picturesque queued Chinese gardeners. The tourists were especially attracted to the evergreen-shielded maze, which is an intricate network of paths where people were sometimes so confused they were unable to find their way out.

Del Monte Hotel was opened by the Pacific Improvement Company on June 3, 1880, which was the 110th anniversary of the founding of

---

11 Joyce and I believe when W.R. referred to a "convention" he meant the Chautauqua gatherings, which were held during the summertime, and which ended with a Chinese lantern festival on the final day. Chautauqua was an adult education movement, started on the east coast of the United States during the 1800s; communities would come together to enjoy music, entertainment, and cultural learning. Chautauqua Hall, built in 1881, where many of these events would take place, is still standing and located at 16th Street and Central Avenue in downtown Pacific Grove.

Monterey. The hotel, in 1942, was leased to the Navy as a flight school. In 1951 it became the Naval Post Graduate School.

Outstanding bands were hired to play on the bandstand a hundred feet from the Del Monte Hotel itself. One year, Sousa's band from New York came to play for us, an occasion I will always remember.

On the last day of the convention, Chinese lanterns were strung, lighted by thousands of candles, [and] hung from the oaks throughout the gardens. The outside refreshment bar was located about four-hundred feet south of the main entrance of the hotel and a continuous stream of well-dressed people were going and coming from the bar in the evening until late at night.

Where the airport is today, there was a racetrack owned by the P. I. Company. Some of the hotel guests or members brought their race stock with them and stabled them at the racetrack. It was not uncommon for those at the hotel to bet on the races before breakfast.

P. I. Company maintained the largest stables in the U.S.A. These were connected with the hotel where riding horses, carts, buggies, and a large Tally-Ho—a four-in-hand coach with a footman in the rear blowing a horn—took guests around the 17 Mile Drive.

The drivers of the Tally-Ho were experienced horsemen and safe drivers who went around the curves and the straight roads on a dead run. The most breathless part of the Tally-Ho 17 Mile Drive in Pebble Beach was the Loop at Cypress Point—now closed off. It is close to the edge of cliffs with a twenty-foot drop into the Pacific Ocean.

I took my spring wagon on this route many times, but I would never ride it in a Tally-Ho. Besides, these rides were reserved for the wealthy guests of the Del Monte Hotel! Even President Teddy Roosevelt would not ride a Tally-Ho. "Give me a horse and saddle," he said. I saw my favorite President, Teddy Roosevelt, many times, once when he gave a speech on Lighthouse Avenue and Forest in Pacific Grove. His picture is hung prominently in the downstairs front room at 769 Lighthouse Avenue.

A Tally-Ho boarded its passengers at the Del Monte Hotel, went through New Monterey, then through Pacific Grove, through the Forest Hill Gate, around the 17 Mile Drive, returning to the hotel via the gate on top of Carmel Hill, and through Monterey on a dead run!

One day, Clarence and I were slowly riding in a borrowed "seat cart" drawn by a heavy white horse. As we neared Seal Beach, a Tally-Ho came upon us from the opposite side. It did not slow down. Instead, we were run off the road into the ditch as the Tally-Ho speeded away.

I knew Ellick, a Tally-Ho driver, well. He was a great storyteller and took time to entertain his passengers. On the way from the hotel to the 17 Mile Drive, he would stop at Smith's Curio Shop in New Monterey, in front of which was a large tree trunk, about twenty-five feet high, with abalone shells fastened on it so thick that the trunk of the tree did not show. Ellick told his riders that abalone grew there. It was the Abalone Tree.

=

I developed an urge to preserve the natural beauty and resources of our coast. As a boy I'd spend hours by the Monterey Bay shore. One day I spotted Japanese fishermen harvesting the abalone that lay thick on our coast. I began fighting for its preservation about 1917.

=

The city of Monterey, for years was an old sleepy town. Its streets and adobe buildings, some still lived-in, built during the Spanish and Mexican days, were all in very, very bad condition.

Tents were scattered here and there. The Indians lived in them with all their domestic animals. When the tents were laden with fleas, they moved their tents.

Indian bucks came to town. I only saw the squaws in the acorn season, when one hundred or more of them picked acorns off the Del Monte property. They then disappeared. I never did find out where the squaws went to.

=

Outside of stock raising in Monterey, there was a small fishing industry controlled for years by the Decarte family, Spanish people. Fishermen were mostly Portuguese or Chinese.

The Monterey Old Wharf was controlled by the Motley brothers. They operated the South Coast Steamship Company. Their ship, the *Gypsy* plied the coast from San Francisco to Los Angeles, stopping at ports along the way to pick up and deliver cargo. In Monterey, the *Gypsy* landed her cargo on shore by cable from an anchorage point, about where the Coast Guard warehouses are.

The *Gypsy* was wrecked at McAbee Beach, off the center of Cannery Row.

There was another ship, the *Saint Paul*, bought by the Southern Pacific Company from the Alaska Commercial Company, owners of trading posts and stores in Alaska for fur trading and general merchandising. My mother's sister Lettie was married to M. L. Washburn, manager of the Alaska Commercial Company.

For years the *Saint Paul* visited coastal ports as she sailed from San Francisco to Los Angeles. She was wrecked between Restless Sea and Cypress Point near Joe's Point in Pebble Beach.

=

I knew Joe, a middle-aged China man, his long hair worn in a plait. He settled on the coast away from his fellow men in Chinatown. He built his house of driftwood and raised about twenty-five chickens. He gathered shells and seaweed to fill his baskets once a month, which he took to sell in Chinatown, carrying them from a bamboo pole over his shoulder as he walked from Pebble Beach to Monterey.

On the beaches near where Joe lived, there were thirty-foot banks of smooth, shiny, colored pebbles about 1 to 1-1/2 inch in diameter. People came in wagons to haul them off to make garden walks, walls, and even sidewalks, until the banks of pebbles were gone.

=

Sidewalks on Alvarado were boardwalks. At intervals there was a step to cover up the unleveled parts of the street. In winter and when it rained, mud reached to the hubs of our buggies or wagons. Rocks were placed at corners for us to step on to cross the street.

=

Deep colored ice plants bank Pacific Grove's view of Monterey Bay. Over sixty different varieties of wildflowers grow in the Monterey area with poppies everywhere when in season.

Point Lobos Reserve with its perennial shrubs, two or more feet high, with wood bases, and herbs usually less than two-feet high, and its beautiful growth of wildflowers and trees overlooking the Pacific Ocean is an unforgettable vista.

==

When I was a boy, Pacific Improvement Company owned the Del Monte Hotel. When it burnt, they built El Carmelo Hotel with 100 rooms in Pacific Grove. The dining room seated up to 100 people. They also owned and operated the water company that supplied the entire Peninsula with water from the lower dam on Carmel River, the large and small reservoirs that are still in use.

The watermains on Lighthouse Avenue have been used these many years [and] have never been replaced. [They are] still used to service Monterey.

We were seven in the family when we first moved into 769 Lighthouse Avenue. Of course, considering the few people on the Peninsula then, there were no water meters. We had water for the entire block to raise alfalfa for our two cows and four horses; the charge was $1.25 a month, which included the running of sprinklers for twenty-four hours in the summertime, with an extra charge for each cow and horse.

Then we used cesspools, 6x6 ft. and 8-ft. deep.

==

The stagecoach went from Monterey to Big Sur once a week. I was about sixteen when I took this trip. Two or more lady schoolteachers, a Chinese who lived on the coast, and I were the passengers.

About halfway to Big Sur, going over the steep mountain road, the teachers asked the driver to stop the coach so they could pick the golden wild poppies along the road in the bushes. After a short time they returned and we continued our trip to Big Sur.

Half a mile later, the Chinese asked the coachman to stop. "I want to pick poppies!" The driver paid no attention to him and kept going! In a little while the Chinese hollered out to the driver, "If you don't stop and let me get out to pick poppies, I'm going to pick poppies right here in the stage!"

The driver stopped. The Chinese hopped off the coach. I followed him in a hurry. We disappeared into the bushes on the mountainside covered with golden poppies.

What a relief! We returned to the stage and it went on its way to Big Sur.

—

I roamed the whole of Monterey County. The salt lagoons between Seaside and the Salinas River were most of the time covered over with wild fowl that the water was not visible. It was as though a sheet was thrown over the Salinas River! On the banks of lakes were flocks of wild fowl in different shades, the canvas-back ducks, mallards, and other species.

—

I love The Carmel Valley. There were thousands of quail. At every hundred yards I drove with horse and buggy, large covey of quail scattered for the hills on the side.

Coyotes, fox, raccoons, and other varmints were plentiful, but it did not affect the wild game. No man-made rules to protect the abundance of wild game, nature took care of the supply!

Deer was in abundance everywhere, since the Indian days. It was hunted mainly for its hide. On rare occasions its meat was used.

The elk was brought to the Peninsula. They became plentiful. They destroyed people's yards and plants. These huge elks, the head the size of a double door, were herded into boxcars at the Pacific Grove cemetery, and sent away from the Peninsula.

==

In my early days, there was no Carmel, and a few scattering of tents and small resort cabins in Pacific Grove, a beautiful virgin of forests with wild birds and animals, by the thousands, now extinct.

Fish and abalone were in abundance on our coast and the Monterey Bay.

I learned to know every mile of this lovely territory and its nearby towns, the Moss Beach, Seaside, Carmel, and Carmel Valley.

To me, Pacific Grove was a lovely large field of trees, wildflowers, birds, butterflies, chickens, cats, dogs, cows, horses, mountains, beaches, and the beautiful bay of Monterey.

W.R. Holman as a young man.

Mr. and Mrs. Holman with their daughter Patricia on Lovers Point Beach, 1915. Patricia Holman is the young girl in the foreground in white on the right, Mrs. Holman sits behind her, in a white hat and gloves, Mr. Holman is behind her, wearing a black hat.

Shoppers visiting Holman's Durant garage.

Portion of the first floor of Holman's Department Store, June 1938.
Credit: Heidrick & Heidrick.

Holman's interior, garden department.
Credit: McKay Photo.

Holman's Department Store Ladies Ready-to-Wear display.

Three generations at Holmans, from left to right: Laurie (Barter) Stanley, Clifford Jeffrey Stanley, Mrs. Holman, Cynthia Joanne Stanley, Harriet (Holman) Barter.

PART II

Newspaper and Magazine Articles,

and the Steinbeck Letters

W.R. Holman

10

From "The Holmans in America," by David Emory Holman, M.D.

ORIGIN OF THE NAME[12]

AN INTERESTING FACT IS THE DERIVATION OF THE NAME HOLMAN. THE root word is "holme," meaning a flat meadow land lying between the windings of a valley stream, therefore the people who lived in such places were called "holmers," or "dwellers in the holmes." One man would be called a "holmer or holman," hence Holman. The name Holmes being a contraction of it. The old English records show distinctly this origin and change.

In ancient times on the Scandinavian Peninsula, the word "Holm—gang" signified that two men would go to an island and fight for possession of it until one died. Then, the other would live in possession of the land, and was a Holmer or Holman.

---

12 "Origin of the Name" and "Preface" from *The Holmans in America*, by David Emory Holman, M.D., appeared in the preface of W.R. Holman's original publication. (Holman, David Emory, M.D. *The Holmans in America*, New York, The Grafton Press, Genealogical Publisher, 1909).

Holman may be a contraction of "Holyman," but is more likely to be "whole man,"—a man of sterling mettle. It must be recollected that in medieval English, whole was spelt without the "w," and the commonest form of the name in the XIV. and XV. Centuries was Holeman.—*Patronymica Britannica*.

It has been suggested that the name Holman is of Dutch origin. This is borne out by a list of foreigners who settled in London in 1567-8. It was necessary for all foreigners who settled in London and other towns to be registered and have permits. The original of this list is at present among the Landsdown, M.S.S., Vol. x, No. 62, British Museum. See also proceedings of Huguenot Society, Vol. 1, pp. 21-24. Dutch Denizens—Hendrick Holman, resident three years; Mary Holman, resident two years (p. xv).

PREFACE

From Pilgrim days of our country's birth, stalwart and honorable men by the name of HOLMAN have cast their lives and energy into the fabric of this great Republic. To-day the Head of the Nation[13] comes of this family through his most noble and gracious mother.

The South has sent out the name to all of the states of the South and West, since the early landings in the beautiful valleys of Virginia at Jamestown in 1607.

The North has spread its character and influence through the name from pulpit, bench and honest ploughshare—from Dorchester, Boston, Salem and the fertile and lofting "Holman Hill" at West Newbury, Mass.

---

13 "Head of the nation" is President William H. Taft, who was in office when David Emory Holman's book was published.

The descendants of the name have passed through every hardship of pioneer life—fought in the battles of hostile Indians—shared in the struggles of early Colonial days—the strife of the Revolution, when sixty-five young men by the name of Holman were on the field from the State of Massachusetts—the War of the Secession, with its long list of sons of the name who conscientiously fought on either side—and even on the Battleship *Maine*, there was on active duty at the time of her destruction in the Harbor of Havana, Cuba, Lieut. George Frederick Warren Holman.

The name has gone out to the New States—to the very mountain-tops—and by the seas, to the ends of the Earth. Out of all the rush of life and its thousand calls upon one's time, some may wish to look backward to their ancestral home and the beginning of their race in America, and to the place where the very tree bending in the wind seems to point the way to the last resting-place, where lie the bodies of Solaman Holman and his wife Mary (Barton) Holman; whose "Beautiful life barques speed on over the rippling seas of Eternity." (p. xi)

The first generation of Holmans in America: concerning the Descendants of Solaman Holman (1671-1753), married (1) Mary Barton (1673-1753), (2) Elizabeth Kelley (1680-1753). All are buried at West Newbury, Massachusetts. Solaman Holman's grandson, Col. Jonathan Holman, 1732-1814, famous hero of the Revolution, is the great-grandfather of Rensselaer L. Holman.[14]

---

14 *The Holmans in America* by David E. Holman, M.D., pgs. 138-139.

11

Game & Gossip Coverage
of the Holmans

GAME & GOSSIP: TODAY & YESTERDAY ON THE MONTEREY PENINSULA, was a magazine published in Monterey, California. Articles featured local citizens and businesses, as well as advertising throughout.

Game & Gossip JUNE 10, 1966, VOLUME 14, NO. 10

THE HOLMAN STORY

As he rode in a surrey, before the turn of the century, along what is now one of the main streets in Pacific Grove, low-growing underbrush tickled the spokes of the wheels.

The spring odor from wild lilac and tall pine trees perfumed the air and the eye looked out on the sparkling blue waters of the Pacific Ocean, curling into a froth of white on the sandy beaches or spraying the ocean rocks along the coast.

Wild birds by the thousands . . . finches and linnets . . . quail so numerous that it took fifteen or twenty minutes before they were disbursed as one hiked through the chaparral near the lighthouse . . . Truly virgin country . . . "so beautiful is it hard to explain."

Truly a bit of paradise. And the earliest memory of Wilford R. Holman whose life has been dedicated to this, his home and family, his community and his work, principally the store that bears his name.

There probably isn't a home on the Monterey Peninsula that doesn't have a bit of Holman's somewhere in its rooms, cupboards or closets, be it draperies, dishes or diapers.

The country store, the old general store, and now the department store, providing the everyday needs of everyday living, is one of the strong links of a community.

As many similar businesses throughout American do, Holman's satisfies most of the needs of today's living. But there's a difference, too, which sets it apart from any other store.

The stark white three-story building is a beacon. It has served as a landmark for seamen, sailors or fishermen, to a get a bearing and recently for airmen, too.

It has been immortalized in literature. John Steinbeck in *Cannery Row* makes several references to Holman's, one of the amusing incidents being the desire of the "homemaker" living in the boiler who isn't happy until she buys curtains at a Holman's sale.[15]

Among its former employees is Richard Boone of "Have Gun Will Travel" who, at one time, was a Christmastime Santa Claus.

Holman's has not only served customers on the Monterey Peninsula but has mailed merchandise abroad, to France, Germany and other European countries, as well as to the Far East. And always with a "hometown" feeling.

It's been that way and growing more so every year since 1891 when the

---

15 In Chapter 8 of *Cannery Row*, the character Mrs. Malloy's desires curtains from Holman's.

first Holman store was opened in Pacific Grove by the father of the present owner.

Only then, the principal item was dry goods—calico, muslin or percale, to be fashioned into milady's gowns, aprons or beribboned lingerie.

W.R. Holman's eye crinkle up at the corners as he laughs: "Well do I remember that as a lad of 10 or so in knee pants I had to roll all that gingham or percale. The yardage came by the case in long folds a yard wide. We'd lay paper on the floor and start to roll, making the yard-wide into a single fold, 18 inches wide. There'd be hundreds of yards and pretty soon one felt like a machine . . . rolling, rolling, rolling."

He also recalls that one of his important tasks was to dash from school to the store. There was no bank in Pacific Grove so young Wilford was delegated to hitch up the horses and ride to Monterey with the day's receipts.

"Mr. Henry," he continues, "would open up for me after banking hours. This was Charles D. Henry, father of Lou Henry who was married here in Monterey to [President] Herbert Hoover," he reminds.[16]

"Alvarado Street was often a sea of mud. Many times the hubs had a tough time through that mud."

He laughs heartily: "I remember one time especially. I used to hitch the rig lines around the brake. Well, there I was, lines in my hand as the horses took out on a run. I was jerked and then dragged through all that mud as though I were on a sled."

Wilford Rensselaer Holman was about four years old when the family moved to Pacific Grove from Sacramento.

"The trip took three days," he told. "We came in a surrey drawn by two black horses, Nell and Puss. The first night we stopped at our ranch in Stockton and the next night we stopped at Bell Station before coming over the old Pacheco Pass."

---

16 Lou (Henry) Hoover was First Lady of the United States from 1929-1933.

His father, Rensselaer Luther Holman, a successful Sacramento businessman, had come to Pacific Grove for his health. The invigorating air soon brought recovery. He surveyed the lush country and the fifteen acres of campgrounds of the Methodist retreat, realizing the potential.

His son laughs, "Father used to say that in a few years one couldn't buy property here unless he covered it with gold. People came to die but got well."

Rensselaer Luther Holman was a sixth generation descendant of Solaman Holman of Newbury, Mass., whose ancestry is traced to Baron John Holman, standard-bearer in the battle of Bosworth Field which terminated the War of the Roses between the houses of York and Lancaster in England. The family tree also includes President William Howard Taft.

Born in Vermont and hearing tales of the wonders of the West as a boy, R.L. Holman came, as a young man, around the Horn to San Francisco, where he first worked in a bakery.

The aftermath of the gold fever was pulsing at an increasing rate. Opportunity for enterprising young men was spelled in capital letters. Not only the prospectors, but planters—those who would work and harvest— saw gold in the earth of California. And all of these would need supplies— another golden chance for the purveyors of goods.

So R.L. Holman went back to New England where he not only married a Vermont girl but also brought back to California some of the first farm machinery put into use in the Sacramento Valley.

He traveled by buckboard, up and down the Sacramento, Salinas, and San Joaquin valleys, and by boat up Oregon's Columbia River, selling cultivators and combine harvesters to the growers of hay and grain. He also opened the Holman-Stanton wholesale and retail hardware company, selling gold pans, bolts, nails, axes, plow and plowshares to the miners and farmers or ranchers who came in their four-horse wagons to buy goods.

Hard work at his business as well as managing the ranch which he acquired at Stockton impaired his health, resulting in the rest at Pacific Grove. He sold his hardware business to the Sacramento firm now known as Thompson Diggs and settled in Monterey County.

Pacific Grove's tent city was changing from just a summer retreat to a permanent settlement. The Pacific Grove Retreat Association in 1875 had purchased land at Point Pinos from David Jacks and in 1877 had begun to sell lots to its members for homes. In 1881, Mr. Jacks sold 7,000 acres of the Pescadero and Point Pinos ranches to the Southern Pacific Railroad, known as the Pacific Improvement Company, at five dollars an acre. Three years later, prices were advancing and the land boom began. Lucy Neely McLane in her *Piney Paradise*, quotes from the Del Monte Wave of 1885:

> *"The demand for lots from all quarters is wonderful. During the last sixty days the sale of company lots amounted to over $20,000 while real estate transactions among individual property owners amount to nearly half as much."*

R.L. Holman observed this and responded to another opportunity. He made plans for a supplies firm which would sell cement, plaster, lath and similar necessities for obvious building. But he was informed by the Pacific Improvement Company that because he had not obtained a business right permit he would not be allowed to operate and was threatened that if he persisted, all his property would be confiscated.

Disappointed though undaunted, he had also observed that there were other needs to be filled. He entered into a partnership with G. W. Towle, Jr., in the dry goods business.

Before the opening of Towle's, the ladies coming to the summer retreat from their homes in Fresno, Bakersfield or San Francisco for the cooling breezes of the inspiring Chautauqua lectures, bought their thimbles, needles, calico or percale from peddlers who brought their wares in wagons to the campgrounds.

Describing the dry goods store, Mrs. McLane quotes: "A Towle display window of 1890—ox blue oxfords with bulldog toes and suit draped on a dummy which looked like a corpse with painted cheeks. Those responding to the lure were often persuaded by an alpaca-coated clerk to buy a bowler hat or an outspreading collar which showed mauve daisies on saffron ground."

Came the great Klondike strike with another gold fever. Towle took off for Alaska, leaving his partner with the stock, which, according to one report, was assessed for $1,580 and $1,400 on consignment.

W.R. Holman took charge of the business and changed the name to The Popular Dry Goods store.

It was then located at the Lloyd building on the south side of Lighthouse Avenue and it was here that young Wilford was introduced to the world of business.

"We carried men's and boys' suits, too," W.R. Holman recalls. "Some of them sold at $7.50, and you could get a good suit, an Oregon cashmere, for instance, for $12.50.

"We had home delivery, too, traveling all over Monterey and Pacific Grove in a spring wagon with one horse. Oh, and I remember carrying those sewing machines! We'd hoist them up on the shoulder and sometimes had to carry them up several flights of stairs."

The merchandise was moved twice, first to the Robinson building, then to the store now occupied by Wright's hardware store before being moved into the building on the Work-Gross property where the bus depot and the Grove Theater are now located.

It was at this location that W. R. Holman took over the store in 1914 and began enlarging it into a department store. The influx of more residents and distance from larger buying centers created the need for home furnishings, furniture and rugs, as well as clothing and kitchen needs.

He had the expert help of his attractive wife, the former Zena Patrick, who came to Pacific Grove from Hollister, where she had previously lived with her family. She had graduated from the Oakland Polytechnic Business College, had been a stenographer for the Fisk Teachers Agency at Berkeley and had learned merchandising at the Capwell company in Berkeley.

When she joined the Holman store, before her marriage to its owner, it was to manage the ladies' ready-to-wear department. Her eyes sparkle with the recollection: "The fabrics were so beautiful. The suits were made of beautiful broadcloth with fancy braid or soutache trimming and Skinner satin linings."

It was literally a shoulder-to-shoulder job. Stories have been told of how the young Mr. and Mrs. Holman took their babies along to sort or arrange stock after closing hours.

She smiles: "Oh, yes, it's true. We'd put the girls—Patty and Harriet—into a buggy, wheel them from our house down to the store. They'd often fall asleep while W.R. Holman and I would be working. Friends would rattle the door: 'Wiff and Pat,' they'd call, 'you'll get no fun out of life, working like that,' and then they'd go to a party. But we were happy. In love. Strong and well. We loved everybody and doing for the community. You can't beat that combination."

She tells one story, with a characteristic bit of a smile and a twinkle: "People asked W.R. Holman to put in a line of groceries. In fact, they signed a petition, because they said he had saved them so much on their dry goods.

"It was quite a decision. So we put up a galvanized building," she began. "Corrugated," W.R. Holman explained at this point and she nodded.

"Well, one day we found that someone had broken in and took chewing gum, candy and such and cached it under some pine needles in Washington Park. It was a group of youngsters. The great joke around town was that they had used can openers on that corrugated building to make their way in."

W.R. Holman chuckled: "Another experiment, definitely not successful though, was the garage which we opened in 1920. We took over an agency for Studebaker trucks, the Durant and Star automobiles—ill-fated as you know.

"We had mechanics to work on the cars and kept open twenty-four hours a day. We carried wholesale and retail parts and had the first service station, selling gasoline from pumps at the sidewalk. Up over the entrance was a huge sign: 'Square to the Cent.' Well, the automobile companies went out of business and we sold the garage to Spoon who had the Ford agency in Monterey."

In the early 1920s signs of a post-war boom were appearing. The El Carmelo Hotel, which had been built in the 1880s to handle the overflow from Del Monte Hotel, located on Lighthouse Avenue between Fountain and Grand and the scene of much elegance, had been torn down about 1917. Its furnishings had been sold and its lumber was used for the construction of new homes. The property was vacant.

W.R. Holman purchased the land and began construction of the present store. "When we started building, it was rumored that I was building my monument. There were prophecies that creditors would be lucky if they received ten cents on the dollar within six or eight months.

"But we opened in 1924. The main object was to show the community that we had confidence. It was estimated at the time that only 10,000 people lived within twenty miles of Pacific Grove.

"Oh yes, we had a grand opening. In fact, each time a floor was completed, we held a dance before the stock was moved in. We advertised a dance and people came from all over. We decorated the pillars with pine branches. We had an orchestra and served refreshments."

Apropos of dancing and the social life, W.R. Holman reminded that in earlier days, Pacific Grove's curfew required that shades not be drawn until a certain hour, to make sure that the patrolling officer could look into homes to see that neither cardplaying nor dancing was being pursued in one's home.

"It was the Holmans, the Oyers and the Jubbs who built Mariposa Hall, outside the city of Pacific Grove (Rudolph's), for dances and for use as an assembly hall," he reminded.

Continuing, W.R. Holman said: "And during the Depression, in 1932, we put on the upper floor and the Solarium. I paid every workman and every mechanic the same scale that he had received before the crash and the Depression. Many offered to work for $1 or $1.50 a day but I believed that we should pay what the man had received previously. We never cut a salary or let any employee go during the Depression."

Mrs. Holman, who added training employees, writing advertising and buying to her duties, was literally her husband's "right hand." When, during the war, she added going to the furniture markets in Chicago, New York and other points, she became "the traveling man of the family."

Although she had to retire earlier, it was after a four-and-one-half month trip to Europe that she did go into "semi" retirement, today being the executive vice president and secretary of the firm. W.R. Holman, since his "semi" retirement, serves as president of the board. The management of the store and its more than fifty departments is in the hands of their son-in-law, Arthur Barter, their nephews, and nephews-in-law, Vernon Hurd, Hugh Steven and Gordon Knowles.

Mr. and Mrs. Holman maintain the original family home on Lighthouse Avenue, which has been described by Mrs. McLane via the Pacific Grove

Review of 1891 as "the magnificent residence of R.L. Holman. The residence (16 rooms), outbuildings and grounds, including improvements, cost about ten thousand dollars. W.R. Holman has a neat stable with accommodations for four horses."

Of course, the reference was to R.L. Holman. When his son and family took it over, after the estate was settled some fifty years ago, they took off the top floor, removed much of the Victorian "gingerbread," extended to the dining room, and added a solarium and picture windows.

From here they look out over their lovely garden, colorful in the spring with iris and many other flowers, with always the stately holly for a protective screen. The introduction of holly by the Holmans to the Monterey Peninsula is another story.

So is the seven-year battle which W.R. Holman waged for a road to be cut through the hills so that the people of Pacific Grove could have easier access to Carmel rather than the roundabout route through Monterey.

This and support for many conservation and historical projects devoted to preservation of the Peninsula's natural beauty and heritage were some of the community efforts which Mr. and Mrs. Holman have devoted their leisure time to.

As for hobbies, what is more natural than that merchants should indulge in buying? With Mr. and Mrs. Holman, though, it was a lifetime study and collection of Indian relics—a priceless reminder of this country's heritage which they recently presented to the State of California and which is now housed in Monterey's Pacific Building.

For seventy-five years the Holman name has been important to the Monterey Peninsula, with a spirit of "friendliness" which they and their friends cherish.

Mrs. Holman recalls one touching incident. "A blind man came into the store with his attendant," she says, "he raised his head and said: This is a friendly store. I can feel it."

Game & Gossip OCT. 1, 1974, VOL. 18, NO. 12

HOLMAN'S 83RD ANNIVERSARY
by Helen Spangenberg

From kerosene to fluorescent lighting, from mission oak and mohair, to chrome and Naugahyde sofas, from granite ware to Teflon cooking ware—these are just some of the very few changes in the 83 years of merchandising which Holman's, Monterey Peninsula's first store, is observing in September.

For more than three-quarters of a century, the Holman family has owned and operated The Store. First, a small general store for the growing community on the shore of the Pacific Ocean and then a department store which today covers a large portion of downtown Pacific Grove in its five stories, including a solarium which affords a panoramic view of Monterey Bay.

From a staff which consisted of the originator, R.L. Holman, and his family to approximately 215 employees (the staff grows to 275 at holiday time), Holman's has always maintained a hometown, family atmosphere with stress on quality. Here, the customer is a neighbor and usually on a first-name basis with the owners. It's this warm, personal relationship which has always been maintained at Holman's, one which, in some areas, has evaporated in the clack of computers, machines and relay systems from suburban shopping centers to city offices.

Though the decorating changes have kept pace with today's trends, the genuine purpose remains the same. In reference to the old nostalgia theme, Art Barter, merchandising manager, was asked if the old-time touch in the carriers—the metal cylinders in which cash was sent to the cashier—was missed.

"Well," Mr. Barter replied: "They would have been a novelty today, but it just got too hard to get parts when something broke down. And then," he laughed, "they would sometimes fly open and the cash would come tumbling down on the counters or the floor. There was also the worry of one of the carriers flipping off onto the head of some unsuspecting customer."

Today's Holman's is managed by some of the men who married into the family: Mr. Barter[17]; Vernon Hurd[18], who is the general manager; Gordon P. Knoles[19], personnel director; and Hugh Steven[20], comptroller, since Mr. and Mrs. W. R. Holman retired from active participation.

They had assumed direction of the company in 1914. Rensselaer Luther Holman had come to Pacific Grove for his health from Sacramento where he had been a successful businessman, and became a partner of G. W. Towle, Jr., in the dry goods business when Towle took off for the Alaska gold fields in 1891. R.L. Holman took charge of the operation and proceeded to change the name from Towle's[21] to The Popular Dry Goods Store. At that time it was located in the Lloyd building on the south side of Lighthouse Avenue and it was there that Wilford Holman was introduced to the world of business.

This meant helping to wind and unwind bolts of cotton and percale yardage, to deliver purchases, driving a wagon drawn by horses over the dirt roads, which were lined with wild-growing lupines and bracken.

Wilford and his young wife, the former Zena Patrick, operated the business through the economic ups and downs of two world wars. They bought the property of the present site after the old Del Monte Hotel annex had

---

17 Arthur Barter, Jr. was Harriet Holman's husband.

18 Vernon Hurd was married to Marion Luella (Holman) Hurd, Clarence Holman's youngest daughter.

19 Gordon Knoles was married to Audrey Estella (Holman) Knoles, Clarence Holman's eldest daughter.

20 Hugh Steven was Minnie (Holman) Steven and Andrew Steven's son.

21 It was called Towle & Holman before it became The Popular.

been torn down and the new store was opened in 1924. It, too, has been expanded and renovated to keep up with the expansion of the community and its environs, plus the mail orders from distant places—even foreign countries.

The Holmans and their family as well as the employees have always been interested in the good life on the Peninsula. W.R. Holman worked for many years to bring about a shorter route from Pacific Grove to Carmel and thus Route 68, or now as it is known, the Holman Highway, became a reality. Both he and Mrs. Holman have been vitally interested in historic preservation and have collected a great number of Indian artifacts which they have presented to the State of California. They have also collected great first editions and books on California.

The theme for this year's anniversary celebration in September is "The Way They Are," stressing the achievements of Holman "people." Vernon Hurd, who has been general manager since 1944, has served on the Community Hospital board, the Monterey Peninsula Chamber of Commerce, and the Rotary Club board. His son, Gordon Hurd, has just completed a two-year term as president of the Pacific Grove Chamber of Commerce.

Tom Drakes, traffic manager, has been a Pacific Grove councilman for five years; LaVern Blikre is past worthy matron of the OES, and Noreen Woodfin is the president of the Business and Professional Women's Club.

In the 83 years of keeping shop, Holman's has seen thousands upon thousands of items brought into the warehouses to be unpacked, then arranged on the shelves and then to flow out into the community's homes and businesses, and with a success that has surmounted competition from chain stores and specialty shops.

To quote an overheard comment from a customer who had found an item she had been looking for a long time, "I guess you could say, if you can't find it at Holman's, forget it."

Mr. and Mrs. W.R. Holman standing beneath the boughs of a flowering cherry tree in their garden.

Right: *A portrait of W.R. Holman.*
Left: *A portrait of Zena Holman.*

Holman's Department Store exterior, October 23, 1963.

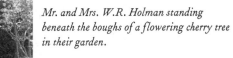

In 1956, the 65th anniversary of Holman's, W.R. Holman cuts the huge cake depicting the growth of the store. Mrs. Holman stands on the ladder, on the left.

The "Big Four" managers at Holman's (left to right): Gordon Knowles, Arthur Barter, Vernon Hurd, and Hugh Steven.

12

Advertising at Holman's

Probably nothing in the way of promotion Holman's Department Store
ever did attracted so much favorable comment as the engagement of the
flag-pole skater.

—John Steinbeck, *Cannery Row*

ON MAY 22, 1977, W.R. HOLMAN SHARED HIS MEMORIES OF THE STORE
with a woman named Annette Erwin. While this enjoyable aside was
not in the original manuscript, I'm including it here:

===

Of course we advertised. We used fun tactics if possible. I had fun
thinking them up—yes, it was fun.

We had an exhibit in our window that attracted the attention of the
papers: a strange creature shown in Holman's Men's Furnishing Department window. The attraction was a strange animal in a wire cage

labeled "Peruvian Swamp Hound," that lives on green grass and saw-dust, sleeps with one eye opened and is two hundred and eighty years old, which is attested by the rings on its tail. Al Norton, noted savant, who captured the animal said that after perusing half a dozen works on natural history, it proved truly to be a Peruvian Swamp Hound (Geomisbursarius). If it lives, it will doubtless be sold for a handsome price to Al Barnes Circus, which comes to Pacific Grove soon. If it dies, it will no doubt be placed as a permanent exhibit in the local museum.

Yes, I had a lot of fun with that display, because it was a gopher I had trapped right in my backyard. It was played up in the papers without my asking.

There were other advertising stunts. There was Penny Day, when I went to the roof and threw pennies to people below. Come to think of it, some of those pennies must now be priceless.

Then there was the Chicken Day when I let chickens fly into the street. There was Kite Day. Kites advertising Holman's flew from the roof of Holman's. Then there was the Balloon Day, when I let balloons fly off the roof advertising Holman's.

The most exciting ad Holman's had was Mr. X roller skating on a flag pole erected on the roof of Holman's Department Store. He danced, jumped rope, dined, etc. on roller skates on a 5 foot disk for 50 hours. He rested on a couch in the main window of Holman's, masked from 8 to 10 AM on a Saturday.

Cameramen from nationally known newsreels were on hand to photograph this hazardous feat! Lighthouse Avenue was thronged with people from all over the country that morning, when the daredevil, the son of a friend of mine, a harness maker for years in Monterey, began his stunt.

I enjoyed my advertising stunt, and so did a lot of people of all ages.

"MISTER X"

Monterey Peninsula Herald FRIDAY, JUNE 17, 1932

SKY SKATER

—mysterious marvel who will thrill and entertain spectators at tomorrow's bathing suit revue in Pacific Grove by gyrating on a tiny platform far above the top of Holman's department store.[22]

Monterey Peninsula Herald SATURDAY, JUNE 18, 1932

SKY SKATER HAS HIGH AMBITIONS, NO COMPETITION

There's at least one man who is not afraid that he'll lose his job. Nobody wants it. This man stands on skates. And he stands alone on skates on a tiny 60 inch wooden disc atop a pole built out over the sidewalk from the edge of the Holman department store roof. 120 feet above the sidewalk he just skates. His skating rink is perhaps the smallest in the world; it is just 60 inches across. He's a good skater. He jumps rope, does fancy backward steps, a tap dance and a heel and toe number, not to mention a dizzy spin.

From the street level the stunt is hair-raising, but from any point on the Holman roof it is guaranteed to develop a good case of jitters in even the most hardened watcher. Especially when 24 year old "Mr. X" does that fancy heel and toe step to the edge of his platform. Or when he jumps rope, roller skates and all.

Judging by the number of feet of film Jack McHenry, of the Universal

---

22 A handwritten note on the original manuscript reads: "Joe Cramer's son from San Jose, California." Cramer was Holman's friend from San Jose who introduced him to " . . . buying small shops and stores through the Board of Trade," as mentioned in Chapter 8. Apparently, Joe Cramer's son was the infamous Mr. X.

newsreel, took of Mr. X and his skating tricks it is a real stunt, unusual and daring to the extreme. McHenry also photographed Mr. X saying goodbye to Mayor Julia B. Platt, City Manager Erwin Dames, Chief of Police Sam Bashline and Mr. W. R. Holman before he climbed to the perch that he is to call "home" for the next fifty to sixty hours. Mr. X ascended to his flagpole perch at 11 o'clock this morning and will remain up there until sometime Monday in an effort to establish the newest flagpole skating endurance record. Lighthouse Avenue was thronged this morning when the daredevil began his stunt.

==

SANTA CLAUS SPECIAL

Monterey Peninsula Herald SATURDAY, DECEMBER 12, 1959

TICKETS MONDAY FOR SANTA CLAUS SPECIAL

Tickets will be handed out at Holman's Department Store Monday for youngsters to ride on this year's Santa Claus Special.

For the fourth straight year, the store is sponsoring a free train from Monterey to Pacific Grove for carloads of Peninsula youngsters, who'll meet Santa, be entertained, and receive some goodies.

The Santa Claus special will make its run next Saturday, leaving the Southern Pacific Station in Monterey at 9:45 a.m., making a leisurely journey out the coast, and arriving at the Pacific Grove depot at 11 a.m.

Parents may pick up free tickets for their children Monday at the special ticket booth on the ground floor of the Holman's store in Pacific Grove. Some tickets will also be available for parents to accompany children too young to take the ride alone.

Kids up to 11 years old are eligible to ride the Santa Claus Special.

Part of the Pacific Grove High School band will be at the Monterey station to play Christmas music before the train arrives. Clowns will be there to pass out balloons and entertain the kids.

All Aboard

Aboard the train, besides Santa, will be Mrs. Claus, clowns, elves, animals and other entertainers. The train will move slowly enough for Santa to walk through all the cars, passing out free candy.

Parents whose children are riding the train are advised to see the youngsters off in Monterey then drive to the Pacific Grove station in time to collect the kids when the train arrives there at 11 o'clock.

In past years, Holman's has used the regularly scheduled Del Monte Express in the evening for its Santa Claus train, but a change in schedule made the Del Monte arrive too late for small children. Southern Pacific is sending a special train from San Francisco for this year's Santa Claus run.

In 1956, the year it started the annual event, Holman's won the National Retail Merchants Assn. "Best Christmas Attraction" award in a national contest. Last year about 2,500 children rode the Santa Claus Special.

Pacific Grove Tribune FRIDAY, MARCH 8, 1935

HOLMAN'S STORE ATTAINS WORLD-WIDE REPUTATION

Linking Pacific Grove with every state in the Union and every country in the world is a merchandising institution which holds a unique position in the commercial world—Holman's. Probably nowhere else in the world is a store of its scope to be found in a community with as small a population as Pacific Grove.

Records of its shipping department indicate customers in most towns of California, in every one of the 48 states and in many foreign countries, including Morocco, Alaska, England, Russia, Australia, China, Norway,

New Zealand, Belgium, Central America, Puerto Rico, and the Hawaiian Islands.

Letters from past or prospective patrons arrive daily, some of them vaguely addressed but all indicating Holman's has impressed them. For example, in the correspondence file can be found a letter addressed to "The Big Dry Goods Store at Pacific Grove."

Many facts concerning the store's dimensions and the extent of its merchandising are regarded by businessmen everywhere as little short of miraculous. For example, it is one of the largest dealers in Catalina pottery anywhere in the United States, shipping this currently popular product to patrons throughout the east and middle-west.

Its floor space is the largest between San Francisco and Los Angeles. It consumes 100 tons of wrapping paper annually and has on its year-around payroll 120 people. This number is greatly increased in the pre-Christmas season.

Founded in 1891 by R.L. Holman, father of the present owner, it occupied originally the corner where the Grove Pharmacy now stands. Subsequent moves included a store in the Lloyd building adjoining what is now Fortier's drug store; then the center of the block where the First National Bank stands; the corner at Sixteenth Street and Lighthouse, present site of Jones' market. For twenty years following this, Holman's business flourished in the location of the present Grove Theatre.

When in 1924 W. R. Holman had the present structure erected on the site of the old Carmelo hotel, it was to the gaping wonderment of the community and skeptic chorus of many. The first year of the Depression he demonstrated further confidence in the Peninsula as a business location by adding the furniture department and building the Solarium for the public.

Mrs. Holman, who, since her marriage to W. R. Holman almost 22 years ago, has been associated with the store in many different capacities and who is at present one of its executives, explains the miraculous growth of the store in her philosophy that "smallness is only in one's mind." The good will of one person is as valuable, she believes, as that of 1,000 patrons.

==

HOLMAN'S 75TH BIRTHDAY
COMMEMORATIVE NEWSPAPER

[Editor's note: For Holman's 75th Birthday, the store created a sixteen-page newspaper in 1966, commemorating the past and looking to the future. The following are select articles W.R. Holman chose for his original book which appeared in that paper.]

Phenomenal Growth of Store
under Guidance of W. R. Holman

By 1914, when son Wilford took over full management, "Holman's," as it was now called, had come a very long way from the simple general store of its beginnings. It was a large, full-fledged department store and the complexities of its operation were enormous.

Wilford Holman needed help and he was lucky enough to find it close at hand. Zena Patrick was an exceptionally pretty and vivacious Hollister girl and she came to work at the store in the ladies ready-to-wear department. She and the boss fell in love and before long were married. From then on, the running of Holman's was a joint affair.

Zena Patrick Holman was not only pretty but she was energetic and hardworking as well. Furthermore, she had had sound merchandising training in San Francisco, so it was only natural that in addition to rearing a family, she was also involved, head over heels, in helping her husband run the store.

Her duties were many and she shouldered them joyfully and capably. She put on yearly fashion shows, designed interior decor, soothed employees' ruffled feelings, tested merchandise, and made frequent buying trips East for many of the store's departments. Zena Holman was truly her husband's good right arm.

Further Changes

By 1922 the store had once more outgrown its location and a change was in order. With an eye to the future, Holman had some time previously purchased the entire block of land bounded by Lighthouse and Central Avenues between Grand and Fountain. This had been the site of Pacific Grove's most famous, hostelry, the El Carmelo Hotel. On this property Holman decided to build a really enormous store.

Two years before this decision, he had erected a big garage on the lower part of the land. Evidently with a firm belief that gas buggies were here to stay, he had taken over the franchises for Studebaker trucks as well as for the Durant and Star automobiles. Holman's assessments of business trends were supremely accurate. However, neither the Durant nor the Star caught on and the building subsequently housed the overflow from the main store which went up.

New Building

This new building, into which all the stock was moved in 1924, was the largest store of its kind between San Francisco and Los Angeles. For many years it was known to bankers, credit men, and others in the world of business literally from coast to coast, as "Holman's monument," or "Holman's folly." Perhaps they had valid reasons for their dire predictions. There were scarcely 10,000 people in the entire immediate area.

How was such a gigantic store going to pay for itself? But pay for itself it did. Wilford Holman's judgment was sound. The store prospered over the years, and additional small "branches," one in Carmel for household wares, and one in Monterey handling shoes, were put in operation. These were sold eventually to devote more attention to the big store in Pacific Grove.

Floor Added

In 1932 the store was expanded again by the addition of a large third floor entirely devoted to the sale of furniture. The construction of this floor did much to help alleviate the effects of the Depression into which the country was sinking deeper and deeper.

It is to Mr. and Mrs. Holman's everlasting credit that their faith in America and the American people never wavered during these difficult times. This faith took concrete form, in ways that had meaning. All the workmen employed in building the new addition were paid pre-Depression wages. In addition to this, no employee was ever laid off due to the Depression, nor were wages lowered. True, hours had to be cut, but somehow the work was spread so that everyone still had a job and income.

The store still remains at the location where Holman put up his "folly." Further expansion has taken place to various nearby annexes, and in keeping with the times, additional empty property close at hand has been turned into parking lots.

Special Events Are Fun at Holman's

Every store has its sales and Holman's was no exception. However, like Carlo[23] and the Santa Claus Special, and many, many other things, Holman sales are old traditions and are a lot of fun.

---

23 Carlo the Clown was at nearly every Holman's event. Charles Hilderra (aka, Carlo), was a circus performer with Barnum and Bailey, the B.F. Keith Circuit, and Sells Floto Circus, among others. Originally a trapeze artist, he took a fall, ending his career as an aerialist. He couldn't stay away from the circus, so he became a clown, eventually settled in Pacific Grove, and was a part of the Holman's family bringing laughter and balloon animals wherever he went.

Twice a year, there's the HOLMAN DAYS SALE, when practically everybody in Monterey County heads for Pacific Grove to see what's new at the big store and to pick up bargains.

And there's the PARKING LOT SALE. The staff of the store dolls up in bandannas and straw hats and the merchandise is stacked on big tables outdoors. This is a good time to renew old acquaintances because you'll see everybody there you ever knew, including Mr. Wilford Holman cracking jokes and having the time of his life.

Also, don't ever miss the CAT AND DOG SALE. Every once in a while, Holman's gets a little desperate to clear its shelves of odds and ends that haven't sold.

The buyers who made the mistakes may have been sent to Siberia but chances are the mistakes are to your advantage. In the market for teapot lids? A purple vest? Twenty-thousand ball bearings? Mason jars without tops? A gross of small, beautifully colored gizmos made of plastic and nylon . . . Holman's doesn't know what they are but maybe you do and maybe they're exactly what you need. You can be sure Holman's is striving mightily to get rid of them and they'll come cheap.

Holman's services

Home delivery has always been featured at Holman's. A horse-drawn spring buggy made the first rounds. Today a fleet of trucks delivers to virtually the entire county of Monterey including Big Sur, Carmel Valley, Salinas, the Monterey Peninsula and adjacent areas. Salinas residents may also shop Holman's by dialing toll-free 424-0201.

Left: *Advertisement run by Holman's, encouraging people to come watch Mr. X.* Monterey Peninsula Herald, Saturday, June 18, 1932.

Right: *Mr. X atop Holman's.*

The Santa Claus Special. [Editor's note: One evening years ago, my mother-in-law, Genie Santini, brought out a binder full of Holman's clippings from various newspapers, photos taken by W.R. Holman, and other historical documents. As we looked through them together, this photo captured my attention— of course the white bear was something to look at, but my eyes went right to the little girl in the foreground on the left, the one with her hand to her lips. That is my mother, Cathleen Marie Spindler. My aunt, Kimberly

Spindler Wright, sits next to her. Out for the day from their home in Carmel, my grandparents Warren "Tor" Spindler and Katherine Therese Donahue Spindler would drop off their four children at the train depot in Monterey, and pick them up for special Christmas shopping at Holman's in Pacific Grove.]

The "front page" of the newspaper published by Holman's.

HOLMAN'S CELEBRATES 75TH BIRTHDAY

Wilford R. Holman, under whose capable management the store achieved its greatest growth.

Photo from a Holman's ad for the Santa Claus Special in the Monterey Peninsula Herald, *Friday December 9, 1960.*

Vernon Hurd, Holman's General Manager at the time, and W.R. Holman speak at a parking lot sale, July 1960.

W.R.'s "Holman's Card."

W.R. Holman in a cowboy hat at the parking lot sale, 1962.

[Editor's note: This text and photo appeared in the Holman's commemorative newspaper.]
"The old gentleman driving this Ford 1926 hit the wrong pedal and hauled down hard on the hand throttle. This is the result. The famous little Flivver gave Holman's some of the best advertising it ever had. Roped off, it was an attraction for more than six weeks, drawing crowds from near and far."

Holman's Department Store postcard, published by the M. Kashower Co., Los Angeles.

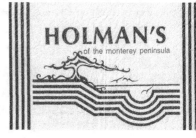

A shopping bag from Holman's.

Holman's Department Store postcard. Pub. by Lee Blaisdell, Monterey California.

HOLMAN'S DEPT. STORE FOR OVER 68 YEARS — PACIFIC GROVE — CALIFORNIA
WHERE THOUSANDS SHOP FOR QUALITY MERCHANDISE AND SAVE

Holman's card. If you brought this in, you could receive a "Free delicious wine cocktail or coffee and roll in our Solarium Restaurant."

With the most beautiful view on the Monterey Peninsula

THE BETTER HALF — **By Barnes**

"Quick! Tell me that Holman's Department Store has contracted to rent our living room as a warehouse annex!"

Cartoon from the Oakland Tribune, *Tuesday, September 24, 1974.*

THE BETTER HALF — **By Bob Barnes**

"She says she's afraid to go home."

Cartoon from the Oakland Tribune, *Monday, June 20, 1960. The box says Holman's.*

13

Holly Hills Farm

Game & Gossip DECEMBER 8, 1950, VOL. 4, NO. 12

THE HOLMAN HOLLY STORY
by Shirlie Stoddard

Today is the day W.R. Holman starts harvesting his holly, and within a week or so, mantelpieces and dining room tables throughout the United States will be serving as settings for his shiny green leaves and bright red berries.

What was once just an absorbing sideline for the Pacific Grove department store executive has become, he will admit modestly, a big business. His 140-acre Holly Hills Farm, five miles out of Watsonville, is now considered the largest individually owned single planting of holly in the world. As far as the eye can see from a promontory near the Holman barn are holly trees, marching in symmetrical rows up the gently sloping hills and, for all you know, down the other side and on and on, *ad infinitum*.

Always interested in "growing things," W.R. Holman was bitten by the holly bug about 45 years ago. At that time, his home was the seat of his hobby. "I remember when I had 22,000 trees in cans around the house," he says. "We couldn't move without stepping on one."

When he decided to go into holly growing on a large scale, W.R. Holman bought some land near Ukiah in Mendocino County, planting several hundred trees. "I had been told that holly would do well where redwood trees grow," he recalls. "But the deer got 'em and the trees weren't good from a commercial standpoint; they spread out like fir trees. Eventually I gave it up. Now we use the Ukiah ranch as a summer place."[24]

His second attempt at starting a ranch had its disappointments, too. When he purchased the Watsonville land, W.R. Holman imported several half-grown trees from his Pacific Grove collection to form the nucleus of his crop. Every single one of those trees was destroyed by gophers within six months. "It broke my heart," says Holman.

But Holman was a hard man to discourage. Planting new cuttings and figuring out ways of protecting them from pests was an exciting game to him, and he played it with all the concentrated verve of a canasta fan. He placed his trees in plots of land 20 by 25 feet square; worked out a system, with the help of the University of California, of effectively poisoning gophers; bought some bees for pollination purposes, and fought the mealy bug and scale, traditional enemies of holly, with almost military skill. The result is 50 acres of commercially mature trees (holly is not harvested until a tree has reached its 18th year, plus thousands of younger trees whose potentialities are practically limitless, since a holly tree, if properly cared for, may live 250 years.

Apart from pest control and some application of fertilizer, a holly tree does not require much care during its first 16 years of life, according to Holman. If you don't irrigate young trees—and he purposely doesn't—they

---

24 The log cabin in Low Gap, written about in Chapter 6.

will be the hardier for the lack of forcing, though they will, admittedly, grow more slowly.

Mature trees, however, must be watched and washed. With the help of his caretaker, W.R. Holman works the soil around his trees constantly, disc-plowing it at least four times a year but taking care to avoid touching the delicate feeder roots. To keep the foliage bright and glossy and to give the trees the proper amount of water, he uses an overhead sprinkler system. Growers of single trees should, he says, wash their trees "with the full force of the water," except at blossom time. The full force, he adds, will not knock off the berry crop. "In summer months let the hose dribble at the base of your tree for half an hour at a time to keep the close roots well supplied with water."

W.R. Holman sprays his trees for mealy bugs and scale twice a year—in June and September—choosing an oil emulsion which loosens the black coating known as "honeydew" and causes it to fall off.

As the visitor to Holly Hills Farm strolls between the trees on soil as soft as a heavy pile rug, his attention is attracted by several wooden structures identified as bird-feeders. "We've got 120 of them," W.R. Holman explains. "The idea is to keep the birds from eating the holly berries. And besides, they have to have *something* to eat. Certain kinds of birds like holly trees to nest in, mainly because the thorns on the leaves protect them from their enemies. My trees are full of linnets and quail."

After spending almost $1,000 a year for several years on the single item of gopher-poisoning, W.R. Holman thinks he has almost licked the problem. "I haven't seen a gopher this season," he says. "But you never know. You never know a gopher's been at work on a tree until too late to save it. The little rascals chaw on the roots and do their killing gradually. Several months later you notice a tree is dead.

"Last year we were invaded by field mice—thousands of them! It was very, very severe, that invasion. They swarmed up the trees and ate the bark off the branches. We routed 'em, though, and they haven't returned."

Producing berries on holly trees has something in common with raising chickens. "You need only one male tree to about 20 females," says Holman. "Since it's only the female tree that bears the berries, you need a male tree within a few hundred yards to fertilize the female blossoms. And that's where my 20 swarms of bees come in."

Certain varieties of certain species of holly trees bear heavier clusters of berries than others, and certain types, apparently with an eye to the florist trade, seem to specialize in groupings from which boutonnieres and corsages can easily be made. Holman is constantly breeding for "larger clumps of berries and larger berries of a deeper shade of red."

"I wouldn't even dare to say how many varieties we have now," he says. "You see, every time we find a sport—that's a branch or section of leaves which appears to be different from and often better than the tree on which it grows—we take a cutting and plant it, thus starting a new type. That way we're constantly improving. Many of my trees are of the Dutch type, I guess, but I've never had them classified.

"A peculiarity of holly is that you're apt to find several types of leaves on one tree. Usually, there'll be heavily thorned leaves down below— that's nature's way of protecting the roots from animals, I suppose—and smoother leaves toward the top."

In addition to harvesting just previous to the holidays for the retail and wholesale trade, W.R. Holman harvests his foliage all year 'round. This is sold to a concern which has worked out a foolproof method of preservation. After soaking in a large tank, the holly leaves emerge rubberized and olive green. Sprayed with holly green paint, they look, says Holman, "like real holly," and they'll last, as "artificial" holly corsages and decoration, for several years. "It's quite a trick," says Holman.

Because they thrive on sea air and fog, holly trees are found in large numbers in Pacific Grove, Monterey, Carmel, and up where the fog belt ends in the Carmel Valley. Many of these are descendants of W.R. Holman's earlier trees.

The Holman house on Lighthouse Avenue is a holly showplace, fronted and flanked with a 460-foot long, 25-foot high hedge—an effect obtained by planting the trees very close together.

W.R. Holman, understandably, is a sentimentalist about his holly trees. As he shows a visitor around the ranch, he is given to exclaiming, "Now isn't that a pretty one! And see that tree over there! Isn't it a little beauty?"

And when a conducted tour comes to an end, he sighs happily. "It's just like a park, isn't it!" he beams. And it certainly is.

1. In mild coast climates where the temperature seldom exceeds 80 degrees, holly may be planted in almost any location—open, shaded, or half-shaded. In interior sections where the temperature rises above 80 degrees during the summer, holly should be planted where it will get the early morning or late afternoon sun.

2. Holly should be planted in well-drained sandy loam.

3. Holly should be mulched with leaf mold, straw or peat moss to a depth of about three inches to protect its very fine top feeder roots from heat and cold and to help retain moisture at all times.

4. Never dig or cultivate close to a holly tree or you will destroy its feeder roots and cause a setback.

5. Never cut lower branches close to trunk as lower branches should spread close to the ground to protect fine roots from elements and help maintain moisture, as well as to preserve the symmetrical form of the tree.

6. Do not fertilize in planting soil or hole where tree is planted. Fertilize on top of mulch and allow moisture to carry fertilizer to the feeder

roots. Chicken, pigeon, sheep, rabbit or cow manure are the best fertilizers and can be used on top of mulch once a month away from trunk of tree with safety. Once a year only, fertilize in early spring with sulfate of ammonia.

7. A holly tree is a heavy feeder and needs lots of moisture at all times, but the soil must be well drained to prevent it from becoming sour.

==

CATS AT HOLLY HILLS FARM

[Editor's note: In examining Holman's archive, I found a booklet of clippings about W.R. Holman and the cats on Holly Hills Farm. It appears W.R. Holman asked the SPCA for 50 cats as can be seen in the headlines and articles on the next two pages. When they declined to provide the cats, he placed the following classified ad:]

Monterey Peninsula Herald TUESDAY, OCTOBER 30, 1951

CLASSIFIED AD

PARADISE for unwanted cats on my 300-acre holly farm near Watsonville. Will provide housing for 50 felines and all the field mice they can catch and eat. The good mousers can take care of themselves. Poor hunters who are not as yet biologically fitted to seek their own meals will be properly fed until their hunting instinct is developed. I will pick up the cats. Phone W.R. Holman at 5-5037 to make arrangements.

Register-Pajaronian WATSONVILLE (CALIF.)
WEDNESDAY, OCTOBER 31, 1951

SPCA SAYS NO SOAP

HOLMAN'S HOLLY FARM OVERRUN WITH MICE—NEEDS 50 CATS

Monterey Peninsula Herald OCTOBER 31, 1951

QUESTION OF SLAVE LABOR?

SPCA REFUSES REQUEST FOR 50 CATS TO CATCH MICE ON HOLLY FARM[25]

"We decided that the move was not in the best interest of the cats," Countess Claude Kinnoull of the SPCA said today . . . "Our view is that it would not be humane to put that many cats on the ranch. Some cats are not good mousers. They would be very unhappy there and would probably starve to death . . ."

Holman said that Frank Halter, manager of the SPCA shelter, had suggested a compromise deal whereby the SPCA would supply him with 'just a few cats at $1 apiece.'

"But I'm not going to pay $1 apiece for cats," he said. "I'm going to Salinas, where I know they will let me have all the cats I want."

Monterey Peninsula Herald[26]

ANYBODY WANT CATS?

HOLMAN HAS PLENTY BUT BATTLE OVER CAT COLONY CONTINUES
by Ritch Lovejoy[27]

---

25 Rather than reprint this article in full, I've extracted a few paragraphs that exemplify both views.

26 This article was not dated, but I believe it is from October 31, 1951.

27 We'll see him later in Chapter 19.

Register-Pajaronian WATSONVILLE (CALIF.)
FRIDAY, NOVEMBER 2, 1951

GONE GOPHERS NOW

MICE RETREAT AS CATS HAVE HOLIDAY AT HOLLY FARM HERE

Monterey Peninsula Herald FRIDAY, NOVEMBER 2, 1951

CAT AND MOUSE BATTLE CONTINUES

PENINSULA PETS DIVIDED

Monterey Peninsula Herald SATURDAY, NOVEMBER 3, 1951

HOLMAN ANSWERS CRITICS OF HOMELESS CAT PLAN

Register-Pajaronian WATSONVILLE, (CALIF.)
TUESDAY, NOVEMBER 6, 1951

NO MORE CATS PLEASE

HOLMAN'S UP TO HIS NECK IN CATS AND CONTROVERSY

If what their former owners say about them is true, then W.R. Holman has half a hundred of the toughest, meanest and most self-sufficient cats in existence on his San Andreas Road holly farm.

Last week he offered free room and board to rough and ready felines with the idea of ridding the farm of gophers and field mice. He got about 50 in assorted colors and sizes—all mean-tempered.

"I turned down offers of about 100 Santa Cruz county cats because I had appealed first for Monterey area animals. Besides, I have more than enough now," he added.

In the process he precipitated a minor war between cat fanciers of the Monterey Peninsula area.

Judging from reports, many people are in a state of high dudgeon over the whole thing—mostly at each other.

All concerned seem to be pro-cat, but members of the Monterey SPCA are lined up solidly against adherents of Peninsula Pets, Inc., the membership of which is reportedly split down the middle.

And right in the middle is where Holman has found himself.

"Unfair to cats," proclaimed the SPCA and rebel members of the Peninsula Pets. "Fine idea," countered the loyalist faction of the latter group.

Incidentally, this is National Cat Week, and the American Cat Society reports that there are ten million homeless cats in the country.

Whether the society is up in applause or up in arms over Holman's Haven for Homeless Cats is unknown at this time.

Meanwhile, Holman was laying out supplies of cat food for those who didn't make that adjustment to rural life, but said that of the 50 animals which had been turned loose, only six were hanging around looking for food.

"Most of them are working out pretty well," Holman declared.

Asked how long he expected to need the cats, Holman said that it looked like a permanent thing. "There are about 300 acres out here, some of it in grain, and the mice will keep migrating in and breeding, so the cats have a steady job ahead of them."

Each cat will do away with two or three gophers and four or five mice a day, Holman estimates. It has cost him as much as $1,000 a year to poison the gophers and so far they have multiplied faster than he could do away with them. The cats were a last resort.

To opponents of his plan, the owner says that Holman's Happy Hunting

Ground for Hungry Homeless Cats offers abundant food for animals which might otherwise starve or be neglected.

Also, he contends, no cats are being thrown into the battle which are not used to taking care of themselves, and that there is plenty of room for the 50 and even more to roam without scrapping with each other.

Kittens and young cats have been turned down.

Neighboring farmers think the idea is good, Holman declared, adding that they, too, have been bothered by the mice.

"Back in 1888 when I came over here, there were cats all over—each farm had half a dozen to keep pests out of the barns. There was plenty of wild game, but now the cats are gone and so is most of the game," Holman said.

"Mice like eggs and eat any laid by birds in the fields. The cats will combat this and I don't believe they will bother the birds too much," he added.

Final score: Happy, Holman, some Peninsula Pet members and presumably cats. Unhappy, the Monterey SPCA and rebel Petters, also the mice.

Monterey Peninsula Herald FRIDAY, NOVEMBER 16, 1951

HOLMAN'S CATS ARE DOING FINE BUT NO REPORT YET FROM MICE

Monterey Peninsula Herald THURSDAY, FEBRUARY 26, 1953

REPORT TO ANIMAL LOVERS: CATS DOING FINE ON HOLMAN HOLLY RANCH

W.R. Holman of Pacific Grove, who started a controversy of volcanic proportions a couple of years ago, when he imported an army of cats to Watsonville to fight mice, says the cats are doing just fine.

"They're as fat and sleek as seals," Holman told *The Herald* yesterday. "People thought they'd be sick, yowling, and killing all the game, but they're not."

Holman took the cats to his Watsonville ranch because field mice were gnawing the bark off his prize holly trees and killing them.

Animal lovers as well as haters joined in a pitched battle over what would become of the 65 domesticated felines.

Cat lovers feared the domesticated cats would die of starvation if left to their own devices on the ranch; bird lovers feared they would kill all the birds.

But Holman says the cats are doing fine; the birds are more plentiful than ever, and the holly trees have more bark. Only sufferers are the mice, and that was the whole idea anyway.

When Holman drives his car in the farm driveway, cats come from all over to meet it. They don't come to meet other cars.

"The quail are thicker than they were before," Holman declares. "Pigeons thrive better.

"Wild mice will eat the birds' eggs and destroy the young; cats kill the mice.

"There are thousands of cat tracks around in the morning, and those cats were the best idea I ever had. I put food out for some who are too tame, and there are several fine springs for their drinking water.

"The trees are doing better. I don't know how many cats there are; they hide around in the brush in the daytime.

"But those cats are doing just fine," Holman reported.

A FINAL WORD ON HOLLY HILLS

Salinas Californian SATURDAY NOVEMBER 29, 1980

W.R. HOLMAN TAKES PLEASURE IN PRICKLY PLANT
by Jim Barrett, *Californian* Staff Writer

PACIFIC GROVE—This time of the year, the holly berries glow ripe-red outside Wilford R. Holman's picture window.

He takes pleasure in the sight. Holman, 96, bedridden most of the time and seriously ailing, had his bed moved close to the window so he could see the holly trees.

Holman is regarded as the leading expert in California on holly cultivation. Soon the harvest will start at his stately home, but he can only watch.

In an interview with the Californian, Holman, once chief executive of Holman's Department Store, described his love affair with holly and the heartbreak it caused in his latter years.

As a boy, Holman would pick the red berries on the holly that grew at Del Monte Park. For reasons he cannot explain, he set out in his adult years to cultivate holly.

"It's just something," Holman said of his avocation. "A person likes a certain plant, a certain tree."

He bought 20 acres of land five miles west of Watsonville and called it "Holly Hills Farm," once said to be the largest holly grove in the world under cultivation of an individual.

At Holly Hills, Holman said he proved holly would grow to saleable quality in California. He also said he proved holly could be grown from sprigs instead of seeds, which required lengthy germination periods.

For decades, Holman worked the groves and became a major commercial holly supplier on the West Coast.

The dates are uncertain in his mind, but Holman gave the land to a relative who subsequently sold Holly Hills to an heir to the DuPont chemical fortune.

"It was red with berries the year he bought it and he never cut a sprig," Holman said.

Holman said the grove became overgrown from lack of cultivation. He last saw the grove five years ago.

"It broke my heart to see it go to pieces. It hurt me so," said Holman.

The last of his holly trees grow at Holman's stately home down the block from his father's first store on Lighthouse Avenues. Holman said he was disturbed that this year's holly has few berries, the most important feature of marketable holly.

"This is the smallest crop I've had in years. The berries are not ripening. There's green and they should be red by now," he said.

Holman will sell boughs of holly. His secretary, Louise V. Jaques, conducts the business for him.

Holman suffers from an asthmatic condition that tires him quickly and diminishes his ability to speak, according to Jaques. "He is such an extrovert and he wants so much to be outgoing," she said.

His speech strained at times, Holman described how to start a holly tree: "There's not much to it," he declared.

"You can start from a cutting. Keep it in a cool place where the sun doesn't hit it. Cover it with a blanket or burlap, such like that. Water it through that and after it gets started, plant it in a one-gallon container. "When somebody wanted to know about holly, they'd say, 'You go down to Holman. He'll tell you about it'," he said.

Holman said holly is disease resistant. Birds eat some of the berries, but he said not to worry. Wild pigeons visited his groves for years and helped pollinate the trees, according to Holman.

Holman said he derives the most pride from proving holly would grow from cuttings. Horticulturists from Stanford University once told him he was crazy to try.

"They said I was just wasting my time and money," Holman said.

When the grove thrived and he began to sell commercially, the experts changed their minds, he said.

W.R. Holman in front of the holly at his home in Pacific Grove.

Mr. and Mrs. Holman examine a holly tree at Holly Hills Farm.

Business card from Holly Hills.

Some varieties of holly produce ready-made boutonnieres and corsages, apparently with an eye to the florist trade. W. R. Holman displays such a berry cluster in this photo.

California House and Gardens DECEMBER 1946, VOL. V, NO. 11

CALIFORNIA HOLLY GOES TO MARKET[28]

What began as a hobby has become a commercial enterprise. W.R. Holman supervises harvesting and packing, doing much of the work himself.

Clipping holly for wreaths amounts to pruning. These trees grow few berries and by Christmas, the cuttings will look like artificial sprays and wreaths. Artificial berries will be put on the finished decoration. The trees seen on the distant hill are berry producing and will be clipped in December.

After the holly is clipped from the trees it is hauled to the packing point and prepared for shipping. When not harvesting, the "cat" is busy cultivating the area between the trees and clearing new ground for more extensive plantings.

---

28 This article's content is similar to the *Game & Gossip* article, but since W.R. Holman included these photos in his book, I include them here.

14

W.R. Holman Highway

FOR SEVEN YEARS, W.R. HOLMAN, ALONG WITH MANY OTHERS, FOUGHT to have a highway built between Pacific Grove and Carmel. The W.R. Holman Highway seems like a natural link between Pacific Grove and Highway 1, but before its construction, Holman would have to ride his horse or walk through the woods to get to Carmel. Indeed, to create the highway we now use, W.R. Holman walked the surveyors along his route.

The first article below is an extract from a much longer editorial.

Carmel Pine Cone SATURDAY, NOV. 24, 1923; VOL. IX, NO. 45

HOLMAN WRITES OF P.G.—CARMEL ROAD

To the Citizens of Carmel, Seaside, Del Monte, Oak Grove, Marina, Corral De Tierra, Highlands, Monterey, New Monterey and Pacific Grove . . .

There are those who will say that a new state highway is not required by any public necessity, as there already is a state highway between the cities of Los Angeles and Monterey which is amply sufficient for all traffic requirements of the present time. These same factions will try to tell the taxpayers of California that this road will greatly increase taxes; and with almost tears in their eyes for the 'poor public' will tell them of the burden of taxation. But the sky is the limit to their efforts to obtain their wants, and taxation is forgotten. How easy it is to tell others to be economical when tax money is not spent as they would like to see it spent . . .

Who can say that the Pacheco Pass highway is not as valuable to the citizen who lives in the remotest section of Pacific Grove or Carmel, as it is to the citizens of Fresno? Who can say that the Castroville highway is not as important to every citizen in Santa Cruz County as it is to the citizens of the Peninsula?...

A few of the opposing side would have the public believe that the new proposed road from Carmel to Pacific Grove and New Monterey is solely and exclusively for the benefit of Holman. One group has gone so far as to have a map drawn up of the proposed road and have labeled it—from Holman's in Pacific Grove to Holman's in Carmel. They evidently forgot that Holman was in business in Monterey also, and is just as interested in seeing any portion of this Peninsula grow as another . . .

This road would have a tendency of drawing the travel through the entire Peninsula, rather than lose 80 per cent of the benefit of this traveling public, which under the present conditions and under the plans of the Highway Commission will only touch the outskirts of the Peninsula. If the present plans for the Highway Commission and the opposition to the new proposed road are carried out, the entire business sections of Monterey, New Monterey, and Pacific Grove, as well as the residential sections will not derive the benefits to which they are entitled for their efforts and their expenditure.

W. R. Holman

Monterey Peninsula Herald TUESDAY, SEPTEMBER 19, 1972

CARMEL-PACIFIC GROVE CUTOFF RENAMED
W. R. HOLMAN HIGHWAY
by Everett Messick, *Herald* Staff Writer

THE CARMEL-PACIFIC GROVE HIGHWAY TODAY OFFICIALLY
BECAME THE W. R. HOLMAN HIGHWAY.

Some 30 officials, relatives and friends gathered at the northern terminus on Asilomar Avenue near Sinex Avenue in Pacific Grove to honor the man credited with bringing about construction of the four-mile road almost 40 years ago.

Another sign had already been erected at the southern terminus on Carmel Hill, and a third sign was presented to Holman, president of Holman's Department Store since 1912.

Seven-Year Effort

Holman, 88, recalled how he led a seven-year campaign that included unseating longtime County Supervisor John L.D. Roberts and resulted in completion of the highway in 1930.

By coincidence, the spot picked for the sign is across the road from the site of the Holman historical library[29] and the date picked is the 81st anniversary of the opening of the store and the 60th anniversary of the marriage of Mr. and Mrs. Holman.

Among officials present were Assemblyman Bob Wood, R-Greenfield, and Sen. Donald L. Grumsky, R-Watsonville, who coauthored a legislative resolution authorizing the naming; county supervisors Willard

---

29 More about the Zena Holman Library in Chapter 20.

Branson and Loren Smith; County Road Commissioner Bruce McClain; and Pacific Grove Mayor Robert Quinn, and city manager Gary Bales.

Also present were Holman's wife, Zena, and their two daughters, Harriet Holman Barter of Carmel and Patricia Holman O'Meara of Watsonville.

Gardner Credited

Branson and Wood credited Neill Gardner, publisher of the *Pacific Grove Tribune*[30], with initiating and promoting the drive to rename the highway.

Branson noted that there were 18,000 traffic movements daily at the highway's intersection with Highway 1 on Carmel Hill last year, compared to 2,000 per day in 1947.

Lending atmosphere to the ceremony was a restored 1924 Dodge touring car owned by Earl Lopes of Pacific Grove.

In the state resolution, Holman is credited with being the "motivating force" behind the road, now part of State Highway 68.

Fenced In

Today, Holman recalled how he began his campaign in 1923 because "Pacific Grove and New Monterey were fenced in by government land (the Presidio of Monterey) which we were afraid might be closed in case of trouble."

When he was told by Roberts that no highway would be built while he was supervisor, Holman organized a drive to collect 2,500 names on a petition, which was taken to Salinas by 1,100 people, Holman said.

When Roberts remained adamant, a successful campaign was launched to unseat the long-time supervisor and elect A.A. Carruthers in 1928.

Then he told the county he wanted the highway to be included in an

---

30 Two pieces he published about W.R. Holman follow this article.

$85,000 bond issue or "we'll beat the bonds, and that's how we got the highway," Holman said.

Pacific Grove Pebble Beach Tribune AUGUST 28, 1979

THIS MAN'S OPINION
by Neill Gardner

BACK IN the fall of 1971, W. R. Holman was gracious enough to invite me out to his estate behind all that holly on Lighthouse Avenue. He was gonna give me an "interview."

We had just barely finished our "howdies" when Mrs. Holman appeared on the scene. Her arrival had a somewhat dampening affect on the informal nature of the proceedings. W. R. is an old shoe kind of guy and y'all know how loose I am.

First off, Mrs. H had to show me stacks of memorabilia that filled to overflowing an upstairs room. It was a little like trying to get a handle on the *Encyclopedia Britannica*. I gave up trying to take notes.

WHEN THE man and I got together again, his lady kept a close ear on the conversation. Every now and again she'd either tell him that he shouldn't have said that or caution me that I mustn't print it.

The lady diluted her restrictions with an inexhaustible flow of coffee and cookies. Although I may have been leaping to a conclusion, I couldn't shake the feeling that if W. R. and I had been left alone, the refreshments might have been more conducive to the free exchange of ideas.

ONE OF the scrapbooks contained a detailed history of Holman's seven-year battle to get a road built between The Grove and Highway One. At that time, Grovians could get to Carmel only via what the local paper called a route "through the old Spanish town laid out in somewhat careless fashion."

His plan for a new road ran into formidable opposition. Over in Monterey, merchants didn't like the idea of Carmelites bypassing their stores on their way to Holman's. Carmel businessmen didn't want to lose customers to either of the two Peninsula cities.

Among Carmel protestants was a merchant who noted that soup was selling for 10 cents a can while it was bringing in nine cents in the Grove.

SAMUEL F. B. Morse wasn't all that enthralled with Holman's idea, either. He didn't want to lose traffic from his 17 Mile Drive. In later years, Morse was to tell Holman that the new road hadn't done business any harm.

Col. Allen Griffin, publisher of the Monterey paper, was caught in the middle. He took a full page ad in *The Grove at High Tide* to explain that 90 percent of Monterey didn't want the road while an equal percentage of The Grove did want it.

Things came to a head when the county wanted to float a large bond issue. The Holmans got together a caravan that included nearly every car in town, including a lot of tourists. Garages offered free gasoline to anyone who'd drive over to Salinas.

W. R. was in fine form before the supervisors. He told them they could either build his shortcut or forget about that bond issue. They capitulated and it wasn't long before surveyors were on the job. When an incumbent supervisor wanted to renege, road supporters got behind A.A. Carruthers at the next election, thus insuring the road's construction.

WHEN THE late Assemblyman Bob Wood read about Holman's road battle, he pushed a resolution through Sacramento renaming that stretch of Highway 68 "W. R. Holman Highway." Wood brought a flock of local politicians down to the Masonic Hall for the Holman's Day breakfast. Later everyone went out to Asilomar to install the new signs.

W. R. celebrated his 95th birthday yesterday. By golly, it's about time we asked for another interview.

Pacific Grove Pebble Beach Tribune SEPTEMBER 19, 1979

W. R. HOLMAN PIONEERED UNIQUE COMMUNITY

THIS MAN'S OPINION
by Neill Gardner

Y'GOTTA write fast when you sit down to talk with W. R. Holman. Although he turned 95 a couple of weeks ago, that old rascal is able to recall most of what's happened around here since he arrived at the age of four.

Most of what he has to say deserves to be printed in something more permanent than the town weekly. Names that should be nailed down in a book come rolling off his tongue, along with interesting tidbits about their personalities.

That sort of thing may not be worthy of preservation by the Smithsonian. But it wouldn't hurt to have it down at the library. For instance: Did you know that the city's post office was once located on Fountain Avenue[31], that W. R. still owns the building, and the postmaster was one Robert Mitchell? Or that the postmaster was known as "Whistling Bob" because he always blew a merry tune while on the street?

Isn't it a shame that Aloha Schaefer left town without learning about her predecessor?

LATTER day environmentalists might have a different impression of W. R. if they knew that he went to bat against the canneries when the sardine harvest was at its peak. Holman recalls telling the big wheels on Cannery Row that they were going to kill off the sardines.

"They were using them for pet food, for fertilizer and even for paint

---

31 It was actually 216 Grand Avenue, as confirmed by W.R. Holman in a recording in October 1976.

oil," says Holman. "When I complained to the Fish and Game Commission they wanted to know what the hell I knew about sardines."

From four to 95, I doubt anyone ever heard W. R. utter an "I told you so." He ain't that sort of an animal. But he looks you square in the eye and delivers the message. He may not have been an authority on sardines, but he knew a thing or two about nature on the Central California Coast.

"If the sardine fishing had been properly managed, we'd still have a million dollar industry on the Monterey Peninsula," says W. R.

ABALONE were nearly as imperiled as the sardines at one time, according to Holman. He remembers when the coast was thick with them. "All you had to do was walk out at low tide and pick them up."

Then, he says, the Japanese—he uses the short form—came in and commercialized the abalone. They harvested the shellfish as far south as Gorda, processing them by the ton in Monterey before shipping the dried meat to Japan.

THE YEAR'S crop of planning commissioners may not know that Holman served seven years on the commission. Or that the town's feisty lady mayor—Julia Platt—headed the city government during that period. She was, W. R. says in tones tinged with pride, the very first female mayor in California.

IT'S EASY to come away from a session with Holman wishing you could get him closeted with folks from Greenpeace, the Historical Society, and the Women's Caucus.

It would likely do them all good to discover just what sort of guy it was who pioneered this quaint community that so many seem to believe they have just discovered.

The Pacific Grove Tribune and Pebble Beach Green Sheet,
WEDNESDAY, SEPTEMBER 27, 1972.

W.R. HOLMAN: AS USUAL, A JOB WELL DONE[32]

Left: *Daughters Patricia Holman O'Meara of Watsonville, left, and Harriet Holman Barter of Carmel, posed with Mr. and Mrs. W. R. Holman. It took the girls several minutes to persuade their mother that the dedication of the sign was indeed being held on their 60th wedding anniversary. Photo by David Eaton.*

Bottom Left: *Mrs. W.R. Holman, Mr. Holman, State Senator Donald Grunsky, Assemblyman Bob Wood, and Monterey County Supervisors Loren Smith and Willard Branson posed with new sign before 1924 Dodge belonging to Pacific Grove antique car buff Earl Lopes. Photo by David Eaton.*

Cartoon that ran in the Pacific Grove Tribune, *September 20, 1972.*

---

32 W.R. Holman included the photos from this article but not the article. He did include the *Monterey Peninsula Herald* article. Both articles had much the same information.

15

Patricia and Harriet Holman in the News

Monterey Trader MONTEREY, CA. FRIDAY, JUNE 22, 1934

PATRICIA HOLMAN WINS GILROY ROUNDUP QUEEN TITLE BY EXPERT HORSEMANSHIP: ENTIRE PENINSULA BACKS LOCAL GIRL FOR SALINAS RACE

Riding her way into the hearts of seven critical judges, on a wiry, plunging little cayuse controlled only by a hackamore, "Pat" Holman of Pacific Grove literally ran away with the show at Gilroy's Gymkhana and Round-up last weekend.

Pat was late. All the other girls had been through their riding tests, and had gone to the hotel to put on final touches for the evening's banquet, where their riding costumes and their "poise and personality" were to be rated.

The judges were tired . . . all but one were eating supper. It was too bad, but Miss Monterey Peninsula was too late to get in the running. Then this judge caught sight of a tall, yellow-clad figure swinging by under a ten-gallon hat, headed for the corral, and he changed his mind, buzzing back into the hotel dining room with the news that the candidate from Monterey had something . . . .

Picks Real Hoss

"What difference does it make if we ARE late," inquired Miss Monterey. "I came to ride. I can ride anything." And she turned down several of the hoss-wrangler's best mounts and chose a mean, short-coupled little bay whose teeth and heels rated him a pen by himself.

"But he won't take a bit," the hoss-wrangler said, "he's used to a hack-amore."

"O.K.," said Pat.

"Did you ever ride with a hackamore?" inquired the h.w.

"No," answered the girl who was going to ride before the judges. This left the bay's startled owner with an open mouth and a glassy expression until she was almost out of sight . . . then he yelled: "Hey, here . . . wear my silver-mounted spurs!" But Pat was on her way.

Judges Get Thrill

There was nothing to it. The judges, napkins in hand, filed out from the dining room to see Pat ride in the lot behind the hotel. Through all her cay-use's plunges and turns she stuck to him like burr, never losing the square-ness of her shoulders, never using leather.

"One hundred percent by me," called out one judge. "That's riding!" And the others echoed his verdict

That night came the banquet, attended by the fourteen girls representing San Francisco, Burlingame, San Jose, Salinas, Watsonville, Santa Cruz, Hollister, San Martin, Monterey Peninsula, Santa Clara, San Juan, Sunny-vale, Palo Alto and Morgan Hill. Following the banquet, a Round-Up dance was held, the candidates being introduced one by one, and greeting the huge audience through a microphone from the stage.

Stunning Costumes

The riding costumes of all the entrants were attractive . . . some tan, some black and white, some dark brown. All included chapareros, high-heeled riding boots and ten-gallon hats. Miss Monterey provided a new and interesting note in cowgirl costumes, appearing in a canary yellow roll-necked sweater and riding breeches under her tan chaps. Black stitched boots, shining spurs and a regular concho-and-jewel decorated cowboy belt completed the outfit, and set off to advantage the tall, slender, erect figure topped by a ten-gallon hat from under which appeared a wave of bronze hair, a pair of golden-brown eyes and a dazzling smile. In about three shakes Miss Monterey was announced "Girl of the Golden West," to rule over the thousands of Gymkhana guests and contestants.

Tevis Ranch Guest

Sunday morning she was the guest of Will Tevis, riding over the hills of his ranch for several hours, flying from his landing field to the ranch, inspecting his polo ponies and the perfect rodeo bowl among the hills where his famous "little rodeos" are held.

That afternoon she presided over the Gilroy Round-Up for the second day's events. Even the sponsors of the great event were amazed at the crowd present, which filled 1000 extra seats after the 5000 grandstand seats were all taken. More than one thousand horses and riders took part in the Sunday parade led by Miss Monterey as the Girl of the Golden West.

Where will she go from here? . . . well, she may have a screen test by Universal Pictures if she wishes. But it is riding, not pictures, that our Miss Monterey is interested in, proving once more that the seven Gilroy judges were right when they found her "different."

Enters Salinas Event

However, if Miss Holman decides to have the fun of a trip to Hollywood, with a screen test and a round of entertainment as her reward for winning the title of Queen of the Round-up at Gilroy, it is hers.

She has also been asked to enter the lists as Miss Monterey Peninsula for the Salinas Rodeo in July, sponsored by the *Monterey Trader* and backed by the Monterey and Pacific Grove chambers of commerce and the *Peninsula Herald*. She has asked Mrs. Antoinette Gay to be her official chaperone at the Rodeo as she was at the Gymkhana.

Miss Patricia Holman, chosen Queen of Gilroy's fifth annual roundup last weekend, with "Colonel Bell," a favorite mount, owned by Col. F.B. Hennessy, U.S.A., Retired, of Pacific Grove. Photo by Heidrick & Heidrick, Monterey.

Times-Herald VALLEJO, CALIFORNIA WEDNESDAY, MAY 1, 1935

RODEO QUEEN CANDIDATE

Miss Harriett Holman, pretty Pacific Grove High School student, is one of the entries competing for queen of the annual Salinas Rodeo. The horse is Rajah, winner of the Kentucky Derby and numerous other awards.

16

Gifts and Donations

[SOURCE UNCLEAR] OCTOBER 10, 1932

HOLMAN'S DONATES TOYS TO FIREMEN FOR POOR KIDDIES

Holman's department store, Pacific Grove, today became a heavy contributor to the Christmas joy to be scattered among children of needy peninsula families through efforts of fire departments of Monterey and Pacific Grove. The store sent a heavy consignment of toys to each department to be added to the stock already on hand.

The contribution consisted of leftover stock from last year and slightly damaged items which, while not saleable, will bring joy to many a child. The toys are to be refurbished in the toy shops being operated by the two departments in preparation for distribution at Christmastime.

Officials of both fire departments expressed deep appreciation of the Holman contributions to the forthcoming Christmas parties.

Meanwhile the Monterey firemen were planning a window display which will be shown in the window of the Monterey bank. Representative toys being manufactured in the toy shop operated by members of the department will be included in the display.

Four cash contributions to the Monterey fire department's toy fund were announced today: Miss Maria Antonia Field $1, Lions Club $5, Twenty Thirty Club $5, and "Anonymous" $1.

Monterey Herald WEDNESDAY, OCTOBER 11TH, 1950

PENINSULA DIARY

MANY RARE GIFTS

by Mayo Hayes O'Donnell

Today we will devote the Diary to a "thank you" to the people of Monterey, the Peninsula and Salinas, who have been so kind to us—historical Monterey. In the three state-owned buildings there are numerous and valuable gifts and loans, all of which make up a collection of furniture, costumes, pictures, documents, etc., which attract not only the interest of our own citizens but the interest and admiration of our tourists.

The Monterey History and Art Association, at a meeting held Monday afternoon, accepted with the deepest appreciation the gift of a rare map of the West when California was considered to be an island. Mrs. Sidney Fish is the generous donor and the gift has been made in memory of her late husband. Also on display is a very old and large camphor chest, leather covered and studded with brass—the gift of Mrs. W. R. Holman.

At the meeting of the association on Monday, the directors voted to send a resolution to the council of the City of Monterey, commending the excellent manner in which Colton Hall had been restored and the interpretation which has been presented to the building as it looked in 1849, and the purpose for which it was used more than 100 years ago. They wished to extend a vote of thanks to Mrs. Guy Curtis and the members of the museum board who have carried out the restoration program.

NATIVE AMERICAN COLLECTION

Game & Gossip JANUARY 30TH, 1962, VOL. II, NO. 12

TREASURES OF AMERICA'S PAST

by Helen Spangenberg

MONTEREY'S WEALTH OF AMERICANA will be enriched immeasurably with the outstanding collection of Indian artifacts, gathered and owned by Mr. and Mrs. W. R. Holman and recently presented by them to the State of California, to be housed in the Pacific building.

No amount of money could measure the value of the collection—the apparel; work, hunting or war tools; ceremonial garb; the designs, colored and woven into the remnants of a culture that nurtured this country. Far more than their material assessment is the educational and historic worth to be derived by future generations in viewing and studying these precious relics of America's past. The Holman collection, without a doubt, is one of the most notable in the United States, containing rare articles such as woven rush moccasins, evaluated by experts to be 4,000 years old, and pre-Columbian pottery, judged to be 1,000 years old.

The appreciation and gratitude of the state of California was acknowledged recently in a resolution which Mr. and Mrs. Holman received and which reads:

WHEREAS, the State Park Commission recognizes and realizes the need for historic items and artifacts to properly interpret California's historic heritage; and

WHEREAS, authentic historic items for interpretative display are extremely hard to obtain and in many cases obtainable only at an unrealistic price; and

WHEREAS, the Holman collection of early California Indian artifacts and historical objects is considered one of the outstanding collections of its type in existence; and

WHEREAS, Wilford and Zena Holman have graciously and generously offered this collection to the State of California at no cost to the State; and

WHEREAS, this collection will greatly enhance the historic interpretation of the Monterey area;

NOW THEREFORE, BE IT RESOLVED that the State Park Commission wishes to thank publicly Wilford and Zena Holman for their public spirited generosity in offering to make this outstanding collection to the State of California and recommends that mutually acceptable terms be negotiated between the Holman family and the proper State Agencies for transfer of this collection and assurance of its proper display.

Working with the Holmans in transferring the collection from their home in Pacific Grove to the Pacific building will be Allen Welts of the state division of beaches and parks. The almost 1,000 items will be listed, catalogued and photographed before they will be arranged for exhibition.

The Holmans' interest in the American Indian stems from W.R. Holman's ancestry, which is traced to Pocahontas, and to Mrs. Holman's parents, who were pioneers in North Dakota. Her father homesteaded a claim 40 miles from where Theodore Roosevelt began his career as a Rough Rider, built a sod house, and managed a ranch bearing the Teacup brand. He collected many Indian relics, among them the knee cap of a buffalo still imbedded with the arrow with which it was shot.

As a child Mrs. Holman learned Indian lore and the appreciation of artistic skill.

"We have treated the Indians so badly," she comments. "We've called them savages, uncivilized and ignorant. But look at this basket, for instance," she continued, pointing out a Hopi wedding basket, "see the mathematical precision of the design. This was done by a woman who had no printed pattern to follow. It is precise, symmetrical and perfectly done.

The Indian was not ignorant. This will attest to artistic artisanship of the highest caliber."

One of the rare items is a buffalo hand-painted rug, of which there are only 82 in existence, according to Mrs. Holman. On a whitened hide there appear a herd of buffalo and figures of Indians in brilliant colors, executed with a delicate touch and fine detail that challenge any criticism of crudity.

Testimony to the Indian woman's artistry and love for her children are the papoose carriers, one completely covered with tiny beads sewn individually on a piece of hide, another covered completely with dentalium shells which resemble thin, long, pointed teeth, sewn into rows and highlighted with a pattern. These were special occasion carriers since the everyday transportation for an Indian baby while his mother worked was a cradleboard, a flat piece of wood or wickerwork, sometimes with an awning or hood.

The Holman collection has several rare kachina dolls, given by the Hopis to their children not as playthings but as symbols of their religion, usually made of balsa or cottonwood and elaborately painted to represent a particular god. One which the Holmans have is the sacred rain god which they acquired from Maynard Dixon, noted Indian authority and painter, and which dates to 1850. The wedding baskets of the Hopi in which gifts were exchanged and consequently became the dowry of the bride are woven with designs of the flight of birds, running water, the sun's rays, the snake and the earthworm. The Holman collection has about 14 examples of this craft.

There is an enormous storage basket which, it is estimated, took the Apache at least a year to weave. There are several examples of baskets with "false embroidery," the weaving so fine that it resembles needlepoint. The camel basket has an interesting legend which is being incorporated into a book on Indians of the southwest. The story is that a young girl out on the plains one day actually saw several of the camels which had been imported into the desert. After being scoffed at by elders upon telling the tale, she wove a basket with the image of a camel to prove her story.

There are cornhusk bags made by the Nez Perce Indians of Idaho, as finely woven with corn to look like fabric with decorative borders. And perhaps the most valuable are the feather baskets of the Pomo Indians who lived around Ukiah. The interior is so tightly woven that it is completely waterproof and on the exterior, the colorful feathers of mallards, gold-finches and red-winged blackbirds have been woven into the reeds and rushes, several bordered with topknots from quail.

No one has been certain as to the exact antiquity of several woven straw plaques which are included in the Holman collection, other than to agree that they are "very, very old."

Among the 47 pieces of pre-Columbian era are several which have been on exhibit at Tulane University, which compare with the collection of Vincent Price and have been catalogued by Oliver LaFarge[33].

There are numerous examples of jars for storage, for carrying water and to hold the ashes of the dead, several of the Holman pieces dated as 1,500 years old.

Arrowheads? There are about 3,000 examples of war and hunting arrows. Among the tomahawks, one was acquired from William Grover, former Indian fighter. The story is that Grover took the war club in the early 1870s from Spotted Tail, an Indian brave. It was eventually stolen from Mr. Grover but he discovered it again 40 years later, identifying it because he scratched his initials on the handle.

Porcupine quills decorate the handle of a peace pipe, of which there are several, including one of red sandstone. Examples of salmon spears will be on exhibit at Sutter's Fort, according to Mrs. Holman.

---

33 In addition to acting, Vincent Price was a well-respected art collector. Oliver LaFarge, anthropologist and writer, was awarded the Pulitzer Prize in fiction in 1929.

There is an Indian kayak, complete with decorated ceremonial paddles. There are several back rests which the Indian squaw made for her brave so that he could relax between his hunting or warring expeditions.

Among the colorful blankets and rugs are several Bayeta blankets, tightly woven squares that are completely reversible, and several sand painted rugs.

Beadwork decorates not only the festive costume for the women, some so heavily embroidered that they must weigh between 40–50 pounds, but saddles for horses and breastplates for the medicine men. One example of the latter is covered with delicate pink beads and contains a pocket for the medicine man's tobacco. To carry tobacco the Indian also sometimes had a buckskin bag covered with beads and when he wanted to transport his possessions he placed them in a "trunk," the Indian parfleche, made of buffalo or horsehide, shaped while wet and decorated with vegetable dye designs.

One of the Indian dresses which the Holmans have was made of Civil War flannel and decorated with shells from the South Seas. It is not only the workmanship which can be admired, but the speculation as to how the shells got to the Indians from the South Seas contributes to the romance of these articles.

In addition to wampum belts there are numerous conch belts, necklaces made of seeds, "the beginning of our costume jewelry," Mrs. Holman adds, bracelets and ceremonial headdresses made of eagle feathers, mink and ermine tails. One headband was made entirely of quills.

There are artifacts from practically every Indian tribe that walked through this country—the Apaches, the Sioux, Pima, Mono, Fresno, Tulare, Maidu, Yokut, Tlinget from Alaska, the Washoes of Nevada, the Mission or Digger Indians, etc.

And for the student who wants to read as well as look, the Holman collection contains not only a set of Smithsonian reference books but three valuable volumes on the History of the Indian Tribes of America by James

Hall and Thomas L. M'Kenney, published by Edward Biddle in 1837. These contain 122 full-page color plates of Indian personalities with biographical sketches and anecdotes.

It took many years of study, travel, and establishing contacts which meant visiting out of the way places and monetary remuneration. It has meant the satisfaction to the collector of finding a choice article and the enjoyment of sharing it, not only with friends, but with young people, too. And as the collection grew so did the demands for housing it, so the people of California and particularly Monterey are being given a truly great opportunity to see America's treasure house of its first citizens.

On a plaque on one of the shelves is an Indian prayer which symbolizes this lifetime avocation of Mr. and Mrs. Holman:

"Great Spirit, help me never to judge another until I have walked two weeks in his moccasins."

[Editor's note: The following photos appeared in *Game & Gossip*, January 30th, 1962, Vol. 11, No. 12. Captions have been edited from their original source for clarity.]

Game & Gossip JANUARY 30TH, 1962, VOL. 11, NO. 12.

About forty pounds of turquoise colored beads, accented with a white border and touches of red design form the yoke of this fringed-hide ceremonial robe worn by women.

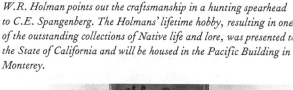

W.R. Holman points out the craftsmanship in a hunting spearhead to C.E. Spangenberg. The Holmans' lifetime hobby, resulting in one of the outstanding collections of Native life and lore, was presented to the State of California and will be housed in the Pacific Building in Monterey.

Mrs. W. R. Holman, shown with one of three rare volumes on the history of Indian tribes, performed the monumental task of itemizing the almost 1,000 books and artifacts.

This huge storage basket took a year to weave. Its precise geometric pattern is a tribute to the Native artist's great skill.

Hundreds of tiny shells and beads, sewn into hides, were the Native woman's way of providing a carriage for her papoose, the carrier complete with hood to shield the baby from the elements.

Two examples of the many baskets in Holman's collection, which includes work of Hopi, Pomos, and other tribes. These show a variety of designs employed by the weaver.

This buffalo hand-painted rug, of which there are only 82 in existence, is considered one of the choicest articles in the collection. Using a whitened hide as canvas, the Indian artist painted the buffalo herd and a band of pursuing hunters above a scene of village life.

One of the rare kachina dolls in the collection (left), this has religious significance for Hopis. Seen also are Medicine Man breastplates of head and bone.

Left: *Chief Sitting Bull. A rare tintype in the Holman collection of Indian relics.*
Middle: *Wearing a woolen cap, Chief Otto Snow Storm holds a peace pipe in this rare picture.*
Right: *In full regalia, Red Cloud is shown with an older chief, before he became a chief.*

This skull, believed to be that of one of Monterey's early Indian inhabitants, was discovered near Del Monte Lodge property.

ESKIMO COLLECTION

Peninsula Herald SUNDAY, DECEMBER 3, 1978

ART AND ARTISTS

HOLMANS GIVE ESKIMO COLLECTION TO MUSEUM

An important section of the Monterey Peninsula Museum of Art's folk art collection was enriched this past week with a donation of 150 early 20[th]century Eskimo ivory carvings from Mr. and Mrs. Wilford R. Holman, longtime Peninsula civic leaders.

At the same time, the two Pacific Grove philanthropists donated 850 ancient pre-Alaskan Eskimo artifacts to the museum's permanent collection.

The artifacts, Holman indicated in a recent interview, were excavated by a university professor who was attempting to locate the first migration of peoples from Siberia to Alaska.

The carved ivories, on the other hand, were created by a self-taught St. Lawrence Island Eskimo named Florence Chauncey and her family.

"Several of Florence's ink drawings," Holman stated, "are in the University of Washington collection and we became acquainted with her work through a university professor who had been in close touch with the St. Lawrence Island people.

"After the professor introduced us to Florence, whose Eskimo name is Melawatkuk, we [Holman and his wife Zena] began to buy her carved ivories.

"That started a long friendship, kept up through letters for years. We also sent Florence's family some clothing from time to time.

"In fact," Holman recalled with a smile, "we clothed some of Florence's children from the time they were babies."

Although the Holman's interest in Eskimo art dates back to a time when an uncle-in-law, named Washburn, maintained trading posts in many of the Alaskan islands, they preferred to have their collection of Alaskan Eskimo artifacts and folk art remain on the Monterey Peninsula for the enjoyment of local residents.

Thus their decision to donate their collection of carved ivory animals, dolls, scrimshaw pieces and artifacts to the Monterey Peninsula Museum of Art.

Expressing delight over the Holman gift, museum director June Braucht tells how, "Mr. and Mrs. Holman invited us (museum president Kate Dietterle and herself) to visit them and see if the material would be of interest to us. Kate and I did so the very day we received the call and when we saw how beautifully the Holmans' collection would fit into the museum's educational and visual program, we alerted the museum's accession committee."

Mrs. Braucht continued, "After all the necessary business procedures were taken care of, we moved the material into the museum and are now constructing a new cabinet for displaying a portion of it in the Folk Art gallery."

Peninsula Herald SUNDAY, DECEMBER 3, 1978.

INK DRAWING. This inhabitant of the far north was drawn in ink by Florence Chauncey of St. Lawrence Island and is included in the collection of Eskimo art donated to the Monterey Peninsula Museum of Art by Mr. and Mrs. Wilford R. Holman of the Peninsula.

ARTIFACTS. A selection of the 850 pre-Alaskan Eskimo artifacts in the Holmans' collection, presented to the Monterey Peninsula Museum of Art, is used in the organization's educational and visual program. Drawings, ivory carvings, dolls, and scrimshaw pieces also were donated.

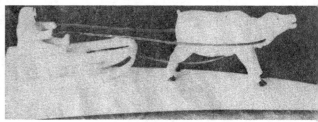

CARVING. Ivory is the medium of this Eskimo traveling across the frozen landscape. The tiny figure is one of 150 ivory carvings from the early 20th century which were given to the art museum's folk art collection by Mr. and Mrs. Holman.

Monterey Peninsula Herald TUESDAY, MAY 7, 1968

A priceless cane that once was the pride, joy and baton of authority of the first alcalde of Monterey, Walter Colton, was presented to the Monterey History and Art Association in honor of Mrs. O'Donnell by Mr. and Mrs. W. R. Holman.[34]

Mrs. W. R. Holman, right, makes Mayo Hayes O'Donnell, Monterey's beloved historian, custodian of a cane once owned by Walter Colton, the first American alcalde of Monterey. Mr. and Mrs. Holman presented the valuable bit of Americana to the Monterey History and Art Association as a way of honoring Mrs. O'Donnell on her birthday.

---

34 The following typeset note is not a part of the article, but was pasted next to it. I believe Holman asked Ms. Jaques to place it where it made the most sense: "Back in the 1920s, Charles McFadden gave a cast iron kettle owned and used by Robert Louis Stevenson to W. R. Holman, who gave it to the Stevenson House. The kettle was used to cook deer meat."

17

Elks Membership

Monterey Peninsula Herald THURSDAY, APRIL 17, 1980

VETERAN ELK

"I am very proud and delighted with my seventy-year pin and to be the oldest member of the Elks in Monterey. I recall the time I went in a spring wagon to be initiated at the Elks Club in Salinas. I became a very active member in Monterey in building our new club here.

"I am very proud to be a member of the 'BPOE' (Best People on Earth)."

W. R. Holman (center), 96-year-old honorary chairman of the Holman's Department Store organization in Pacific Grove, was honored this week with his 70-year pin as a member of the Elks. Presenting the pin to Holman was Murray Vout (left), past exalted ruler of the Monterey Elks lodge, and Everett Williams, a life member. Holman's membership number in the Elks is Number 70, and with his 70-year affiliation he is the oldest living member of the lodge. He was initiated in the Salinas Elks Lodge August 4, 1909, and transferred to the Monterey lodge four years later.

18

Abalone Conservation

The Sunday Peninsula Herald JUNE 13, 1976

WEEKEND MAGAZINE

ONE MAN'S FIGHT TO SAVE THE ABALONE

by John Woolfenden, *Herald* Special Writer

"When I was a boy in Pacific Grove in the late 1880s and 1890s, the abalones were so thick on the shoreline rocks that you couldn't walk out at low tide without stepping all over them," said W.R. Holman.

"In some places, beginning a few miles south of Monterey and continuing south along the coast, abalones would sometimes be several deep, covering whole crevices of rock canyon and extending over 100 feet out into the water when exposed at low tide. Some of them were very big.

"Anybody without any experience could gather all the abalone he wanted without getting his feet wet. Hundreds of people used to come from near and far for the sport of prying these shellfish off the rocks, and for the feast that followed.

"That was before we learned how to slice up the tough foot that adheres to the rock and pound it to make it tender. Instead, it was diced up fine or put through a meat grinder, and made a wonderful chowder.

"Every man and woman hereabouts had some sort of a hook or metal bar to pry the abalones loose. A favorite tool was a broken wagon or automobile spring with one end filed down.

"Of course, we're doing what the Indians had been doing for generations before us. Abalones were a prime source of food for them, too. The tribes from the interior used to make regular trips to the coast for the purpose of gathering them, drying them and taking them back to their villages. And the coastal Indians used the dried abalones for a source of trade. Every Indian burial ground and midden that is dug into today is full of shells and shell fragments."

While acknowledging that sea otters have an appetite for abalone, so do other marine animals, Holman remarked, adding that any attempt to make the otter a scapegoat for the present dwindling supply of the shellfish is ridiculous.

"When otters existed here in much larger numbers, before they were hunted for their furs and nearly wiped out during the first half of the 19th century, there was certainly no lack of abalones, judging by the huge numbers of shells discarded by the Indians," Holman said.

Erwin G. Gudde, in his "California Place Names," states that the names of about 10 points and coves along the coast testify to the presence of the large California mollusk "valued for its meat and for its shell lined with mother-of-pearl. The name originated probably in Rumsen territory of the Costanoan Indians, on the south shore of Monterey Bay, where Point Alones and Point Aulon still testify to the abundance of the mollusk of the genus Haliotis."

The Rumsen word for the red abalone, aulon, became in Spanish aulone or avalone, according to Gudde, who points out that Bayard Taylor, in 1849, gave a detailed description of the "avalones" near Point Pinos.

"They were a marvelous natural resource that should have been thoroughly protected," said Holman. "But thanks to man's greediness, they have almost disappeared, just like our sardines.

"The first commercial fishing of the abalones was by the Chinese colonies which had settled at Point Joe, between there and Seal Rock, at Pebble Beach and in the Chinese village on the present site of Hopkins Marine Station," Holman said. "I remember seeing them with poles on their shoulders and a big rice basket on each end, in which they carried their catch before laying it out in the fields for drying, like squid. Most of the catch was shipped to the Orient," he continued. "However, all of the gathering was from shore, and at low tide, and little if any effect was noticed on the supply.

"Then in 1898 a small band of Japanese—about 10 men—made a survey around Monterey Bay and down the coast.

"In about two weeks many more arrived here. Some of them settled in two large barns where the Coast Guard installation is now. Other occupied barns at Point Lobos and a few small cabins or former coal sheds. Other locations were at the mouth of the Big Sur River and down the coast near Gorda."

A letter written by Holman to George D. Northernholt, state director of natural resources, in June 1935, protesting the reopening of the shores between the Carmel River mouth and the Monterey Wharf to commercial abalone fishing, reviews the situation at the turn of the century and gives his view of what happened to the once abundant supply. It reads in part:

"The fishermen immediately started a systematic campaign of gathering every available abalone of suitable size, which could be gathered at half tide or low tide by wading up to the waist, from one end of county to the other. As soon as boat loads were secured, there were taken to a central location where they (abalones) were taken out of their shells, boiled and dried and placed in storage in great piles."

The kettles, Holman told this writer, were the huge cast iron "try pots" left from the whaling industry which once flourished at Point Lobos. As soon as a sufficient supply of the dried shellfish had been put in trays, "stacked like dried fruit" and had filled the barns, freighters arrived from Japan to pick up "thousands upon thousands" of the delicacy.

As the shoreline supply of abalone dwindled, Holman recounted in his letter to Northernholt, more sophisticated methods were developed to allow hunting at great depths further off shore. Finally, hard-hat diving suits were used in the harvest.

In 1917 there were two diving outfits operating in this district and by 1935, when Holman wrote his letter, that number had grown to 11.

But as early as 1917, the people of Monterey and surrounding counties were concerned about depletion. They unsuccessfully sought controls through the California Fish and Game Commission, but a petition signed by 2,800 prompted action by the legislature. Commercial fishing of abalone was banned in the district between Monterey's Fisherman's Wharf and the Carmel River.

Holman recalled that he and members of the Monterey Peninsula Sportsmen's Conservation Club subsequently obtained 1,500 names on a petition asking the governor and the legislature to stop the drying and exporting of abalone. As a result the fish and game commission came to Monterey and two hearings were held in the chamber of commerce building.

"It was a standing-room-only meeting," he said recently, "with people out on the sidewalk when the building was jammed to capacity. I was on the stand all the first morning and part of the afternoon. We met again the next day, when the commission members were also to be guests of the Allan Abalone Cannery. A. M. Allan, who owned Point Lobos then, gave them a banquet at the cannery, and then took them out in the glass-bottom boats, showing them tens of thousands of shells at the bottom of Carmel Bay, which, they were told, were from abalones which had died of old age and starvation. I was told that the commission swallowed this, hook, line, and sinker."

In his letter to Northernholt, Holman had said: "The facts were that for years, either to cover up the amount of abalones which they were taking from our shores, or for the purpose of keeping the prices of the shells up, which at that time were in great demand for shell jewelry, the abalone cannery management, after extracting the meat, dumped these shells into the bay. The same system of dumping was used at Big Sur, at Gorda, and to a certain extent from Monterey headquarters.

"At the time of our trying to put a protective law through, Prof. Harold Heath, who had been connected with the Stanford Marine Station, made the statement that the abalone had not disappeared from the shores of Pacific Grove and Monterey on account of commercial fishing, but on account of the oil boats coming into our bay, and that this bay under any circumstances would never repopulate.

"This statement was contradicted by me at the time, and with the protection we were able to get—commercial taking prohibited in water less than 30 feet deep between the Wharf and Point Lobos—there was considerable repopulation, but not to compare with the amount of abalones which existed before commercial fishing.

"The remainder of the district has never come to anywhere near the point that existed before this wholesale commercial fishing, when thousands of them were being taken in a single day to be dried or put up in cube form.

"After the area was closed from the wharf to Point Lobos, the law wasn't really enforced. The courts turned loose, for lack of sufficient evidence, divers who had been brought in for disregarding the regulations. It was a crime. We could have saved this resource forever if it hadn't been for political chicanery.

"'Pop' Ernst, who introduced the method of pounding abalone steaks and quick frying them in breadcrumbs and batter, and who became famous as a restauranteur in both San Francisco and Monterey as a result, fought the reserve bitterly in 1917. But in less than six months after it had gone into effect, he came into my office and told me he had been wrong, and that if this law had not gone through to protect the abalone there would not have been one abalone left on the shores of the Monterey Peninsula.

"'Pop' employed his own divers and made a study of abalone life and habits for many years.

"Just a couple of months prior to his death in December, 1934, he called on me to say that there was a move afoot to reopen the area between the wharf and the river, and begged me to use every effort to prevent it. Otherwise, he said, within three weeks every abalone of commercial size would have disappeared from our coastline, leaving Monterey County without any spawning grounds whatever.

"He also said that up to about a year previously, his diving crews had had no trouble going out and getting boatloads of abalones, but now they would frequently come back with not more than a dozen."

The Holman letter to Northenholt, written the following year, said,

"As it requires approximately seven years before an abalone becomes of spawning age and 14 years for an abalone to become of commercial size, you can really understand how this continuance of taking abalones without restrictions in their breeding beds is bound to deplete and exhaust the source of supply . . .

"The commercial fishers operate in water from 20 feet out, which covers all of the main breeding beds. Abalone life starts in on the coast wherever sea algae is located, and extends to a depth of 300 feet, the end of sea algae, the main beds of abalone naturally being in the area which is easily covered by the commercial fishers . . .

"The abalones do not remain stationary, as stated by some of our professors, and some of our commissioners. Schools of abalones travel with the tide back and forth, the same as fish. I have, personally, before the limit, years back filled barley sacks with abalone as they were swimming through the water like fish, and have actual proof of this condition, as others were with me gathering them as they were coming in with the tide."

In the Thanksgiving Day storm of 1919, when much of the Monterey fishing fleet was wrecked, hundreds of abalone were washed up on the beaches, Holman interpolated.

The letter concludes with the statement that requests to the governor to veto the bill reopening the district, had been made by the Pacific Grove City Council, Mayor Sheldon Gilmer, the Monterey Junior Chamber of Commerce, the Pacific Grove Chamber of Commerce, sportsmen's clubs of the Monterey Peninsula, also of Salinas, Watsonville and Santa Cruz; the Lighthouse Club, the Lions Club of the Monterey Peninsula, City Atty. Reginald Foster of Pacific Grove and the Santa Cruz Chamber of Commerce.

Their joint efforts were successful in obtaining a veto for what was actually a rider to a bill that would have opened up not only the river-wharf area, but also a section of coastline in Santa Cruz County.

Ten years later, in March, 1945, Holman was told that consideration was being given to opening up large abalone beds to commercial fishing in the Mendocino County coast. He wrote to the *Ukiah Republican Press*, giving in great detail the history of what had happened along the Monterey County coast. The Ukiah newspaper gave front-page space to the letter.

In it, Holman quoted Phil Oyer, deputy fish and game commissioner stationed on the Monterey Peninsula in 1916, as reporting that 40,000 abalones were harvested by a single outfit in the waters between Pacific Grove beach and Carmel River during the month of August.

"In 1927," Holman wrote to Ukiah, "Monterey Bay alone produced three million pounds of dressed abalone, and a much larger tonnage was taken from many other ports along the Monterey County coast." Most of the catch was exported.

Mendocino County, Holman said recently, was successful in banning commercial fishing of abalone. Marin County was left open. As a result, he said, Mendocino County still has abalone. Marin County went the way of Monterey Bay.

In 1973 came what is now referred to as "the biggest abalone bust in California history," when the State Fish and Game wardens arrested 11 men accused of illegally picking the shellfish from the rocks at Santa Rosa Island, in the Santa Barbara Channel. Other poachers got away, but the 11, after court trial, were convicted and either fined or jailed. "It's easy to run afoul of the law on fathering the shellfish," the *Wall Street Journal* reported in a recent feature article. "It's illegal to take undersize abalone or catch more than five a day for a sportsman or 20 dozen for a commercial operator. 'Beachwalking,' or hunting abalones at tideline during extremely low tides, is illegal at some places, such as Santa Rosa Island. Other rules govern the type of diving equipment permitted. Finally, the entire northern half of the California coast is off limits to commercial abalone gathering."

What was a $5 million a year commercial catch has plummeted, the *Journal* stated. Annual landings are less than half what they were in the late 1960s.

As a result, the price per pound has jumped sky-high, to $8.50 wholesale and $12.50 retail, at last reports. Small wonder that abalone has disappeared totally from many Monterey Peninsula restaurant menus.

Today there is virtually no commercial abalone fishing on the central coast north of Point Purisima in San Luis Obispo County, according to Ken Boettcher, marine warden for the Monterey division of the Department of

Fish and Game. There is none on the Monterey County coast and there is almost no abalone industry remaining in Morro Bay, formerly a center of the activity, he said. "But there are still some good catches in the Purisima area and at some spots south along the San Luis Obispo County coast."

"It's too bad," said W.R. Holman, "but, just as with the sardines, here's a resource that should have been policed and protected years and years ago. Some of us spent a lot of time and effort trying to get this idea across."

[Editor's note: Abalone fishing remains illegal in Monterey Bay. The Monterey Abalone Company currently operates an in-ocean, sustainable, abalone farm off of Wharf #2 in Monterey, where live abalone can be purchased by home cooks and chefs around the country.]

19

The Steinbeck Letters

THESE LETTERS WERE NOT INCLUDED IN W.R. HOLMAN'S BOOK, BUT were in the Holman boxes. I include them for their historical value, with respect to John Steinbeck. Mrs. Holman was an avid reader and book collector, as well as a writer of poetry and fiction. (She self-published a novella, *My Monterey.*) As we know, John Steinbeck mentioned Holman's in his novel *Cannery Row*. Beyond that, Steinbeck knew the Holmans and corresponded with Mrs. Holman over the years. Following are several letters from Steinbeck to Mrs. Holman. Two were typewritten; two are handwritten. For ease of reading, I've typed the contents of each letter, and have also included a photo of each. For the two hand-written letters, I have the corresponding envelopes, which is how I've been able to include the dates they were written.

=

The following letter is John Steinbeck's first personal contact with Mrs. Holman. He writes to ask for her assistance with getting his friend, William Alston Ritchie Lovejoy, a job at Holman's. Ritchie Lovejoy, a writer, was part of Steinbeck's inner circle, and is best known as the writer to whom Steinbeck donated his $1,000 Pulitzer Prize for *The Grapes of Wrath*.

Los Gatos, California,
March 10, 1938.

Dear Mrs Holman:

I feel a little self conscious in writing to you
in as much as I have never met you. However, it may be that
this communication may be of some value to you. And I do
know that you knew my parents when they were living and
that you████ know of my work.

Ritchie Lovejoy has, I believe, applied for
a position xx in the advertising department of Holman's.
I know that he is capable and energetic and trained the
the field. He knows not only advertising layout, selling
but is in addition a very fine commercial artist. I am
quite sure that he could fill the position and be of
peculiar and rather extraordinary value. I have known
him for many years.

There I have done it and it was difficult because
I have never done any such thing before. There must be rules
for recommending a man to a job, but I have never learned them.
I hope that you will seriously consider Mr. Lovejoy for this
position.

In my own interest, may I thank you, Mrs. Holman,
for your interest in my work and for your efforts in
creating an interest in my books on the Penninsula. I hope
I may meet you some time.

Sincerely,

John Steinbeck.

Steinbeck letter, March 10, 1938.

Los Gatos, California
March 10, 1938

Dear Mrs. Holman:

   I feel a little self conscious in writing to you in as much as I have never met you. However, it may be that this communication may be of some value to you. And I do know that you knew my parents when they were living and that you know of my work.

   Ritchie Lovejoy has, I believe, applied for a position in the advertising department of Holman's. I know that he is capable and energetic and trained the the field. He knows not only advertising layout [and] selling but is in addition a very fine commercial artist. I am quite sure that he could fill the position and be of peculiar and rather extraordinary value. I have known him for many years.

   There I have done it and it was difficult because I have never done any such thing before. There must be rules for recommending a man to a job, but I have never learned them. I hope that you will seriously consider Mr. Lovejoy for this position.

   In my own interest, may I thank you, Mrs. Holman, for your interest in my work and for your efforts in creating an interest in my books on the Peninsula. I hope I may meet you some time.

   Sincerely,

   John Steinbeck

===

With Steinbeck's endorsements, Ritchie Lovejoy was hired at Holman's. In Mrs. Holman's next correspondance, she must have asked Steinbeck to have an autograph party or reading at Holman's. His response is on the next few pages.

Los Gatos, Calif.

March 14, 1938

Dear Mrs. Homan:

It was not only courteous but very pleasant
of you to write. And I am sure that you will be pleased with
Mr. LoveJoys ability and acumen. I feel better about it, having
had your letter. It seemed a highly presumptious thing to do.

When you are in this neighborhood, I should like
it if you would come to see us. The place is difficult to find,
but you could telephone and we could give you directions.
Please do.

You know if I ever had an autograph party, I would
have to leave the country. I have never done it, have
refused everyone from Brentano's on , on the ground that the
proper work of a writer was to writer. I've used the same
argument about speaking. There is safety in never having
done a thing. If I borke it once then I could never mend the
breach again . And I wonder if you know the extent, the
American desire for speaking has. People who don't at all
want to read books, want to listen to speeches. It's awful.
And about autographing-- I shall never forget a terrible
picture of Mr. Woolcott with a fat pen in a chubby hand
standing in back of a pile of books. There was a sweet
social smile ob his face, and(knowing mr. Woolcott,)
a string of black curses in his heart. And there he stood
signing books with little phrases he had made up the night
before. You know I would rather sell fewer books . Besides that
I don't think it is very good business. A man or a woman who
admires a book, may very well have his liking turned to contempt
of an author who will jump through little literary hoops.
Its like the feeling you get for a dog who knows too many

Steinbeck letter, March 14th, 1938, page 1.

2.

tricks. If he hunts birds or kills rats, you like him much
better. I've gone on at a great rate about this. It is a
sore point, this tendency to make of writers little trick dogs.
I think a book should do its own work without the writer
acting as ring master.

If you have had as much rain as we have, the
upper streets must have run down and piled up on
Lighthouse. We have had two months of rain and we are very
sick of it.

Again thank you, Mrs. Holman for your courtesy, and
please do come to see us.

Sincerely

John Steinbeck

Steinbeck letter, March 14th, 1938, page 2

Los Gatos, Calif.
March 14, 1938

Dear Mrs. Holman:

It was not only courteous but very pleasant of you to write. And I am
sure that you will be pleased with Mr. Lovejoy's ability and acumen. I feel
better about it, having had your letter. It seemed a highly presumptuous
thing to do.

When you are in this neighborhood, I should like it if you would come
and see us. The place is difficult to find, but you could telephone and we
could give you directions. Please do.

You know if I ever had an autograph party, I would have to leave the country. I have never done it, have refused everyone from Brentano's[35] on the ground that the proper work of a writer was to write. I've used the same argument about speaking. There is safety in never having done a thing. If I broke it once then I could never mend the breach again. And I wonder if you know the extent [of] the American desire for speaking. People who don't at all want to read books, want to listen to speeches. It's awful. And about autographing—I shall never forget a terrible picture of Mr. Woolcott[36] with a fat pen in a chubby hand standing in back of a pile of books. There was a sweet social smile on his face, and (knowing Mr. Woolcott) a string of bleak curses in his heart. And there he stood signing books with little phrases he had made up the night before. You know I would rather sell fewer books. Besides that I don't think it is a very good business. A man or a woman who admires a book, may very well have his liking turned to contempt of an author who will jump through little literary hoops. Its like the feeling you get for a dog who knows too many tricks. If he hunts birds or kills rats, you like him much better. I've gone on at a great rate about this. It is a sore point, this tendency to make of writers little trick dogs. I think a book should do its own work without the writer acting as ring master.

If you have had as much rain as we have, the upper streets must have run down and piled up on Lighthouse. We have had two months of rain and are very sick of it.

Again, thank you Mrs. Holman for your courtesy, and please do come and see us.

Sincerely,

John Steinbeck

---

35 Brentano's was a bookstore chain.

36 Alexander Woollcott (I've retained Steinbeck's spelling) was a nationally known critic and commentator for *The New Yorker*.

Wednesday

Dear Mrs. Halman:

Sorry to delay answering your letter, but as a look at my account will show, I have been painting and fixing the little cottage my father built on 11th St before I was born. Then last night what with paint smells and windows open, I got a bad chill which persisted. I haven't time for a cold so I hit the sack and will try to break it up quickly. But at least I can write a letter although upside down.

Surely I will read your manuscript but against every advice of agents and publishers. The reasons professional writers will not read manuscripts are two and neither has anything to do with you — or maybe the second has a little. It is a common practice for certain people (I am convinced they are groups) to sue established writers. These either deal with a locale or with a kind of generalized plot. There is some correspondence on the matter. Later if the writer touches that locale or that plot (and there are only 12) there is a plagiarism suit and a correspondence to back it up. So if you think a writer is snooty about work of an unknown — it isn't true. He is just cautious. Few nonprofessionals know this but it is a very common practice. I said this did not apply to you.

The second is this — A nonprofessional usually wants not criticism but reassurance and compliments. I notice that the things you quoted were all favorable.

2

Now the only healthy effect of criticism of unpublished work is destructive because through that, changes are indicated. But this kind of creative criticism is usually detested.

I said there were two but there are four reasons. A friend or an acquaintance is incapable of good criticism since his judgement is warped by association. A thing should stand on its own. With an editor or an agent it has to. I would never think of showing work to some one I knew or who knew me before it was published.

The fourth is a little bit complicated but none the less true — there is no writer who is any good as a critic. It just very rarely happens if at all.

If in the light of these things you still want me to read your book, I will but the advantage to you will be practically non-existent. I don't know what publishers will buy. Neither do they. Writing is a trade and a craft like plumbing or printing or say merchandizing. The possibility of your first book being good is very remote just as the possibility of opening a successful store without training is remote. I threw away five novels and should have thrown away five before my first book was printed. This year I threw out two plays and part of a novel — last year a play, a picture script and a long essay.

Steinbeck letter, September, 1948, page 2.

I'm writing this all to show you that this craft never gets easy and you never get used to it. But after years of work, you yourself know what is wrong with it. If you don't believe this, read the divergent opinions of critics (professional) on the same material.

This sounds like a lecture and I suppose it is. But I value the friendship of your family very highly. And I insist I will read the book if you want me to in the light of what I have said.

My head is reeling from the fever that followed the chill, and the violent antifebra quinte but the whole thing.

I shall hope to see you.

Very sincerely

John Steinbeck

Steinbeck letter, September, 1948, page 3.

==

In her previous letter Mrs. Holman asked Steinbeck to read her manuscript. He gives her the reasons he doesn't think that's a good idea. When Steinbeck refers to his "account," he means at Holman's.

147 11th Street

Pacific Grove, California

Dear Mrs. Holman:

Sorry to delay answering your letter, but as a look at my account will show, I have been painting and fixing the little cottage my father built on 11th St before I was born. Then last night what with paint smells and wide open windows, I got a bad chill which persisted. I haven't time for a cold so I hit the sack and will try to buck it up quickly. But at least I can write a letter although upside down.

Surely I will read your manuscript but against every advice of agents and publishers. The reason professional writers will not read manuscripts are two and neither has anything to do with you—or maybe the second has a little. It is a common practice for certain people (I am convinced they are groups) to send a m.s.s.^{37} [to] established writers. These either deal with a locale or with a kind of generalized plot. There is some correspondence on the matter. Later if the writer touches that locale or that plot (and there are only 12 plots) there is a plagiarism suit and a correspondence to back it up. So if you think a writer is snooty about work of an unknown, it isn't true. He's just cautious. Few nonprofessionals know this but it is a very common practice. I said this did not apply to you.

The second is this—a nonprofessional usually wants no criticism but

---

37 Abbreviation for "manuscript."

reassurance and compliments. I notice that the things you quoted were all favorable. Now the only healthy effect of criticism of unpublished work is destructive because through that, changes are [indicated][38]. But this kind of creative criticism is usually detested.

I said there were two but there are four reasons. A friend of an acquaintance is incapable of good criticism since his judgement is warped by association. A thing should stand on its own. With an editor or agent it has to. I would never think of showing work to someone I know or who knew me before it was published.

The fourth is a little bit complicated but none the less true—there is no writer who is any good as a critic. It just very rarely happens if at all.

If in the light of these things you still want me to read your book, I will but the advantage to you will be practically non-existent. <u>I don't know</u> what publishers will buy. Neither do they. Writing is a trade and a craft like plumbing or printing—or say merchandising. The possibility of your first book being good is very remote just as the possibility of opening a successful store merchant training is remote. I threw away five novels and should have thrown away five before my first book was published. This year I threw out two plays and part of a novel—last year a play, a picture script and a long essay.

I am writing this all to show you that this craft never gets easy and you never get used to it. But after years of work, you yourself know what is wrong with it. If you don't believe this, read the divergent opinions of critics (professionals) of the same material.

This sounds like a lecture and I suppose it is. But I value the friendship of your family highly. And I insist I will read the book if you want me to in the light of what I have said.

---

38 Numerous people looked at this letter and none are sure what this word is. We think this is as close as we can get. Contact me if you have other ideas!

My head is reeling from the fever that followed the chill, and the violent antifeb[39] given to heal[40] the whole thing.

I shall hope to see you soon.

Very sincerely,

John Steinbeck

==

On the next page is the final communication from Steinbeck, though it is likely he and Mrs. Holman's paths crossed at the store or in town.

---

39 Once again, none of us are sure of this word, though we believe he wrote "antifebrile." Thanks to Brittany Brubaker, Glynis Barrett, and Megan Terry, who helped decipher the most difficult words throughout.

40 Another guess at the actual word—this could be "lull" also; unclear.

147- 11ᵗʰ St, P.G.
Friday

Dear Mrs Holman:

As I told you in my other note. I am trying to do three things at once. I won't be able to get to your m.ss. for some little time. I have to go back to Mexico next week and will be gone for about a month before I return. (please advise credit dep't not to worry about my account) I have glanced into the manuscript. It has to my mind the stiffness of sentence structure and the lack of ease that is the result of too little practice. Also the dialogue is not very convincing. However, dialogue is probably the most difficult writing of all. If you set down exactly what people say, it does not sound like talk at all. It is translating it into something that sounds like something people might say that is hard.

The best and truest criticism comes from good literary agents and publishers.

As I say I will go into this more thoroughly when I get back from Mexico sometime near the middle of December. I have to go down to lay out the locations for a film. Then I will be very happy if you will come over and again.

Yours sincerely
John Steinbeck

Steinbeck letter, September 6th, 1948.

October 23, 1948
147 11 St. Street; P.G.

Dear Mrs. Holman:

As I told you in my other note I am trying to do three things at once. I won't be able to get to your m.s.s. for some little time. I have to go back to Mexico next week and will be gone for about a month before I return. *(Please advise credit dep't not to worry about my account.)* I have glanced into the manuscript. It has to my mind the stuffiness of sentence structures and the lack of care that is the result of too little practice. Also the dialogue is not very convincing. However, dialogue is probably the most difficult writing of all. If you set down exactly what people say, it doesn't sound like talk at all. It is translating it into something that sounds like something people <u>might</u> say that is hard.

The best and trusted criticism comes from good literary agents and publishers.

As I say I will go into this more thoroughly when I get back from Mexico sometime near the middle of December. I have to go down to lay out the locations for a film. Then I will be very happy if you will come over one afternoon.

Sincerely,

John Steinbeck

20

Mrs. W. R. Holman

ZENA HOLMAN PASSED AWAY NEARLY TWO YEARS BEFORE HER HUS-
band. While Zena was usually the collector of newspaper clippings,
W.R. saved many articles about her after her passing. I read through
thin pieces of old newspapers, as well as what he had included in his
original manuscript. Following are articles from his manuscript and
what I thought added further layers to her personality.

Monterey American SATURDAY, SEPTEMBER 21, 1912

GROVE COUPLE ARE MARRIED: WILFORD HOLMAN
AND ZENA PATRICK PLEDGE THEIR TROTH

Accompanied by Walter Whitney and Miss Patrick's sister, Wilford Hol-
men and Miss Zena Patrick, for some time past in charge of the cloak and
suit department of Holman's big store in Pacific Grove, went to San Francisco yesterday morning and were married in St. Joseph's church. Mrs.
Holman is the niece of Rev. Mr. Howe of the Grove and the daughter of

Mr. and Mrs. Patrick of Hollister. She is popular and has added much to the success of the business. W.R. Holman, who has lived the greater part of his life in the Grove, is known among men as a rising man of marked business qualities.

Upon their return form [sic] a short honeymoon trip Mr. and Mrs. Holman will take up their residence in the Grove.

The *American*, in common with the many friends of the newlyweds, extends felicitations and hopes their voyage on the sea of matrimony will be peaceful and happy.

Monterey Peninsula Herald AUGUST 16, 1951

MRS. HOLMAN DESCRIBES TRIP: OVER 400 GUESTS HEAR OF EUROPEAN TRAVELS AT DINNER IN PACIFIC GROVE

A fitting climax to the 60th anniversary of Holman's Department Store came Tuesday night when 450 employees and their guests were entertained by the store management at dinner and heard Mrs. W. R. Holman give an informal and witty account of her four months' tour of Europe.

The Pacific Grove Masonic Hall was the scene of the dinner. Vernon Hurd, as master of ceremonies, introduced "that jet propulsion on our mezzanine, the first lady of our store." Dressed in a colorful Norwegian costume, similar to one she had seen worn at a wedding at Hardinger Fjord in Norway, Mrs. Holman took her audience on a whirlwind tour of the continent, touching on the highlights of the trip she had just completed.

"We followed springtime around the world," Mrs. Holman said, as she described the beauties of the Atlantic crossing, the Mediterranean, Italy, France, Holland, Switzerland, the Scandinavian countries and Western Germany.

"I don't know why I felt like Columbus—millions of people have made the trip before me—but nonetheless that's just how I felt," she said. "Here were the things I had studied and heard about since my childhood actually coming to life before me."

Hilarious incidents of the trip, including the amazing costumes and reactions of passengers on the *Independence* when the fire alarm rang, their adventures with their guide, Charlie, and their efforts to solve Italian plumbing, were recounted by Mrs. Holman to the delight of her audience.

She described the tragedy of destruction in Western Germany, the thrilling beauty of the flower markets in Holland, the immaculate charm of the Scandinavian countries and their people and the history of the ages as it is to be seen in the architecture and masonry of Italy.

"Don't fool yourselves for one minute, if we move out of Europe, Russia will move in. A vacuum cannot exist. And if Russia moves in, the fun will begin. We are saving our own necks by rebuilding Europe, and I saw with my own eyes much of the fine restoration of transportation, communication and sanitation that is being effected with our money through the Marshall Plan," Mrs. Holman said.

Preceding Mrs. Holman's talk, Mr. Hurd introduced other special guests, among them W.R. Holman, store president; Dr. and Mrs. Eugene O'Meara (Patricia Holman) of Pasadena, Mr. and Mrs. Arthur W. Barter Jr. (Harriet Holman), the C.E. Holmans, the Victor Patricks, the Charles Olmsteds, Mr. and Mrs. Gordon Knoles and daughter, Adrienne; Gordon Byers, Norman Sharkey, editor of "Holmanac," Harold Green, Mrs. Ida Reed, Mrs. Bertha Lake, Henry and Charles Loughery and Charles Coyle.

Eight veteran Holman's employees whose years of service with the store total 185 received special recognition. They are Anna Brinten, 30 years with the store; Paul Norton, who has been associated with Holman's since 1924; Mrs. Minnie King, an employee of Holman's for 24 years; LaVerne Blikre, 24 years; Genevieve Allen, 19 years; Wilma Vons, 23 years; Florence Lauritzen, 18 years, and Alice Carmody, 17 years.

The ham dinner was prepared and served by members of Cypress Re-
bekah Lodge, assisted by young women of the Rainbow Girls and by boys
from the DeMolay chapter. Rev. T.J. Barkle opened the evening with the
invocation, followed by the national anthem.

The Classmate OCTOBER 1968 VOL. 8, NO. 8

PORTRAIT OF A SPIRITED LADY

by Paige Evans

A visit to the Holman house in Pacific Grove is a fascinating experience.
It is a warm and friendly house, originally built with sixteen gables by
the present W.R. Holman's father. The large library of seasoned woods
is wrapped in rare books on California history and Indians. On a square
grand piano rests a stock of yellow newspapers which headline Lincoln's
assassination, Jeff Davis' trial, the Chicago fire, and Commodore Dewey's
great naval victory at Manila. It somehow seems right that Zena Patrick
Holman was born in the wilderness of North Dakota at the time when
Indians roamed the territory. She was born a woman of spirit, game for
adventure and a lover of challenge. She spent her early days in an adobe
hut, built by her father on their homestead cattle ranch. That childhood
home later inspired Zena Holman to help in the fight to save the adobes of
Monterey.

Religion and Roots

With school teacher parents, the five Patrick children heard nightly lessons from the Bible and the dictionary. Their mother explained God and
religion, roots and derivations. This sparked in young Zena an inspiring
faith and an interest in Latin and the law. When the family moved to Red
Bluff, Calif., at the foot of Mt. Shasta, she was a star member of her high
school's championship debating team. After graduation, she longed to

attend university where she might become a lawyer. Lacking funds for a law degree, she instead entered business college and took up the challenge of a career in merchandising.

There was no eight-hour work law when Zena went to work for a large Berkeley store. It didn't take her long to learn the operation of every department. The next job[41] took her to a small firm in Pacific Grove. Her new boss was the young and handsome Wilford Holman, whose father had begun the business as a one aisle store. Soon she was the boss's bride and his energetic right hand in business.

Times were not always easy and there were numerous setbacks. Mrs. Holman seemed to have an amazing capacity for work and responsibility without sacrificing her contagious optimism. She traveled from San Francisco to New York as a buyer, raised two little girls, and was ready with encouragement when things got rough. The store grew and improved, even though some spoke of the large, expanding store in a small town as "Holman's Folly." Through it all, Zena Holman persisted. "We can do anything that's right."

Always Learning

Continually interested in learning, Zena Holman taught herself Latin for fun and Spanish because she wanted to visit Mexico. Wherever she travelled, she engaged her curiosity by browsing through book shops and often junk shops. Eventually her hand-picked treasures became famed collections. Scholars were attracted for years by her basement of Indian artifacts. The collection now belongs to the people of California. It is so big that only 15 percent of the exhibit can be displayed at Monterey's Old Pacific Building.

---

41 From W.R. Holman's telling, we know that Mrs. Holman worked in Salinas before she came to Pacific Grove.

Author Frank Walker spent two weeks at the Holman dining table, pouring over the Jack London first editions and personal papers. He gives credit to Mrs. Holman's collection as a "real find" towards the completion of his book, Jack London and the Klondike.

It would take forever to tell the countless stories which make up this extraordinary lady's life. There seems to be no end to the vitality and scope of the fascinating Mrs. Holman. She speaks in word pictures of the days when holiday makers came to the raw, natural paradise of Pacific Grove, in luxurious railroad cars. She recalls the gorgeous Del Monte Hotel (now the Naval Postgraduate School). The grounds were a splendor of gardens; there was an orchid house, groomed horses, coachmen with beautiful attire and silk top hats. "It was a grand place and the dances were wonderful."

With all her many facets, Mrs. Holman is a patriotic lady. Every evening, she clips the lead stories and editorials from half a dozen newspapers. She is well informed on all levels of politics and is actively involved in helping her community, state and country. As a writer and speaker, she gives of herself. As a generous citizen, she gives of her time and possessions. She is a remarkable woman who lives what she believes, that "We must give something for the space we occupy . . . some sort of rental to God and Humanity."

Game & Gossip MARCH 10, 1972, VOL. 17, NO. 9

A GREAT CITIZEN: MRS. WILFORD R. HOLMAN
by Helen Spangenberg

"Since living here for so long, I've loved every inch of the Monterey Peninsula. The cities which have sprung up from the early Spanish days have woven a sentiment that is deep in my soul and I am grateful, so very grateful to have been able to serve the people of this locality."

This is the response of Zena Patrick Holman to being named 1972 Citizen of the Year of the Monterey Peninsula. The latest honor by the Chamber of Commerce is only one in the collection of Mrs. Holman, whose efforts in conservation, civic, cultural, and historic endeavors in the area have been recognized by the State of California and numerous commissions . . . "I remember the hard work we had in preserving Asilomar when the YMCA wanted to sell it years ago. It could have become a honky-tonk development," she reminded. "But with the earnest work of the people of the area, Asilomar was saved as one of the important spots on the Peninsula where thousands of people can enjoy its beauty of the shores of the Pacific Ocean. Mrs. Philbrook (director of Asilomar) told me at one time that she had conventions booked for five years ahead!"

. . . Mrs. Holman pointed to a recent letter from Governor Ronald Reagan thanking her for the donation of an Indian basket—one made of feathers by the Pomo Indians—which he had taken as a gift to the Emperor of Japan.

"There are so many exciting changes every day! We are living in revolutionary times. Just think of going to the moon! We used to think of the moon only as something associated with a nursery rhyme or a romantic song. You know," she continued, "a noted woman once wrote that the time will come when men will look down from the moon not up to it!" . . .

. . . "God is master of the universe. We need only to know that and realize that the sun comes up every morning, to sustain us. In appreciation we should take advantage of our good fortune in being able to live in this wonderful country, in this beautiful Peninsula, by working hard to preserve this heritage so that we can pass it on to other generations."

Game & Gossip DECEMBER 1, 1973, VOL. 18, NO. 7

PENINSULA AUTHORS

MY MONTEREY

A charming story of a wealthy family of travelers to Monterey in the 1930s whose stay is disturbed by the odor from the fish reduction plants and canneries on "the row." In the process of having the odor identified and explained, the family is exposed to the story of the fishing industry, the history of the Monterey Peninsula and its customs and peoples. The author very clearly weaves a love story in and out of Cannery Row, fishing boats and Monterey pines.

Mrs. Zena Holman has realized a life-long ambition with the publication of "My Monterey." A native North Dakotan, who has since adopted the Peninsula as her own, Mrs. Holman has become an ardent booster of the area and has chosen her favorite surroundings as a background for her first endeavor as an author.

Mrs. Holman has drawn extensively on her vast knowledge and love of the Monterey Peninsula in the penning of this novella. And, her awareness of the history of the area has been used to good advantage as well as her research and large library.

===

[Editor's note: The Zena Holman Library was a great achievement for Mrs. Holman—in many ways, this was her life's work. While there are photos from the day of the dedication and an article in the Parks and Recreation newsletter for the State of California, I could not find a relevant clipping among the boxes and papers. Instead, I offer snippets from the article I wrote about visiting this library for the *Cedar Street Times* in the 2016 Good Old Days issue.]

February 28, 1974 was the dedication of the Zena Holman Library of California and American History, located on the Asilomar Conference Grounds. For a large part of her life, Mrs. Holman had collected first editions of books; more than 3,000 of these are housed at the Zena Holman Research Library. She called the opening of the library "the proudest moment of my life," according to the April 1974 issue of News & Views, *the newsletter of the Department of Parks and Recreation for California State Parks.*

The crowning glory of the collection is the entire Zamarano 80. Founded in 1928, the Zamarano Club of Los Angeles went through several incarnations before publishing a book in 1945, listing the eighty most important books that a collector of Californiana would have in their library. It's very rare to have the entire Zamarano 80 in one library. You can view first editions of Gertrude Atherton's The Splendid Idle Forties, *Mary Austin's* The Land of Little Rain, *Samuel Clemens/Mark Twain's* The Celebrated Jumping Frog of Calaveras County and Other Sketches, *John Muir's* The Mountains of California, *Robert Louis Stevenson's* The Silverado Squatters, *and seventy-five others that typify (according to the club), California literature.*

Mrs. Holman compiled a collection of works by authors frequently included on an English Literature syllabus: Charles Dickens, Jack London, Robinson Jeffers, John Steinbeck, Ernest Hemingway, Robert Louis Stevenson, Mark Twain, and hundreds more. All of these can be viewed by appointment with the California State Parks Department at Asilomar.

Monterey Peninsula Herald WEDNESDAY, MARCH 3, 1980

WE MOURN THE PASSING OF MRS. ZENA PATRICK HOLMAN, WIFE OF WILFORD R. HOLMAN, AND PAY TRIBUTE TO THE MEMORY OF THIS TRULY GREAT CITIZEN

Mrs. Holman, the former Zena Patrick, was born in Taylor, North Dakota. Her family migrated to California in 1896, residing first in Red Bluff, then Berkeley, Hollister, and Pacific Grove.

Before coming to Pacific Grove, Zena had graduated from the Oakland Polytechnic Business College, and had been a stenographer for the Fisk Teachers Agency at Berkeley, and started learning merchandising at the Capwell Company in Berkeley.

She joined the Holman store, before her marriage to its owner, as manager of the Ladies Ready-to-Wear Department.

In 1908 Wilford R. Holman took over the store his father had founded, and began enlarging it into a Department Store. In 1912 Zena and Wilford Holman were married. In the 1920s, Holman's was known as the "largest department store between San Francisco and Los Angeles."

Meanwhile, the Holmans had two lovely daughters, Patricia and Harriet. During the ensuing years, Mr. and Mrs. Holman worked long hours, shoulder to shoulder. Mrs. Holman once said, "We would wheel the girls in a buggy from our house down to the store, and they would nap while we worked. Friends would tell us that we worked too hard, but we were happy, in love, strong and well. We loved everybody and doing for the community. You can't beat that combination."

Through the years, Mrs. Holman continued "doing for the community" in many ways, and received recognition as "A Great Citizen."

She was the first President of the Pacific Grove P.T.A., a Charter Member of the Pacific Grove Art Center Guild, and for over 50 years had been a member of the Pacific Grove Civic Club, where she had an honorary life membership. She worked diligently to help preserve Asilomar State Conference Center and Park, and also worked with Miss Margaret Jacks to preserve the historic adobe landmarks in Monterey.

Other recognitions include the Monterey History and Art Association's "Laura Bride Powers Award" in 1949 for her endeavors in the fields of preservation and conservation.

In 1971, Mrs. Holman's name was added to the select list of woman on the Honor Roll of the Grand Parlor of the Native Daughters of the Golden West. In January 1972, she was presented the "Golden Bear" award by the California Department of Parks and Recreation, and in February of the same year, she was proclaimed "Citizen of the Year" by the Monterey Peninsula Chamber of Commerce.

Mrs. Holman started and maintained a collection of scrapbooks that combine to make an historical treasure. She once remarked, "Col. Griffin had a wonderful paper in the *Monterey Peninsula Herald* and I found it a tremendous inspiration." She wrote numerous letters, which were printed on the Opinion Page, and had great influence on public thinking.

There is a complete scrapbook of the seven-year struggle to have the Pacific Grove-Carmel highway built in the "twenties" . . . culminating with a framed copy of the Resolution to have that part of Route 68 officially designated "The W. R. Holman Highway," a 1971 act of the California Legislature.

In November, 1961, Mr. and Mrs. Holman donated a valuable collection of American Indian artifacts, carefully gathered over 45 years, to the state of California. At that time the collection was appraised at $50,000 and contained some items 4,000 years old. Over 1,000 of these artifacts, baskets, costumes, cooking and living accoutrements are now on display in the Hall of the American Indian at the Pacific Building State Historical Monument in Monterey.

In November 1973, Mrs. Holman presented a collection of California history books to the Asilomar Conference Grounds. Her gift went then to the new ranger training facility at Asilomar. During a meeting in Sacramento, the State Parks and Recreation Commission adopted a resolution of appreciation, thus expressing official thanks for her generosity.

Mrs. Holman somehow obtained the original symbolic cane of Walter Colton, the first Alcalde of Monterey, and contributed it to the Monterey History and Art Association.

Mrs. Holman played a major role in building the fine reputation of Holman's Department Store, and was the persuading influence in the expansion and remodeling of the store to its present size, to serve the public. Always active in store management, she gave her heart as well as her genius in merchandising to the establishment. Many prominent manufacturers remember her gracious welcome, and her policy of always "seeing their salesmen," realizing that "their time is valuable too." She retired from the Fashion Buying in 1950, and served as Executive Vice-President and Secretary for the Board of Directors for many succeeding years.

Mrs. Holman's strong Religious Belief once prompted her to say "God is Master of the Universe. We need only to know that and realize that the sun comes up every morning, to sustain us. In appreciation, we should take advantage of our good fortune in being able to live in this country, on this beautiful Peninsula, by working hard to preserve this heritage so that we can pass it on to other generations."

Pacific Grove Tribune MARCH 12, 1980

ZENA HOLMAN DIES FOLLOWING LONG ILLNESS

Mrs. Wilford Rensselaer Holman died at her Lighthouse Avenue home on March 4 following a long period of ill health. She was born Zena Georgina Patrick on April 9, 1891, in Taylor, N.D.

Her family migrated to California in 1894, residing in Red Bluff, Berkeley, Hollister, and Pacific Grove.

Her early days in North Dakota were spent in an adobe hut built by her father on his homestead cattle ranch, an experience that inspired her to help in the fight to save Monterey adobes.

During her childhood she heard nightly lessons from the Bible and the dictionary from her schoolteacher parents. It became a source of deep faith and interest in Latin and the law.

After the family moved to Red Bluff, she was a star member of the high school's championship debating team. She had hoped to attend the university, but lacking money she entered business college and pursued a career in merchandising.

Following a brief period with a Berkeley department store, she moved to Pacific Grove to join Holman's Department Store. She married W. R. Holman, whose father was the store's founder, in 1912.

She traveled extensively as a buyer, raised two daughters, and helped her husband with the management of the store. During her travels she visited bookstores and junk shops. Her collection of first editions and other Jack London material is now maintained by the state Department of Parks and Recreation at Sonoma. Her collection of Indian artifacts is on exhibit in the Pacific Building in Monterey. Asilomar Conference Grounds is the home of the Zena Holman Library.

She and her husband were active in community improvement. In the late Twenties they fought vigorously for a more direct highway between Carmel and Pacific Grove. At the time Pacific Grove was virtually a ghost town, so residents formed a caravan, traveling to Salinas to persuade county officials of the need. The road was named for her husband in 1972.

Mrs. Holman was a charter member of the Pacific Grove Art Center and was the oldest living member of the Pacific Grove Woman's Club. She was named Citizen of the Year by the Monterey Peninsula Chamber of

Commerce in 1972. Although born in North Dakota, her name was on the honor roll of the Native Daughters of the Golden West. She was the first president of the Pacific Grove PTA.

Survivors include her husband, at the Lighthouse Avenue family home; daughters Patricia O'Meara of Watsonville and Harriet Barter of Carmel; a sister, Gladys Bonwell of Alameda, six grandchildren and 10 great grandchildren.

=

A Letter to the Editor from the celebrated photographer Ansel Adams.

The Herald MARCH 17, 1980

LETTER TO EDITOR

I am aware of the sad fact that our community has lost several remarkable citizens in a short period of time: Mrs Zena Holman, Giles Healey, and Harry Downey.

Apart from our deep regret at their passing, have we properly acknowledged their enormous contribution—other than the conventional obituary notices? In these we list their life-record in terms of interest and accomplishments, and this is as it should be—for the record.

However, their real achievements are not obvious: who has interpreted Mrs. Holman's part in the life of the community; who has described Giles Healey's spirit and very vital contributions to archeology; and who has adequately described what Harry Downey really accomplished in the great work he did in the restoration of the Carmel Mission?

I respectfully recommend you explore these lives and their achievements at a high plane of interpretation and penetration. These people are the life-blood of any society, and they should not be dismissed with an obituary—no matter how complete—of fact only.

Ansel Adams, Carmel

Monterey Peninsula Herald WEDNESDAY, MARCH 5, 1980

MRS. W. R. HOLMAN, CIVIC LEADER, DIES

Rare Honor

Although Mrs. Holman was not eligible for membership in the Native Daughters of the Golden West because of her North Dakota place of birth, she was one of only 36 persons named to the Honor Roll.

She joined such distinguished persons as Phoebe A. Hearst, University of California benefactor; Jane L. Stanford, joint founder of Leland Stanford Junior University, and the late Eliza P. Donner Houghton, daughter of George Donner of the Donner Party.

Among Mrs. Holman's accomplishments mentioned during the chamber event was her receiving of the California Department of Parks and Recreation's Golden Bear award in appreciation of her gifts of books, manuscripts and memorabilia of Jack London to the state historical park named for the late author at Sonoma.

A decade earlier, Mr. and Mrs. Holman had donated more than 1,000 Indian artifacts, now on display in the Hall of the American Indian at the Pacific Building State Historical Monument in Monterey.

The Zena Holman Library of Californiana and Americana was also established. It is located at the Asilomar State Conference Grounds in Pacific Grove. And the Holman house in Pacific Grove has long been filled with collections of other California historical items.

Mrs. Holman was the recipient of the Monterey History and Art Association's Laura Bride Powers award in 1969 for her endeavors in the fields of preservation and conservation. She was a lifetime member of the association.

In Pacific Grove Mrs. Holman was a charter member of the Art Center

Guild, and was considered the senior member of the Women's Civic Club, having joined the club in 1917. She was a member of the First Church of Christ, Scientist, in Pacific Grove and the Mother Church in Boston.

Long an activist in local politics as well as civic matters, Mrs. Holman and her husband were influential in having the Pacific Grove-Carmel highway constructed.

In 1972, that section of Highway 68 was named W. R. Holman Highway and Mrs. Holman, her outfit highlighted with a huge corsage, proudly helped her husband put the identifying road markers in place while photographers recorded the event.

Mrs. Holman had been one of the sponsors of the Feast of Lanterns, Pacific Grove's annual summer celebration, since its reactivation in 1956 by Mrs. Elmarie Dyke, a longtime friend.

Concert Supporter

Mrs. Holman was also one of the donors of the concert grand piano belonging to the Monterey Peninsula Concert Association. She was a charter member of the association and has been affiliated with it since its founding in 1939.

She was the first president of the Pacific Grove Parent-Teacher Association.

More recently, Mrs. Holman had published a book about the "beginning of the end of Cannery Row." Entitled *My Monterey*, the 95-page book was published in 1972.

Mrs. Holman's generosity was demonstrated again in December 1978, when she and her husband donated 850 ancient pre-Alaskan Eskimo artifacts and other Alaskan items to the Monterey Peninsula Museum of Art's permanent collection.

Private services will be held Saturday at the Paul Mortuary, followed by private entombment at El Carmelo Cemetery in Pacific Grove. The family asks that any tributes be to the church of the donor's choice or a favorite charity.

Zena Holman in front of the Pacific Grove Community Center.

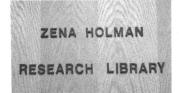

The door to Mrs. Holman's library.

Zena Holman as a young woman.

Zena as a child.

From left to right: *Director Mott, Louise Jaques, Mrs. Holman, Mrs. Harriet (Holman) Barter, at the dedication of the Zena Holman Library.*

Zena in the Zena Holman Research Library.

PART III

The Pacific Grove Charter

*W.R. Holman at the beach with Rodmere
in the background.*

21

Pacific Grove Charter

W.R. HOLMAN FOUGHT PASSIONATELY TO SEE THE PACIFIC GROVE Charter enacted. In April 1927 he joined a citizens group to push through a yes vote for the Charter, thereby creating the foundation for Pacific Grove governance. W.R. Holman went so far as to create a circular, which he distributed throughout town hoping to persuade citizens to vote—and to vote yes. More than 60% of registered voters showed up at the polls, with 614 people voting yes, and 570 voting no. W.R. Holman's comment after was: "Today is my wife's birthday, and this is my present to her."

I could not locate all of the original documents, though the microfilm at the Pacific Grove Library was very helpful in filling in the blanks where words were missing from the mimeographed version of W.R. Holman's book. I have done my best, as has Joyce Krieg in her transcribing, to recreate what W.R. Holman wanted to share.

CHARTER

*Prepared and Proposed for the City of Pacific Grove
by the Board of Freeholders, elected on the 10ᵗʰ Day of January, 1927*

Section 1. Name

The municipal corporation now existing and known as "The City of Pacific Grove" shall remain and continue a body politic and corporate, as at present, in fact and in law, by the name of "The City of Pacific Grove," and by such name shall have perpetual succession.

Section 2. Boundaries

The boundaries of the City of Pacific Grove shall continue as now established and be changed only in a manner authorized by law.

Section 3. Inalienable Rights of City

The rights of the city in and to its waterfront, lands under water, and such public wharves, docks and landings as may be hereafter thereon constructed are hereby declared inalienable.

Section 4. Powers

The City of Pacific Grove by and through its Council and other officials, shall have and may exercise all powers necessary or appropriate to a municipal corporation and the general welfare of its inhabitants, which are not prohibited by the constitution of the state and which it would be competent for this charter to set forth particularly or specifically; and the specification herein of any particular powers shall not be held to be exclusive or any limitation upon this general grant of powers.

Section 5. General Laws Applicable

All general laws of the state applicable to municipal corporations now or hereafter enacted and which are not in conflict with the provisions of this charter shall be applicable to the City of Pacific Grove, provided that the Council may adopt and enforce ordinances in compliance with the provisions of this Charter which shall control in relation to municipal affairs as against general laws of the state.

Section 6. Officers and Employees

The officers of the City of Pacific Grove shall consist of six Councilmen and a Mayor, a City Manager, a City Clerk, a City Treasurer, a City Attorney, a City Assessor, a City Tax Collector, a City Engineer, a Street Superintendent, a Judge of the Police Court, a Chief of Police, a Fire Chief, a Health Officer, a board of five Library Trustees. And a board of five Museum Trustees; provided, the Council may by ordinance provide for such subordinate officers, assistants, deputies, clerks and employees as it deems necessary, and provided further that the City Clerk shall be ex-officio Assessor, and the City Treasurer ex-officio City Tax Collector, and that the council may at any time, when in its judgment the interest of the city so demands, consolidate by ordinance the powers and duties of two or more city officers, and place the same in charge of one such officer. The Mayor, the members of the Council, the City Clerk, and the City Treasurer shall be elected from the city at large. All other officers, assistants, deputies, clerks, and employees shall be appointed as provided in this Charter, or as the Council may provide by ordinance in case no provision for their appointment is herein made, and they shall hold their respective offices or positions at the pleasure of the appointing power, except as otherwise herein provided. Where the appointment of any officers, assistants, deputies, clerks or employees is vested in the Council, Board of Library Trustees, Board of Museum Trustees, or other body, the appointment and removal must be made by a majority vote of the members of such body, except as otherwise herein provided.

Section 7. Residential Qualifications

No person shall be eligible to hold any elective office of the city unless he be a resident and elector herein, and shall have resided in said city for at least one year, next preceding the date of his election.

Section 8. Elections

General municipal elections shall be held in the city on the second Monday in April in each odd-numbered year under and pursuant to the provisions of the general laws of the state of California governing elections in the cities of the sixth class so far as the same may be applicable and except as herein otherwise provided. The first general election in said city under this Charter shall be held on the first Monday in June, 1927. All other municipal elections that may be held by authority of this Charter or of the general law shall be known as special municipal elections. At least twenty days before the day of the election, each candidate for an elective office shall file with the City Clerk a sworn statement containing the following information: (A) his name; (B) the office for which he is a candidate; (C) his present residence and occupation; (D) the public offices he ever held, if any, as principal, deputy or employee; (E) the experience, training or education received which, in the candidate's opinion, would qualify him to fill the office for which he is a candidate.

He shall also file a statement setting forth the principal public improvement or betterments . . . [text missing] . . . shall publish the statement of each candidate in the official newspaper of the city by two insertions therein prior to the day of the election. Each candidate shall be required to pay the cost of publication, to be deposited with his application. No response to any one of the several above-mentioned requirements shall exceed one hundred words in length.

Section 9. Canvass of Returns

The Council of said city shall meet at its usual meeting place on the first Monday after any municipal election, duly canvass the returns of the election and declare the results thereof, and install the newly elected officers, if any.

Section 10. Oath of Office

Every officer shall take and subscribe to the oath of office as provided in the constitution of the state before entering upon the performance of his official duties.

Section 11. Official Bonds

Except as prescribed by this Charter, the Council shall determine which officers shall give bonds for the faithful performance of their official duties, shall fix the amount of said bonds and the mode of approving the same. Such officers before entering upon their official duties, shall execute a bond to the city in the penal sum required, and said bond shall be approved by the Council and filed with the City Clerk.

Section 12. The Mayor

A Mayor shall be elected at each general municipal election and shall hold office for the term of two years from and after the Monday next succeeding the day of such election and until a successor is elected and qualified. The Mayor shall receive no compensation and shall be ineligible to hold any office or employment with the City except as a member of any board, commission or committee thereof of which the Mayor is constituted such member by general law. The Mayor shall be the executive head of the city. In case of riot, insurrection or extraordinary emergency he shall assume general control of the city government and all of its branches and be responsible for the suppression of disorder and the restoration of normal conditions. In the name and on behalf of the city he shall sign all contracts, deeds, bonds and other legal instruments in which the city is a party. He shall represent the city at all ceremonial functions of a social or patriotic character when it is desirable or appropriate to have the city represented officially thereat. In case of vacancy in the office of Mayor or during the temporary absence or disability of the Mayor, the Council shall choose one of its members to serve as Mayor pro tempore.

Section 13. The Council

The legislative body of the city shall consist of the Mayor and six Councilmen, each of whom including the Mayor shall have the right to vote upon all questions coming before the Council. Three Councilmembers shall be elected at each general municipal election and shall hold office for the term of four years each from and after the Monday next succeeding the day of such election, and until their successors are elected and qualified; provided, however, that six Councilmen shall be elected at the first general municipal election under the provisions of this charter. The three councilmen receiving the highest number of votes at said first election shall hold office for the full term of four years each, and the three Councilmen elected by the lowest number of votes shall hold office for two years each. In the event that two or more persons shall be elected by the same number of votes, their terms shall be fixed by lot . . . [text missing] . . . shall be divided into six departments; namely: (1) Finance, (2) Ordinance, (3) Street, (4) Police, (5) Park, (6) Fire, Light and Water, and at the first regular meeting of the Council following the installation of officers after a general municipal election, the Mayor, with the approval of the Council, shall assign each of said departments of the City to the special interest of a particular Councilman, whose duty it shall be to inform himself regarding the conduct of said department both in Pacific

Grove and in other cities, that he may advise the Council relative to legislative acts that tend to the betterment thereof.

Upon request of any Councilman the Council may appoint two citizens chosen because of their knowledge of the department to act with said Councilman, without compensation, as an advisory board; provided that the Councilman interested in the City Parks shall be ex-officio chairman of a City Planning Board.

The Councilmen shall receive no compensation, and no Councilman shall be eligible to hold any other office or employment with the city except as a member of any board, commission, or committee thereof, of which he is constituted such member by the general law of the state.

Section 14. City Clerk and Ex-Officio Assessor

A City Clerk shall be elected every two years at a general municipal election. He shall be ex-officio Assessor of the City and Clerk of the Council and of the Board of Equalization. His salary and bonds as such shall be fixed by ordinance. It shall be the duty of the city clerk to attend all sessions of the Council and of the Board of Equalization, and to keep a full and correct record of the proceedings of each of such bodies. The proceedings of the council shall be kept in a book marked, "Minutes of the Council," and the proceedings of the Board of Equalization shall be kept in a separate book marked, "Minutes of the Board of Equalization." He shall keep a book marked "Ordinances" into which he shall copy all city ordinances certifying that each such copy is a full and correct copy of the original ordinance, and stating that the same has been published as required by law. Said record copy, so certified, shall be prima facie evidence of the contents of the ordinance, and of its passage and publication and shall be admissible, as such evidence of any court or proceeding. Such record shall not be filed but shall be returned to the custody of the City Clerk. He shall also keep a book marked "Resolutions" into which he shall copy all resolutions passed by the Council. Both the books containing ordinances and resolutions shall be adequately and comprehensively indexed. He shall conduct promptly, and keep a systematic record of all correspondence between the Council and third parties relating to city business.

He shall be the keeper of the corporate seal of the city, and shall affix the same to instruments or writings requiring authentication. He shall safely keep all records, documents, ordinances, resolutions, books, and such other papers and matters as may be regularly delivered into his custody or required by law or ordinance to be filed with him.

It shall be the duty of the City Clerk, as ex-officio Assessor, between the first Monday in March and the first Monday in August of each year, to assess all taxable property within the City of Pacific Grove at the time and in the manner prescribed by general law of the state, except as may be otherwise provided by ordinance. The Assessor shall possess such other powers and perform such additional duties, not inconsistent with this Charter, as may be prescribed by ordinances.

Section 15. City Treasurer and Ex-Officio City Tax Collector

There shall be a City Treasurer elected every two years at a general municipal election. It shall be the duty of said Treasurer to receive and safely keep all moneys and securities belonging to the City and coming into his hands, and pay out the same, only on warrants signed by the proper officers and otherwise. He shall make quarterly statements showing the receipts and disbursements for the quarters ending September 30, December 31, March 31, and June 30 in each year. Such statements shall show in detail the condition of each and every fund required to be set apart by him. All statements shall be made in duplicate, one copy of which shall be filed with the City Clerk, and one delivered to the City Manager within ten days after the end of each quarter.

The Treasurer shall be ex-officio City Tax Collector. He shall be charged with, and indebted to the City for all taxes levied upon real and personal property within the City unless the Council determines by resolution that he is unable to collect delinquent taxes by levy or sale of property assessed therefor. The salary of the Treasurer and City Tax Collector shall be fixed by ordinance, and also the amount of his official bond.

Section 16. Meetings of the Council

All meetings of the Council shall be held in the City Hall, unless by reason of fire, flood or other disaster, the City Hall cannot be used for that purpose, and all meetings shall be open to the public. There shall be two regular meetings of the Council in each month at a day and hour by ordinance determined, and any regular meeting may be adjourned to a date and hour certain and such adjourned meeting shall be a regular meeting for all purposes. The Council shall adopt rules for the conduct of its proceedings and shall provide by ordinance the manner in which special meetings may be called.

Section 17. Quorum

A majority of the Council shall constitute a quorum for the transaction of business, but a less number may adjourn from time to time and compel the attendance of absent members in such manner and under such penalties as may be prescribed by ordinance.

Section 18. Ordinances

The enacting clause of all ordinances passed by the Council shall read as follows: "The Council of the City of Pacific Grove do ordain as follows:" The enacting clause of all ordinances passed by the vote of the electors of the City through the exercise of the initiative or referendum shall be: "The people of the City of Pacific Grove do ordain as follows:"

The affirmative vote of a majority of the Council shall be necessary to adopt any ordinances, resolutions or claims against the City, which vote shall be taken by ayes and noes and entered upon the record, and upon the request of any member of the Council the ayes and noes shall be taken and recorded upon any vote.

No ordinance shall be passed by the Council on the day of its introduction nor within five days thereafter, nor at any time other than at a regular meeting, nor until its publication at least once in the official newspaper at least three days before its adoption, provided, any ordinance declared by the Council to be necessary as an emergency measure for preserving the public peace, health or safety, and containing the reasons for its urgency may be introduced and if passed by 5-7 vote shall become effective immediately

A proposed ordinance may be amended or modified between the time of its introduction and the time of its final passage, provided its general scope and original purpose are retained. No ordinance or portion thereof shall be repealed, revised or amended except by ordinance, and all ordinances shall be signed by the Mayor and attested by the City Clerk. Except as provided by general law, or by this Charter, no action providing for any specific public improvement, or for the appropriation or expenditures of public moneys, in any amount over five hundred dollars, or for the acquisition, sale, lease, encumbrancing or disposition of real property of the City, or any interest therein, or for the levying of any tax or assessment, or for the granting of any franchise, or for the establishing or changing fire limits or business or residential zones, shall be taken except by ordinance.

Section 19. The Initiative and Referendum

The initiative and referendum may be exercised in accordance with the constitution and general laws of this state, provided, however, that when any ordinance is referred to the electors either upon an initiative or referendum petition, it shall be voted upon at a special election to be held not less than twenty days nor more than thirty days from the presentation of the petition therefor unless there is to occur a special or regular municipal election not less than twenty days nor more than ninety days from the presentation of the petition, in which event the ordinance shall be submitted at such special or general election.

Section 20. The Recall

The Recall may be exercised in accordance with the constitution and general laws of this State as to municipal officers.

Section 21. Police Judge and Police Court

There shall be a Police Judge appointed by the Council. He shall be the judge of the Police Court, which is hereby established. The Police Court shall have jurisdiction, concurrently with the Justice's Courts of all actions and proceedings, civil and criminal, arising within the corporate limits of the city, and which might be tried in such Justice's Court; and said Police Court shall have exclusive jurisdiction of all actions for the recovery of any fine, penalty or forfeiture prescribed for the breach of any ordinance of said City, of all actions founded upon any obligation created by any ordinance thereof, and of all prosecutions for the violation of any such ordinance. In all civil actions where the fine, penalty or forfeiture prescribed for the breach of any ordinance of the city is not more than one hundred dollars, the trial must be by this court. In civil actions where the fines, penalty or forfeiture prescribed for the breach of any ordinance of the city is over one hundred dollars, the defendant is, upon his demand, entitled to a jury. Except as in this section otherwise provided, the rules and practice and mode of proceeding in said Police Court shall be the same as are, or may be, prescribed by law for Justice's Courts in like cases, and appeals may be taken to the Superior Court from all judgments of said Police Court in like manner and with like effect as in cases of appeals from Justice's Courts.

The Police Judge shall have all powers and perform the duties of a Magistrate and may administer and certify oaths and affirmations and take and certify acknowledgements. All fines, fees, forfeitures and costs collected by him shall be paid into the City Treasury within forty-eight hours from and after the receipt thereof. He shall make such periodical reports as the Council may require.

In all cases in which the Police Judge is a party, or in which he is interested, or when he is related to either party by consanguinity, or affinity within the third degree, or is otherwise disqualified, or in cases of sickness or inability to act, he may call upon any Justice of the Peace residing in the County of Monterey to act in his stead.

The Council may, by ordinance, appoint the Justice of the Peace of the township in which the City of Pacific Grove is located, as Police Judge thereof.

The Police Judge shall keep a record of the proceedings of the Police Court in all matters and cases before said court. Separate dockets shall be kept for civil and criminal cases.

Section 22. Oaths and Subpoenas

The Mayor, City Manager, and City Clerk shall have power to administer oaths, to issue subpoenas, to compel by subpoena the production of the books, papers and documents of the City and to take and hear testimony whenever necessary in carrying out their official duties.

Section 23. City Manager

There shall be a City Manager appointed by the Council who shall be the administrative head of the City government. The City Manager shall be chosen by the Council without regard to political consideration and with reference solely to qualifications for such office.

It shall not be necessary that he reside in the City at the time of appointment, but he shall become a resident thereof within sixty days thereafter and thereafter during incumbency shall actually reside in the City. The salary of the City Manager shall be fixed by ordinance at no less than $2500 per year, payable in equal monthly installments.

Before entering upon his duties, the City Manager shall file with the City Clerk an official bond for the faithful performance thereof, payable to the City of Pacific Grove in a sum no less than $5,000, the premium of which shall be paid by the City. The powers and duties of the City Manager shall be:

(1) To see that all ordinances are enforced.

(2) To appoint, except as otherwise provided, all heads of departments, subordinate officials and employees, and remove the same, except as otherwise provided, and have general supervision and control over the same. Save when in the opinion of the City Manager or the interests of the city otherwise demand, appointees shall be residents of Pacific Grove.

(3) To exercise general supervision over all privately owned public utilities operating within the City so far as the same are subject to municipal control.

(4) To see that the provisions of all franchises, leases, contracts, permits and privileges granted by the City are fully observed and to report to the Council any violations thereof.

(5) To act as purchasing agent for the city in transactions involving expenditure not in excess of five hundred dollars. He shall know the exact condition of the treasury at all times, and shall approve all demands before the same have been allowed by the Council if he is satisfied that the money is lawfully due.

(6) To attend all meetings of the Council unless excused therefrom by three members thereof or by the Mayor.

(7) To examine, or cause to be examined, without notice, the conduct, or the official account and records, of any officer or employee of the city.

(8) To keep the Council advised as to the needs of the City.

(9) To devote his entire time to the interests of the City.

(10) To have general supervision over all City property, including public buildings, parks and playgrounds.

(11) To appoint such advisory boards as he may deem desirable to advise and assist him in his work, provided the members of such boards shall receive no compensation.

(12) To make such recommendations to the Council or Board of Equalization, regarding the assessment roll as he may deem advisable.

Article 24. City Manager Pro-Tem

In case of the absence from the City of the City Manager, or his temporary disability to act as such, the Council shall appoint a City Manager pro-tem who shall possess the powers and discharge the duties of the City Manager during such absence or disability only; provided, however, that a City Manager pro-tem shall have no authority to appoint or remove any City officer or employee except with the unanimous formal approval of all the members of the Council.

Section 25. Interference with or by City Manager

Neither the Council nor any of its committees or members shall dictate or attempt to dictate, either directly or indirectly, the appointment of any person to office or employment by the City Manager, or in any manner interfere with the City Manager or prevent him from exercising his own judgment in the appointment of officers and employees in the administrative service. Except for the purpose of inquiry the Council and its members shall deal with the administrative service solely through the City Manager, and neither the Council nor any member thereof shall give orders to any of the subordinates of the City Manager, either publicly or privately.

Neither the City Manager, nor any appointive officer or employee of the City, shall take any active part in securing or shall contribute money toward, the nomination or election of any elective candidate for municipal office.

Section 26. City Attorney

There shall be a City Attorney appointed by the City Manager, subject to approval by the Council. He shall be an attorney-at-law, admitted to the bar of the Supreme Court of this State, and one who has been in actual practice in the State, for at least three years next preceding appointment. All other things being equal, an attorney who has had special training for this office or experience in municipal corporation law shall be appointed to this office, if practicable. The City Attorney shall be legal advisor of the Council and all other City officials. He shall prosecute all violations of City ordinances, and shall draft all ordinances, resolutions, contracts, or other legal documents or proceedings required by the Council or other officials, except as may be otherwise provided, and shall perform such legal services from time to time as the Council may require, and shall attend all meetings of the Council unless excused therefrom by four members thereof or by the Mayor. The salary of the City Attorney shall be fixed by ordinance.

When from any cause therefrom the City Attorney is unable to perform the duties of office, he may, with the consent of the City Manager, appoint some other qualified attorney to act temporarily as City Attorney. Whenever, in the judgment of the Council, the interests of the City require it, assistant counsel may be employed. The City Attorney shall deliver all books, records, papers, documents, and property of every description, under his control, owned by the City, to his successor in office, and shall possess such other powers, and perform such additional duties, not in conflict with this Charter, as may be prescribed by ordinance.

Section 27. City Engineer

There shall be a City Engineer appointed by the City Manager who at the time of his appointment shall have been a practicing civil engineer for a period of at least three years.

As City Engineer, he shall be the custodian of, and responsible for, all maps, plans, profiles, field studies and other records and documents belonging to the city, pertaining to his office and the work thereof, all of which he shall keep in proper order and condition with full indices thereof. He shall turn the same over to his successor upon relinquishing his office, who shall give him duplicate receipts therefor, one of which he shall file with the City Clerk.

All maps, plans, profiles, field notes, estimates and other memoranda of surveys and other professional work in behalf of the City, made or done by him or under his direction or control during his term of office, shall be the property of the City, and shall be kept in the City vaults. He shall perform all engineering work and surveying in prosecuting public improvements in or for the City, and in relation to public streets, lanes, alleys, ways, places and real property of the City, and shall possess such other powers and perform such additional duties not in conflict with this Charter, as may be prescribed by ordinance or the general laws of the State. His compensation shall be fixed by ordinance. All salaries, commissions, or fees received by the City Engineer as compensation for his official services shall be published quarterly in the official paper of the City.

Section 28. Street Superintendent

The Street Superintendent shall perform such duties as may be prescribed, now or hereafter, by ordinance, or general laws of the State. Nothing herein contained shall prevent the City Manager himself from acting as ex-officio City Engineer and Street Superintendent and filling such offices as herein provided.

Section 29. Chief of Police

There shall be a Chief of Police appointed by the City Manager. He shall be head of the Police Department of the City, and shall have all the powers that are now or may hereafter be conferred upon sheriffs and other peace officers by the laws of the State. It shall be his duty to preserve the public peace, and to suppress riots, tumults and disturbances. His orders shall be promptly executed by the police officers or watchmen of the city, and every citizen shall lend him aid when requested for the arrest of offenders, the maintenance of public order, or the protection of life and property.

He shall execute and return all process issued to him by legal authority. He shall have authority, and it is hereby made his duty, to arrest persons violating any law of the State or ordinance of the City. Those arrested for violating City ordinances may, before or after trial, be confined in the County Jail of Monterey County or in the City Prison of Pacific Grove. He shall have such other powers and duties appertaining to his office as may be prescribed by ordinance or by the City Manager, who shall prescribe tests for the examination of applicants for subordinate positions in the Police Department. The salary of the Chief of Police shall be fixed by ordinance.

Section 30. Chief of the Fire Department

There shall be a Fire Chief appointed by the City Manager. He shall be head of the Fire Department of the City and shall have charge and supervision over all matters relating to the prevention and extinction of fires, and of all measures necessary to guard and protect all property impaired thereby. During the time of a fire he shall have supreme authority over the territory involved herein, and all persons in the immediate vicinity of the fire during such time, including policemen, shall be subject to his orders. He shall appoint and remove all subordinates in the department, make rules and regulations for the government thereof, subject to the approval of the City Manager.

Section 31. City Health Officer

There shall be a Health Officer appointed by the City Manager. He shall be a person who has been licensed to practice medicine in the State of California, or who has received special training in public health work. He or his deputies shall exercise general supervision over the health and cleanliness of the City, and take all necessary measures for the preservation and promotion thereof. He shall enforce all laws, ordinances, and regulations relative to the preservation and improvement of the public health, including those provided for the prevention of disease, the suppression of unsanitary conditions, and the inspection and supervision of the production, transportation, storage and sale of food stuffs.

Section 32. Compensation

The Council shall fix the compensation of all officers, also the compensation of all deputies, assistants and employees of all officers appointed by the Council. The salaries of all officers shall be fixed by ordinance.

The City Manager shall fix the compensation of all deputies, assistants and employees of all officers appointed by him, subject to the approval of the Council.

No officer or employee shall be allowed any fee, perquisite, emolument, or stipend in addition to, or save as embraced in the salary or compensation fixed for such office by the Council and all fees received by such officer in connection with his official duties shall be paid by him into the City Treasury.

Section 33. Pensions

No pensions of any kind or character shall be awarded to any active or retired city official, employee, or member of the police or fire department, unless provided by an initiative ordinance adopted by the electors of the City.

Section 34. Appointment and Removal of Officers and Employees

The City Manager, and the Police Judge shall be appointed by the affirmative votes of five-sevenths of the Council.

A Board of five Library Trustees, and a Board of five Museum Trustees shall be appointed by the Mayor subject to the confirmation of a majority of the Council.

Except as otherwise provided in this Charter, all other City officers and employees shall be appointed, and may be removed by the City Manager.

The Council may remove any of its appointees by the affirmative votes of a majority of the Council, provided, however, that where appointments have been made for a definite term or for an extended period of time, a month's notice shall be given the appointee, except in case of removal for cause based upon one or more of the following grounds: Namely, willful neglect of official duty, gross carelessness in the discharge thereof, misconduct of a disgraceful or scandalous nature, intemperance, malfeasance in office, insanity or conviction of felony.

For such cause the Council may remove by majority vote any of its appointees immediately, but such removal must be accompanied by a verified complaint in writing filed with the City Clerk specifying the cause or causes for removal, and the appointee thus removed shall have the right to demand a public hearing in his own defense under protection of court rules of procedure as regards evidence and testimony.

Section 35. Approving Illegal Claims

Every officer who shall willfully and knowingly approve, allow, or pay, any demand on the treasury knowing it is not authorized by law, shall be liable to the City individually and on his or her official bond for the amount of the demand so approved, allowed, or paid, and if an appointive officer, shall forfeit his office and be forever disbarred and disqualified from holding any position in the service of the City.

Section 36. Vacancies

A vacancy in an elective office shall be filled by appointment by the Council, such appointee to hold office until the next general municipal election and until his successor is elected and qualified. Such successor shall be elected for the unexpired term of his predecessor at the general municipal election next succeeding such appointment. Should the Council fail to fill any such vacancy within thirty days after the same occurs, then it shall be filled by appointment by the Mayor; provided, however, that if the offices of a majority, or more, of the Council shall become vacant, then the City Clerk shall call a special election at once to fill the vacancies for the unexpired terms, and the same shall be conducted substantially in the manner provided for general municipal elections.

If any officer of the City shall remove from the City or absent himself therefrom for more than thirty days consecutively without the permission of the Council, or shall fail to qualify, or shall resign or be convicted of a felony, or be adjudged insane, his office shall become vacant.

Section 37. Vacations

All officers and regular employees of the City after serving at least one year as such, shall be entitled to one week's vacation annually. Such vacation shall be at a time to be fixed by the executive head of the Department wherein the officer or employee is serving, and shall be without loss of pay. The City Manager shall fix such vacation periods for the chief officials and department heads of the City, provided that employees working seven days a week shall be entitled to a vacation of two weeks.

Section 38. Uniform Accounts and Reports

The Council shall prescribe uniform forms of accounts, which shall be observed by all officers and departments of the City which receive or disburse City monies. Whenever an act shall be passed by the legislature of the State providing for uniform municipal accounts or reports, the City authorities shall be governed thereby.

Section 39. Counting the City's Money

The Mayor, City Clerk and City Manager shall together count the money and other securities in the treasury at least once every three months, and ascertain if the amounts on hand tally with the amounts that should be in the treasury according to the books of the City. They shall make a written report thereof to the Council at its first regular meeting thereafter.

Section 40. Monthly Financial Reports

All officers charged by ordinance with submitting monthly financial reports to the Council, shall submit the same in duplicate, and upon their approval by the Council, one of each of such duplicate reports shall be posted forthwith in the office of the City Clerk in such manner as to be readily accessible to the public, and shall remain so posted until the approval by the Council of the next succeeding financial report when the same procedure shall be followed in relation thereto. The Council, in addition to such posting, may, in its discretion, cause any of such reports to be published at any time.

Section 41. Budget

Not later than thirty days before the time for fixing the annual tax levy, the City Manager shall submit to the Council an estimate of the expenditures and revenues of the City departments for the ensuing year. This estimate shall be compiled from detailed information obtained from the several departments on uniform blanks to the furnished by the Manager. The classification of the estimate of expenditures shall be as nearly uniform as possible for the main financial divisions of all departments, and shall give in parallel columns the following information:

A detailed estimate of the expense of conducting each department as submitted by the department.

Expenditures for corresponding items for the last two fiscal years.

Expenditures for corresponding items for the current fiscal year, including adjustments due to transfer between appropriations plus an estimate of expenditures necessary to complete the current fiscal year.

Amount of supplies and material on hand at the date of the preparation of the invoice.

Increase or decrease of requests compared with the corresponding appropriations for the current year.

Such other information as is required by the council or that the Manager may deem advisable to submit.

The recommendation of the Manager as to the amounts to be appropriated with reasons therefor in such detail as the Council may direct.

Sufficient copies of such estimate shall be prepared and submitted, that there may be copies on file in the office of the City Clerk for the inspection by the public, unless the council shall publish the same in the official paper.

After duly considering the estimate as presented in the budget, the Council shall pass an ordinance levying the annual tax.

Section 42. Inventory of City Property

At the time for preparing and submitting the budget, as prescribed by this charter, a complete inventory of all real and personal property belonging to the City shall be prepared and filed with the City Clerk, and such inventory shall be submitted to the Council by the City Manager at the time of the submission of the annual budget. Such inventory shall be prepared under the direction of the City Manager, and all chief officials and department heads of the City shall be responsible for making and transmitting to the City Manager a full and correct inventory of all City personal property in their possession or under their control.

Section 43. The Fiscal Year

The fiscal year of the city shall commence on the first day of July of each year, or at such other time as may be fixed by ordinance.

Section 44. Taxation

Except as otherwise herein provided, the Council, by ordinance, shall provide a system for the assessment, levy, collection and equalization of taxes which, as nearly as may be, shall conform to the system provided by the general laws of the State; provided, that all sales for delinquent taxes shall be made to the City of Pacific Grove. Should the Council fail to fix the tax rate within the time prescribed, then the tax rate for the previous year shall constitute the rate for the current year.

Section 45. Assessment Roll

On or before the first Monday in August of each year, the City Assessor shall make out a list of all the taxable property within the city, which list, or assessment roll for the City, shall describe the property assessed and the value thereof, and shall contain all other matter required to be stated in such list by ordinance. The Assessor shall verify said list by his oath, shall attach his certificate thereto and deliver the same to the Council. Thereupon, by publication in the official newspaper of the City, the City Clerk shall give notice of the meeting of the Council as a Board of Equalization.

Section 46. Board of Equalization

The Council shall meet at its usual meeting place on the second Monday in August of each year at ten o'clock in the A.M. and sit as a Board of Equalization, and shall continue in session by adjournment from day to day until all returns of the Assessor have been rectified and assessments equalized. The Board of Equalization shall have the power to hear complaints, to take testimony under oath, and to correct, modify, strike out or raise any assessment, provided that notice shall first be given to anyone whose assessment it is proposed to raise.

Section 47. License Tax

The Council shall, by ordinance, fix a license tax for the purpose of regulation and revenue, as businesses, professions, trades, callings and occupations carried on within the limits of the City of Pacific Grove.

Section 48. Annual Tax Levy

The Council must finally adopt, not later than the first regular meeting in September, an ordinance levying upon the assessed valuation of all property in the City, a rate of taxation sufficient to raise the amounts estimated to be required in the annual budget and as herein provided, less the amounts estimated to be received from fines, licenses and other sources of revenue. The Council shall then deliver the assessment roll to the City Clerk, who shall thereupon compute and carry out the amount of the tax so levied on each parcel of property contained in the assessment roll. The corrected list for each tax shall be the assessment roll of said tax for said year, and it shall be certified by the City Clerk, as being the assessment roll of said tax.

Section 49. Limit and Apportionment of the Tax Levy

The tax levy authorized by the Council to meet the municipal expenses for each fiscal year shall not exceed the rate of One Dollar on each One Hundred Dollars of the assessed valuation of the real and personal property within the City, except as in this Charter otherwise provided. The moneys collected from such levy shall be placed in the general fund of the City and may be apportioned in separate funds as determined by the Council. No transfer of money shall be made from one fund to another, except of balance in excess of the amount required in a fund or from the general fund to meet deficiencies, or to provide for the redemption of City bonds.

The foregoing limitation shall not apply in the event of any great necessity or emergency, in which case it may be temporarily suspended, provided that no increase over said limit, except as herein prescribed, shall be made in any fiscal year, unless authorized by ordinance adopted by the vote of the electors of the City.

Section 50. Special Tax Levy

The Council shall have power to levy and collect additional taxes sufficient to pay interest on the bonded indebtedness of the City, and to pay and maintain the sinking fund thereof, and for the following purposes only:

For the maintenance and support of a free public library in accordance with the provisions of the state law.

For the maintenance and support of a free public museum in accordance with the provisions of the state law.

For the acquisition and/or construction, as the case may be, of permanent public improvements, or real property, of public buildings and structures including equipping and furnishing the same, and the tax levied for any and all such purposes combined shall not exceed one and one-half mills on each dollar of the assessed valuation of the real and personal property within the City, and no such acquisition or construction shall be charged against the general tax levied to meet current municipal expenses for each fiscal year.

Section 51. Tax Liens

All taxes and assessments levied, together with any percentage imposed for delinquency and the cost of collection, shall constitute liens on the property assessed; every tax upon the personal property shall be a lien upon the real property of the owner thereof. The liens provided for in this section shall attach as of the first Monday in March of each year, and may be enforced by actions to foreclose such liens in any court of competent jurisdiction, or by a sale of the property affected and the execution and delivery of all necessary certificates and deeds therefor, under such regulations as may be prescribed by ordinance; provided that when real estate is offered for sale for City taxes due thereon, the same shall be sold to the City in like case and manner, and with like effect and right of redemption as it may be struck off and sold to the State when offered for sale for County taxes; and the Council shall have power to provide by ordinance for the procedure to be followed in such sales to the City and redemption thereafter.

Section 52. Deposit of City Moneys

All moneys collected for the City by any officer or department thereof shall be paid daily if possible, into the City treasury, credited to the funds to which such moneys severally belong.

Section 53. Payment of City Moneys

Money shall be drawn from the treasury only upon warrants as herein prescribed. Every demand against the City, from whatever source, must be presented to the City Manager. Demands against the free public library or the Museum shall first be signed by the president and clerk of the board of trustees thereof. The City Manager shall satisfy himself whether the money demanded is legally due and its payment authorized by law. If he allows the demand he shall endorse thereon the word "allowed" and sign his name thereto. It shall thereafter be presented to the City Council and if by them allowed shall be signed by the Mayor and City Clerk, and a warrant, numbered and dated the same as the demand, issued and signed by the same officers shall be drawn upon the treasurer. No demand shall be allowed, approved or paid unless it shall specify each item of the claim and the date thereof.

Provided, however, that warrants for salaries, fixed by ordinance, of officers and offices specifically created by this Charter shall be allowed by the City Manager and paid regularly from the treasurer without the necessity of any demand therefor as in this section prescribed for other claims, and at such time, not in conflict with this Charter, as may be prescribed by ordinance.

Section 54. Expert Accountant

The Council shall employ a certified or a thoroughly qualified public accountant annually to investigate and render a report on the transactions and accounts of all officers or employees having the collection, deposit, custody or disbursement of public money or property, or the power to approve, allow or audit demands on the treasury.

Section 55. Franchises

Every franchise or privilege to construct, maintain, or operate any means or method of transportation on or over any street, lane, alley, or other public place within the City, or to lay pipes or conduits, or erect poles or wires or other structures in or across any public way or place, for the transmission of gas, electricity, or other commodity, or for the use of public property or places now or hereafter owned by the City, shall be granted under and in pursuance to the general laws of the State relating to the granting of franchises; provided, no new franchise or the renewal of an existing franchise shall be granted except upon the condition that at least two percent (2 per cent) of the gross annual receipts derived from the use of such franchise shall be paid the City. In all cases the applicant for a franchise shall advance the cost of advertising the same.

Every such franchise shall require the grantee thereof to agree to a joint use of its property with others wherever practicable, and nothing herein shall be construed as prohibiting the Council from requiring other conditions in granting the same not inconsistent with the constitution and general laws of the State. No franchise or privilege so granted shall be sold, leased, assigned, or otherwise alienated, without the express consent of the Council given by ordinance and subject to the referendum.

Section 56. Contract Work

In the erection, improvement and repair of all public buildings and works, in all street and sewer work, and in furnishing supplies or materials for same when the expenditure required for the same shall exceed the sum of five hundred dollars, the same shall be done by contract and shall be let to the lowest responsible bidder, after notice by publication in the official newspaper, and security for the due execution and performance of any such contract may be required of the successful bidder and successful contractor, respectively. The detailed procedure for carrying out the provisions of this section shall be prescribed by ordinance.

Provided, that the Council may reject any and all bids presented and may re-advertise in their discretion, and provided further, that after rejecting bids the Council may declare and determine by an affirmative vote of five-sevenths vote of all its members that in its opinion the work in question may be more economically or satisfactorily performed by day labor, or the materials or supplies purchased at a lower price in the open market, and after adoption of a resolution to this effect, it may proceed to have the same done in the manner stated without further observance of the foregoing provisions of this section; and,

Provided, further, that in case of a great public calamity, such as an extraordinary fire, flood, storm, epidemic or other disaster, the Council may, by resolution passed by a vote of five-sevenths of all its members, declare and determine that public interest and necessity demand the immediate expenditure of public money to safeguard life, health or property, and thereupon may proceed to expend or enter into a contract involving the expenditure of any sum required in such emergency, on hand in the City treasury and available for such purpose.

Section 57. Street Improvements

Proceedings for all public improvements which are to be paid for by assessment upon private property, shall be according to the general laws of the State, provided however, that if within the time for making objections, as fixed by the resolution of intention, the owners of record of a majority of the frontage of the property to be assessed shall file with the Council a written objection to the making of such improvement, signed by such owners, no further proceedings should be had under such resolution of intention, nor shall any new proceedings for such improvement be initiated by the Council within twelve (12) months from the filing of such objection.

If there be included in one proceeding several distinct improvements, the objection herein above referenced to may be directed to any of said propositions, in which event such objection need be signed by the owners of a majority of the frontage of the property to be assessed for such distinct improvement only; provided further that whenever any resolution of intention includes the paving of a street, the owners of a majority of the front footage of the property to be assessed therefor, shall have the right to determine the character and kind of pavement to be constructed, and the Council shall be bound by such determination upon receiving notice in writing thereof, signed by such majority.

Section 58. Illegal Contracts

No member of the Council, or of any board, and no officer of the City shall be or become directly or indirectly interested in any contract, work or business, or in the sale of any article, the expense, price or consideration of which is payable from the City treasury, nor receive any gratuity or advantage from any contract or person furnishing labor or material for the same. Any contract with the City in which any such officer is or becomes interested may be declared void by the Council.

No officer or employee of the City shall aid or assist a bidder in securing a contract to furnish labor, material or supplies at a higher price or rate than that proposed by any other bidder, or favor one bidder over another, giving or withholding information, or willfully mislead any bidder in regard to the character of the materials or supplies called for, or knowingly accept materials or supplies of a quality inferior to that called for by the contract, or knowingly certify to a greater amount of labor performed than has actually been performed, or to the receipt of a greater amount of material, or supplies than has actually been received. Any officer or employee violating any of the foregoing provisions of this section shall be guilty of a misdemeanor and be automatically expelled from his office or employment.

If at any time it shall be found that the person, firm or corporation to whom a contract has been awarded by the City has, in presenting any bid or bids, colluded with any other party or parties then the contract so awarded shall if the City so elect, be null and void and the contractor and his bondsmen shall be liable to the City for all loss or damage which the City may suffer thereby. In such event the Council may advertise for new bids for said work or supplies.

Section 59. City Planning Board

There shall be a City planning board of three members, consisting of the Councilman officially interested in the City parks and two citizens, members appointed by the Council because of their knowledge of City planning, and serving without remuneration. It shall be the duty of such board to make studies and recommendations for the improvements of the City with a view to the present and future movement of traffic, the convenience, amenity, health, recreation, general welfare and other needs of the City dependent on the City plan. All acts of the Council or any other branch of City government affecting the City plan shall be submitted to the board for report and recommendations. The board shall submit to the Council an annual report summarizing the activities of the board for the fiscal year, and presenting a plan for civic improvement year by year during the three years next ensuing, with estimates of the cost thereof and recommendations relative to meeting the cost. It shall be the particular duty of the City Manager to call the needs of the City to the attention of the Planning Board, and of the City Engineer to make recommendations designed to bring all engineering work of the City into harmony as parts of a comprehensive plan. The Health Office shall advise the Planning Board of municipal improvements which would improve the healthfulness of the City.

Section 60. Public Library

The free public library of the City shall be managed under and in accordance with the provisions of the general laws of the State relating to free public libraries. The salaries and compensation of all officers and employees appointed by the Board of Library Trustees shall be paid out of the moneys received by the City from the special levy for the maintenance and the support of a free public library.

Section 61. Public Museum

The free public museum of the City shall be managed under and in accordance with the provisions of the general laws of the State relating to free public museums. The salaries and compensation of all officers and employees appointed by the Board of Museum Trustees shall be paid out of the moneys received by the City from the special levy for the maintenance and support of a free public museum.

Section 62. Equipment

The City of Pacific Grove is hereby empowered to supply all officers and employees thereof with tools, equipment, books, records and other personal property necessary to discharge properly the duties of their respective offices and employments, and it shall by the duty of the City

Manager to acquire or purchase the same at his own discretion, or on advice of the City Council on behalf of offices over which the Council exercises appointing power.

Section 63. Official Records

All books and records of every office and department shall be open to inspection by any citizen during business hours, subject to the proper rules and regulations for the efficient conduct of the business of such department or office; provided, the records of the police department shall not be subjected to such inspection except by permission of the proper police authorities.

Copies or extracts, duly certified, from said books and records open to inspection, shall be given by the officer having the same in custody to any person demanding the same and paying or tendering an established charge.

All officers, boards, commissions and committees shall deliver to their successors all papers, books, documents, records, archives and other properties pertaining to their respective offices or departments, in their possession or under their control.

Section 64. Continuing Officers and Employees

Until the election or appointment and induction into office of the officers and employees in this Charter provided for, the present officers and employees shall without interruption, continue to perform the duties of their respective offices and employments for the compensation provided by existing ordinances or laws.

Section 65. Continuing Ordinances in Force

All lawful ordinances, resolutions, and regulations in force at the time this Charter shall take effect, and not inconsistent with its provisions, are hereby continued in force until the same shall have been duly amended, repealed or superseded.

Section 66. Newspaper Advertising and Printing

The Council shall advertise annually for the submission of sealed proposals or bids from the newspapers of general circulation in the City, for the publication of all ordinances and other legal notices required to be published. The newspaper to which such a contract is awarded shall be known as an Official Newspaper. The rates for publishing public notices shall not exceed the customary rates charged for publishing legal notices of a private character.

The Council shall also advertise annually for sealed proposals or bids for printing and furnishing all letterheads, stationery, tax bills, account books and other printed matter likely to be required during the fiscal year.

Contracts for advertising or printing, as the case may be, shall be awarded to the lowest responsible bidder.

Section 67. When Charter Effective

This Charter shall go into effect upon its approval by the Legislature. All elective officers in office at the time this Charter becomes effective shall hold, and perform the duties of their respective offices in accordance with the provisions of this Charter until their successors are elected and qualified.

Whereas The City of Pacific Grove, a city of more than three thousand, five hundred (3,500) inhabitants, did on the tenth day of January, 1927, hold a special election under and pursuant to the provisions of Section 8 of Article XI, of the Constitution of the State of California, and did thereat choose and elect Lillian G. Ayres, Edward Berwick,

Reeve Conover, George H. Ermann, Walter K. Fisher, W. R. Holman, George Moser, Julia B. Platt, John P. Pryor, Edward Simpson, Eben Cooke Smith, Benjamin F. Sowell, Bertha L. Strong, Lew H. Wilson, and Thomas A. Work as a board of fifteen Freeholders to prepare and propose a charter for said City.

BE IT KNOWN, that in pursuance of said provisions of the Constitution of the State of California, and within a period of thirty days after such election we, the undersigned members of the said board of Freeholders, have prepared and do hereby propose the foregoing Charter as and for the Charter of the City of Pacific Grove, and do fix the ninth (9th) day of April, 1927, as the date for holding a special municipal election in said City at which the said proposed Charter shall be submitted to the electors thereof for their ratification and adoption.

Edward Berwick
President Of The Board Of Freeholders

Lillian G. Ayers
Secretary Of Said Board

George Moser

Julia B. Platt

Bertha L. Strong

George H. Ermann

Walter K. Fisher

Thomas A. Work

Ed Simpson

Lew H. Wilson

Eben Booke Smith

John P. Pryor

Wilford R. Holman

22

Pacific Grove Charter Campaign, April 1927

WHAT FOLLOWS ARE ADS, EDITORIALS, ARTICLES, LETTERS TO THE ED-itor, and circulars, all written for the purpose of convincing Pacific Grove citizens to vote on the Charter. One of the major players was Julia Platt, a signer of the City Charter, along with W.R. Holman. In 1931, Julia Platt (then seventy-four years old) was elected town mayor, though the charter predates that election. Born in 1857, an embryolo-gist and politician, Julia Platt was an exceptional woman. Also included is commentary from Silas Mack, W.R. Holman's attorney; Mack was strictly in the No camp.

=

The following is a circular W.R. Holman wrote and distributed; there's no newspaper attribute as it didn't appear in one.

VOTE YES

The proposed Charter for Pacific Grove is a GOOD CHARTER and a PRO-TECTION to THE CITY TAXPAYERS AND VOTERS; insures Honesty and FAIR TREATMENT in place of INSULTS. A DOLLAR VALUE FOR EVERY DOLLAR SPENT.

My Name Is W. R. Holman

I believe in calling a SPADE a SPADE. I don't work behind a blanket by calling myself a "BUSINESS MEN'S COMMITTEE" or a "CITIZENS' COM-MITTEE" or any other clause to hide my identity, so that I will not, person-ally, have to take the responsibility for what I have to say.

I have lived in Pacific Grove since it was a small camp, or for forty years. I love Pacific Grove and the entire Peninsula and the people on it. I am for advancement on BUSINESS PRINCIPLES and know with our surround-ings, which are unequaled, that this whole Peninsula will rapidly become a GREAT CITY. Your property, no matter where situated on this Peninsula, will double and quadruple in value in the next few years.

BECAUSE I HAD FAITH IN THE PENINSULA I built in your midst the LARGEST DEPARTMENT STORE IN THE WEST situated in a town of THIS SIZE. The word was scattered throughout the entire commercial world that this store could not pay; such a store in such a small town was impossible and sure to fail within six months. Hard-headed business men and some of the largest on this coast said that I was crazy and predicted that I was headed for the rocks. I have given values equal to any City Prices and in thousands of cases, better than City Prices, and today enjoy a busi-ness, not only from the Monterey Peninsula, but from every section of this State and many other States—and we are growing and going to continue to grow. We maintain offices in San Francisco, New York and Berlin.

I have made some enemies and many friends by being OUTSPOKEN, although I have NEVER INTENTIONALLY HURT ANY MAN who has played FAIR BALL. I believe HONESTY AND TRUTH and DOING WHAT IS RIGHT BY YOUR FELLOW CITIZEN AT ALL TIMES is the only principle and I am WILLING TO FAIL OR SUCCEED by these policies. God to be my judge.

How Long?

How long would any business last from a peanut stand to the largest corporation if run as your city?—which represents a thousand times the investment of any single person or corporation within its boundaries. Yet some would have you believe that NO MANAGEMENT IS NECESSARY. That a few citizens who have their business which keeps them occupied six days a week, can direct without pay, through one meeting a month the entire city affairs.

You Pay, Mr. Citizen

The only business on earth THAT COULD KEEP RUNNING under such unbusinesslike principles is a business that is paid for by the TAXPAYERS EITHER DIRECTLY OR INDIRECTLY. You may read between the lines if you desire.

Over 364 Cities

Over 364 cities have adopted the City Charter plan in the past few years and only 3 are on record of discontinuing the Charter form of government and HUNDREDS OF CITIES THROUGHOUT THE UNITED STATES are considering or about to consider Charter forms of government.

City Manager's Pay

The pay for the City Manager HAS BEEN HARPED ON AND USED AS A BLIND TO DECEIVE OUR TAXPAYERS and CITIZENS. Your City

Surveyor has received about $6777.19 for work on ONE graded street, which work should require less than 30 days actual work for any competent surveyor, enough to pay a surveyor a full year—and this amount came from about one thousandth part of the property holders.

Your Present City Government

Your present City Government allows the surveyor 8 cents per foot for every foot of wooden curb replaced in the city of Pacific Grove, if paid for by the property holder through contractor or 7 cents per foot if paid by the City Government. You have over 25 miles of wooden curb and gutter in the City of Pacific Grove, or taking both sides of the streets, you have over 50 miles, which at the present rate will be replaced in 4 to 5 years, and for which at the present adopted rates, you will PAY OVER $21,000 to your SURVEYOR for surveying CURB AND GUTTER WORK only, not including any cement work which comes under a separate contract. WITH THESE CONDITIONS EXISTING DO WE NEED A MANAGER or a BODY GUARD OR ARE YOU SATISFIED to have YOUR MONEY SPENT IN THIS MANNER?

These Conditions

These conditions and many others just as bad—or just as good—as you wish to place it—are existing in your City Government and CAN AND WILL BE REMEDIED if you VOTE FOR THE CHARTER.

Every Street To Be Paved

It has been stated in open meeting by a member of your present Board that EVERY STREET in your CITY is to be PAVED. This means an expenditure by our property holders of about $3,000,000. Three million dollars which would draw interest to the amount of $210,000—Two Hundred and Ten Thousand Dollars per year at the rate of interest the street bonds draw or

7 per cent—and this does not include curb and gutter or sidewalk expenditures.

Are You Satisfied?

Are you satisfied to have your present Government spend this amount of money, which amounts to more than the entire assessed value of all property combined in your City—and without encouraging or soliciting competition through varied specifications, or without giving the property holders any CONSIDERATION as to the KIND OF PAVING WHICH THEY PREFER. And last but not least—5 PER CENT OF THE ENTIRE AMOUNT WILL GO TO THE SURVEYOR UNDER PRESENT CONDITIONS, which will amount to about $150,000—One hundred and Fifty Thousand Dollars, excluding Curb and Gutter work.

Your Charter Protects You

Under the proposed Charter the property Owners have the RIGHT to specify the kind and class of pavement for which their money shall be spent and the majority on any one street HAS THE RIGHT to sanction or reject paving. This clause protects the taxpayer as he should be protected in PRICE, COMPETITION and PAVEMENTS GRAFT BY NOT GIVING THE POWER TO ANY FEW TO SPECIFY THE CLASS OF PAVEMENT THAT MUST BE USED.

Whose Advantage?

Some perhaps, to their advantage, desire these conditions to remain and are using every effort to pull the blinds over the voters' eyes and to mislead them so that the easy money can continue to flow.

Disqualifying Charter

Disqualifying the Charter is the aim of those who would keep conditions as they are. THE GREATEST PORTION OF THE CHARTER WHICH IS TO BE VOTED ON APRIL 9TH, HAS BEEN TAKEN FROM THE LEAGUE OF MUNICIPALITY MODEL CHARTERS WHICH HAVE BEEN LISTED AND APPROVED BY THE BEST EXPERTS ON GOVERNMENT IN THESE UNITED STATES.

Attorney Inspected And Passed

The opposition has stated that the Charter was drawn up without the advice of legal aid, which statement is a COLD BLOODED LIE. Please excuse my expression, but I have no use for this kind. One of the BEST KNOWN ATTORNEYS IN MONTEREY COUNTY assisted in the handling of the charter and went over it from start to finish, previous to its adoption. Every section which materially differed from the Model Charter was read and passed by the prominent attorney and certain sections were written entirely by him.

THIS CIRCULAR WRITTEN AND PAID FOR BY W. R. HOLMAN

(To Be Continued)

The Peninsular Review APRIL 4, 1927

FORWARD PACIFIC GROVE

AN OVERSIGHT?

On Mar. 31 the Citizens Committee published the following statement in both *Herald* and *Review* relative to the proposed charter of Pacific Grove: "No better evidence of bungling can be found than the omission to provide for an auditor. This is excused on the grounds that the model charter prepared by Locke doesn't provide for an auditor. It is not true, as can be seen on page 125, section 12, of the Municipal Handbook. The omission of the office of auditor is one of the most glaring defects. It was caused by haste and failure to employ competent counsel in framing the charter. Possibly the person who compiled the document was not able to see this important paragraph in the model charter."

Yesterday "sentences" were "unintelligible" to "the person." Today paragraphs are invisible—too bad!

Upon the title page of the Municipal Handbook, published in 1926, it appears that the book is for City Officials of the Fifth and Sixth Class Cities of the State of California.

According to our state statutes, cities "having a population of more than six thousand and not exceeding twenty thousand, shall constitute the fifth class; those having a population of not exceeding six thousand shall constitute the sixth class." Pacific Grove is therefore a city of the sixth class.

The said Municipal Handbook contains a model charter. In section 4 (p. 119) of this charter officers are listed and an auditor is not included in the list. The following sections of the model charter define the duties of council, mayor, attorney, etc., until we come to section 12 (page 124) entitled "City Clerk and ex-Officio Assessor." This section is followed by another (p. 125) also numbered 12, which is designated as an "alternate section" entitled "Auditor and ex-Officio Assessor." Immediately thereafter is the following note: "In all cities of the sixth class the auditing is done by a committee of the board of trustees, but where the population reaches 15,000 or over, it is better to have a regular auditor, in which case, as in Alameda, the office is often consolidated with that of Assessor."

Hence the alternate sections. One without an auditor for sixth class cities, and one with an auditor for cities with a population in excess of 15,000. Our proposed charter calls for no auditor, and this we are told is evidence of bungling, a most glaring defect, caused by haste and failure to employ competent counsel (?).

It is suggested to the Citizens Committee that despite their eagerness to disparage the charter, it were well to keep within the bounds of truth.

Julia B. Platt   .

[SOURCE AND DATE UNCLEAR]

Voters of Pacific Grove:

I understand that W. R. Holman procured a telegram from W. J. Locke commending the proposed Charter. I can't understand how Mr. Locke can commend the present Charter. In his handbook he provides a penalty for interference with the City Manager, and in a note at the end of the section he says: "This is one of the most important provisions of a City Manager Charter. A councilman who attempts to dictate appointments or tells the manager where to make his purchases hereby violates the fundamental principles of this system of government." Page 145, Municipal Handbook. The proposed Charter has no such provision.

How can this charter be fundamentally right if fundamental provision is omitted? Mr. Locke evidently overlooked this.

I have a letter from him which he criticizes the provisions of the Charter in regard to the number of councilmen and its street provisions. He also told me personally that the provision as to initiative and referendum, shortening the time for calling special elections, was bad.

Don't be influenced by last minute canards or telegraphic endorsements by people who know nothing of local conditions.

H.G. JORGENSEN, City Attorney

The Peninsular Review MONDAY, APRIL 4, 1927

VOTE NO

NOT THE MODEL CHARTER; W. R. HOLMAN ANSWERED

In a letter published in the local papers issued Feb. 24th last, Miss Platt says of the proposed charter that "in its main outline . . . it is based upon a model charter published in 1926 by Wm. J. Locke, Secretary of the League of California Municipalities," but she also admits that the sections relative to the initiative, referendum and recall and a section governing street improvements were drafted by Attorney C. F. Lacey of Salinas. Mr. Lacey, while in many ways an able lawyer, is not an expert as to any of these subjects and these sections as rewritten by him are mutilation of the general law written to please the client by whom he was paid. To illustrate:

Miss Platt's Charter

The general laws provide that a vote under the initiative and referendum shall be had in not less than 30, nor more than 60 days after the petition is filed. Such provision embodies the combined wisdom of the people of the State of California. In the proposed charter the time is fixed as not less than 20 or more than 30 days. This is not according to Locke.

Again, in the matter of street improvements, if same are on a large scale, the district to be specially benefitted thereby is designated and the cost is assessed against all the property to be benefitted thereby. Miss Platt's charter would give no property holder a voice in the matter except one whose property actually fronted upon the street to be improved. This is manifestly unfair. Lack of space forbids other glaring examples.

The failure to provide for an auditor has already been pointed out, and this although Locke has a whole section covering this important office.

City Manager Unprotected

More important still, while this proposed charter forbids the members of the Council—nothing is said about their 14 advisers—from interfering with the City Manager, it omits to provide any penalty if they do. Sec. 60 of Locke's Model Charter reads as follows: "No member of the Council shall in any manner directly or indirectly, by suggestion or otherwise, attempt to influence or coerce the City Manager in the making of any appointment or the purchase of supplies, or attempt to exact any promise relative to any appointment from any such candidate for the City Manager . . . Any violation of the foregoing provisions of this section shall constitute a misdemeanor and shall work a forfeiture of the office of the offending member of Council," etc.

In a note to this section Locke says: "This is one of the most important provisions of the city manager charter. Councilmen who attempt to dictate . . . violate the fundamental provisions of this system of government. A manager cannot be held accountable for failure unless he is given a free rein. There can be no responsibility without complete authority." Yet in Miss Platt's charter any member of the Council can violate the "fundamental principles" of the city manager form of government with absolute impunity. The city manager may be pledged in advance as to all of his appointments and from whom he will buy his supplies. Yet Miss Platt says that she followed Locke "in its main outline." Perhaps she was looking forward to a day when she might be on the Board in which case, God pity the City Manager.

Locke Again Disagrees with Miss Platt

The Model Charter provides for only five councilmen. Miss Platt would raise that number to seven. In a recent letter to a prominent citizen of the

Peninsula, Mr. Locke writes: "I think the provision of seven members is a mistake. Practically all of the trustees of the cities of the state, large and small, with a few exceptions, manage to get along very nicely with a city council of five." It is even now notoriously hard to get five competent persons to serve and it will be increasingly harder if the charter is adopted. Why raise the number to seven?

Attorney Lacey Disagrees with His Client

In inserting the following stupid provisions in the proposed charter, Miss Platt went contrary to the advice of her own attorney for, according to his own statement, he advised her against requiring candidates for an elective office to include in the sworn statement which they are to file with the City Cerk, the following information: "(D) the public offices he has ever held, if any, as principal, deputy, or employee; (E) the experience, training or education he has received which, in his opinion, would qualify him to fill the office for which he is a candidate; (F) he shall also file a statement setting forth the public improvements or betterments which he favors." Most of our successful business men have no other degreees than such as they have received from the College of Hard Knocks and the women are content to have earned an M.A. The whole provision is undemocratic but characteristic of a pedantic and impractical mind.

Judgment Not To Be Colored by Prejudice

The writer favors Portland cement as against asphalt and holds no brief for any member of the present board. If there is any immediate danger there is a plain remedy and that is the recall. The writer has investigated the cost of street improvements in Carmel, Salinas, Monterey and Pacific Grove and it is nearly uniform. To take but one instance, the charges of the city engineer. In Carmel, he receives 7 per cent of the total cost, in Salinas from 6 to 7 per cent and in Monterey and Pacific Grove only 5 per cent.

In the improvement of such a street as Lighthouse Avenue, including both upper and lower Lighthouse from its extreme easterly to its extreme westerly limits, which was done under three separate contracts and over a period of years, the engineer's charges might reach $6,777.19—we do not know—but the bulk of it would be payroll, blue prints, and maps. That any surveyor could do all this work in 30 days, as alleged by W. R. Holman, is preposterous and he must know it if he is in his right mind. His knowledge of such matters is insufficient for him to qualify even as a witness in court to give testimony to all to the reasonable value of such services. Again the City Trustees allow the surveyor 8 cents per foot for every foot of wooden curb replaced if paid for through the contractor or 7 cents if by the city. This applies to piece work. Very properly, no such work can be done unless the city surveyor establishes the grade and on a 30-foot lot he would receive either $2.40 or $2.10 as the case might be not much more than a plumber would charge if summoned to stop a leak.

W.R. Holman is so blinded with rage that he circulates thousands of circulars wherein he indulges in the use of such terms as "graft," "cold-blooded lies," etc. Whether or not the news of his mercantile venture was scattered throughout the entire mercantile world or what are the offices which he "maintains in San Francisco, New York and Berlin," has nothing whatever to do with the question, and is not entitled to more consideration here than Burbank's idea of God or Henry Ford's views of the Jews. Let the shoemaker stick to his last. The use of such arguments are an old trick to give weight to arguments which are without merit in themselves and seek to blind the voter to the real issues in the campaign.

Citizen's Committee

(To Be Continued)

The Peninsular Review APRIL 5, 1927

VOTE YES FOR THE CHARTER SATURDAY APRIL 9

Beware of those who hide behind a blanket and sign their printed statements with some made-up name that is not known to our general taxpayers and voters. Such statements are not worthy of the consideration of thinking people. They are like anonymous letters received signed by fictitious persons or firms who do not exist.

Think It Over

Just before the election for Freeholders, the voters were warned that if they voted in favor of the Freeholders, THE STREET LIGHTS WOULD BE TURNED OFF AND THE FIRE HYDRANTS LOCKED. HAS THIS THREAT BEEN CARRIED OUT AND WHY NOT?

YOU WOULD JUDGE FROM THE TACTICS OF SUCH PEOPLE THAT THE CITIZENS OF PACIFIC GROVE ARE IMBECILES. The very same "SCARE" methods are now being used in different ways to discredit the Charter, which is to come before you on April 9th for your approval or discard.

"A Snare, A Delusion, Freak Legislation with a Vengeance"

This is what "they" call (whoever "they" may be) the section in the Charter THAT GIVES THE PEOPLE OR TAXPAYERS WHO FOOT THE BILLS THE RIGHT TO DETERMINE THE CLASS OR KIND OF PAVEMENT THEY DESIRE—and the right by MAJORITY on any one street effected to say whether or not that street shall be improved.

I CLAIM THAT THIS SECTION IS A GOOD SECTION AND A

PROTECTION AGAINST SPITE IMPROVEMENT AND AGAINST GRAFT, as it prevents one or a few from "forcing down our throats" anything they desire to force upon us which may be to THEIR advantage. Another thing don't overlook, as the situation now stands NO STREET IS ACCEPTED BY THE CITY and if for any reason a street requires repaving the property owner is again forced to pay the bill.

Genuine Competition

Genuine competition in street paving WITHOUT THE SPECIAL PRIV-ILEGES has never been known to increase cost and any statement to the contrary is ridiculous. With a fee as great as about $6777 (Six thousand Seven Hundred and Seventy Dollars) for the surveyor all on ONE STREET for a short period of work it naturally seems that it would be of great advantage to some to recommend the paving program until every alley and street in town is paved, WITHOUT REGARD TO PROPERTY VALUES, ABILITY OF HOLDERS TO PAY OR THEIR DESIRES.

Why Not Turn All Our Property Over to Their Care and Jurisdiction?

If, as they state (this so-called Citizens' Committee) that we should have no voice as to the improvements of our own property, why would it not be best to turn all of our real estate over in the same manner and allow them to erect our homes, build and stock our stores and to arrange our gardens to suit themselves or turn same to some company whom they particularly favor, and to assess us accordingly and if we were not able to pay at once to bond our property which would serve as first mortgage. ONE IS AS FAIR AS THE OTHER AND JUST AS REASONABLE—still such legislation as recommended and carried out in the Charter to protect the taxpayer and to give you the power to state how your money shall be spent—would be, according to the Citizens' Committee (whoever they may be) a snare—a delusion—a freak legislation with a vengeance to win your votes. They even claim this is used as a "SOP" to win votes.

They Say Your Taxes Will Be Advanced if the City Manager Form of Government is Carried

Just compare your taxes for the LAST TWO YEARS with what you paid previously under your present form of government. These HEAVY ADVANCES have been put on to the property holder in the face of all the building, all the new construction which has been carried on in your city during the past few years, and which in itself has very materially increased revenues. With all the new tax revenue and with the heavy additional advances in taxes during the past two years, the opposition to the Charter claimed the city was broke, and if the Freeholders' election carried they would be compelled to turn off the fire hydrants and the street lights and were ANTICIPATING SELLING THE PAST DUMP GROUNDS FOR THE PURPOSE OF TURNING OVER THE PROCEEDS TO THE PAVING COMPANY. The grounds formerly used for a dump, IS ONE OF THE CITY'S MOST VALUABLE HOLDINGS AND WILL BE NEEDED FOR A PARK PURPOSE WITHIN THE VERY NEAR FUTURE. Its location is central between all sections of the Peninsula. What this city needs is more grounds for the future—NOT LESS.

Increase Taxes Paid

You paid 15 per cent INCREASE IN TAX RATE IN 1925 WITH A PROMISE IT WOULD BE TAKEN OFF THE NEXT YEAR. In place of doing away with the 15 per cent increase your valuation was increased 20 per cent for 1926. All these increases with the same amount of City Employees and the same government under the present form of government, you can continue to look for advanced taxes if you continue our present obsolete form of government.

The following taken from the *Pacific Grove Review*, April 2, 1927: We are told by the Citizens' Committee that the law now provides that a four-fifths vote of the Council can overrule all protests regarding street work, that the reason for this rule is that if protests have merit they should (1) receive the support of more than one-fifth of the Council, and that if a Council does not represent a majority of the people and acts in an arbitrary manner, "the law provides the remedy by recall."

Unfortunately, the constitution of the state also provides that "no recall petition shall be circulated or filed against any officer until he has actually held his office for at least six months." If a member of the city council re-signs, a trustee is appointed to his place by the remaining board, and it is obvious that by repeating this procedure any board of trustees can carry through a PREARRANGED POLICY WITHOUT CHECK BY RECALL.

One more resignation from the city board last fall would have placed Pacific Grove in just this helpless situation. THE CHARTER SECURES TO THE PEOPLE THEIR AUTHORITY.

We are told by the Citizens' Committee that the adoption of the charter will be a decided step backward.

By the grace of God it will be. It will be a step backward towards the days WHEN CITIZENS OF PACIFIC GROVE WERE TREATED WITH COUR-TESY BY A CITY COUNCIL ELECTED TO REPRESENT, NOT TO DEFY, THE PEOPLE. IT WILL BE A STEP BACK TO THE DAYS WHEN STREET CONTRACTS WERE SUBJECT TO REAL COMPETITION, AND NOT IN-FALLIBLY AWARDED AS PREDETERMINED BY THE SPECIFICATIONS OF THE TRUSTEES AND THE MIXING PLANT OF THE CONTRACTOR. IT WILL BE A STEP BACK TO DAYS WHEN THOSE PAYING THE BILLS HAD THE RIGHT TO DECIDE WHETHER THEY WISHED TO MAKE

THE INVESTMENT. IT WILL BE A STEP BACK TO DAYS WHEN IT WAS
EXPECTED THAT PRE-ELECTION PROMISES WOULD BE REDEEMED.
A STEP BACK FROM A LOST TRAIL TO THE GREAT HIGHWAY OF
COURTESY, TRUTH, HONESTY AND JUSTICE.

W.R. Holman

(To Be Continued)

The Peninsular Review APRIL 5, 1927

VOTE NO

Do We Need a City Manager?

We understand that the City of Salinas employed City Manager Ely of
Berkeley, a man of years experience, a great advocate of City Manager
form of government, and President of the City Managers' Association, to
make a survey of their city with the idea of adopting the City Manager
form of government. He reported to them in effect: "You do not need a
City Manager. You have nothing to manage. Your income is solely from
your taxes. You have no public utilities which require the services of a City
Manager, and your Council form of government is just as effective as you
can get in a city of this character."

The City of Pacific Grove is in the same situation. The City of Monterey
is not. It has its municipal wharf and other municipal affairs which we do
not have.

No Effective City Manager Form of Government
Provided by This Charter

This Charter is not a true City Manager form of government nor a commission form of government. It is neither. It will be ineffective as a City
Manager form of government because:

FIRST: No qualifications are provided for its City Manager.

Miss Platt says that she will trust the Council. Now the Council appoints the City Manager and under her Charter both the City Manager and the City Council appoint the City Attorney, and yet very elaborate qualifications are prescribed for the City Attorney. Couldn't Miss Platt trust the Council and the City Manager in the matter of appointment of the City Attorney?

SECOND: While the Charter provides that the City Councilmen shall not interfere with the duties of the City Manager, no penalty for violation is prescribed, so that the Council can dictate the appointments and the whole conduct of the City Manager and make him an errand boy and man-of-all-work.

THIRD: It fails to restrict the Council to legislative duties and permits them to interfere in the administrative duties by assigning each Councilman to a department. Thus the City Manager will have several bosses and if each Councilman adopts the unique idea of appointing two advisors, the City Manager will be the errand boy of the whole twenty-one.

City Manager Form of Government Can be Adopted Under Our Present Law

We are operating as a City of the sixth class under the general laws of the State of California. This form of government is conceded to be one of the best forms of government ever adopted for small cities. At the present time there are over 130 small cities operating under this form of government. Some of the cities range in population from ten to fifteen thousand. This form of government has behind it years of practical experience and the best judgment of men and women who are interested in the improvement of our laws relating to government of cities. Because so many of the cities of our state are of this class the League of California Municipalities at each annual session takes up intensively the study of laws relating to the government of cities of this class, and has introduced at the present session of this Legislature an amendment allowing cities of sixth class to appoint by ordinance a City Manager. The law is so drawn as to make the City Manager an effective officer. This amendment has practically passed both Houses and it is meeting with no opposition, and is assured of the Governor's signature. So that if the Charter is beaten, as it should be, the city can try out the City Manager form of government and if it is ineffective in our city, then the ordinance can be readily changed.

City Manager Form Of Government Will Not
Reduce Paving Cost

W.R. Holman, who we understand took at least $20,000.00 from the City of Pacific Grove last year—probably not all profit—is generally extravagant in his statements. We ask that before you swallow all his line that you take the trouble to check up on him.

The city engineering services in this city cost the same as in the City of Monterey under the City Manager form of government and is about the same as in other cities of this size. Some cities pay more so far as we can tell. None pay less. In spite of having a City Manager, the City of Monterey must have, and does have, its City Engineer. If competent services could have been obtained for a smaller cost, the Council of the City of Monterey and the Board of Trustees of the City of Pacific Grove certainly would have entertained such a proposition.

In a wild and grossly misleading circulator, W.R. Holman tries to make the people believe that graft is going on in our city and our paving cost is expensive.

One case in point will refute such an absurd and libelous statement. The City of Pacific Grove recently awarded the contract for four-inch asphaltic concrete pavement on Ocean View Boulevard for 20 3/4 cents per square foot. The City of Monterey let a similar contract on Larkin and Watson

Street for 21¢ per square foot. The slightly higher rate in Monterey is undoubtedly accounted for by the hauling cost.

This refutes the idea that if we were asking for bids on Portland cement and asphaltic concrete we would get lower bids because in Monterey at the present time they are asking for bids on both Portland cement and asphaltic concrete paving.

Incidentally the people will remember that this same W.R. Holman was very instrumental in electing Mr. Basham, Mr. Gould and Mr. Cosmey to our Board of Trustees and promised the people that they would be able to please 100 per cent of the people 100 per cent of the time in 100 per cent of everything coming before the Board. Evidentially he is a poor prophet.

He promises such a fine performance under the form of City Manager government. Is there any reason to believe that he will be a better prophet this time?

About The Auditor

We do not contend that the Auditor should be a separate office but we do say that the important duties of an Auditor should be performed by somebody. Under the government of cities of the sixth class the City Clerk performs these duties. See Section 873 of the Municipal Corporation Bill. It states among other things:

"The City Clerk shall keep a book marked 'Demands and Warrants' in which he shall note every demand against the city or town and file the same . . . He shall prepare a quarterly statement in writing showing the receipts and expenditures of the city or town for the preceding quarter and the amount remaining in the Treasury."

In other words, he performs relatively the same chores as the Auditor in the City of Monterey and other cities.

We do not say that there should be distinct office, but we do say that taking the duties away from the City Clerk and assigning them to no other office is a striking evidence of bungling, which would never have occurred if a municipal expert had been employed to draft the Charter.

DON'T SUBSTITUTE A FORM OF GOVERNMENT PREPARED IN ONE WEEK BY A BOARD OF THIRTEEN FREEHOLDERS WITHOUT EXPERT ADVICE FOR A FORM OF GOVERNMENT WHICH IS THE RESULT OF FORTY YEARS OF EXPERIENCE AND THE WORK OF MANY EXPERT AND EXPERIENCED MEN AND LEGISLATORS.

Citizen's Committee

(ADVERTISEMENT)

Peninsula Daily Herald APRIL 8, 1927

VOTE YES

Why Does The "Citizens' Committee" Misrepresent To Our Citizens? Read and Judge For Yourself—Refer to Monday's article of April 4, 1927, wherein the "Citizens Committee" stated in their advertisement:

"Not The Model Charter—W. R. Holman Answered"

Also another of their headings:

"Locke Again Disagrees With Miss Platt"

No Wonder They Have Hidden Behind a Blanket

Better Do Some Checking On the "Citizens' Committee" When Using Such Tactics of Misrepresentation

Read Attorney Wm. J. Locke's Own Letter, The Greatest Authority On City Charters And City Government In America

W. R. Holman

April 5, 1927
Mr. B. L. Strong,
568 Lighthouse Ave.,
Pacific Grove, Calif.

Dear Sir:
Yours of March 30th, together with copy of the proposed
charter for the City of Pacific Grove, duly received.

About two weeks ago some of the opponents of the proposed
charter sent word that they would like to have me go down
there and address a public meeting in opposition to the instrument. However, after reading the charter I told them it
would be impossible for me to take a stand against the charter as it embodied so many of the provisions of the charter which I have recommended as a model. The gentleman who
waited upon me at that time is a personal friend and, under
the circumstances, I would prefer not to be quoted one way
or the other.

Thanking you for your letter and appreciating your expression of concern, I am

                           Yours very truly,
                           WM. J. Locke
                           Attorney and Counselor at Law
                           Chancery Bldg., 564 Market St.
                           San Francisco, Calif.

READ THIS TELEGRAM RECEIVED OVER WESTERN UNION THIS
MORNING:

WJL-BL
RECEIVED AT 211 FOREST AVE., PACIFIC GROVE, CAL., PHONE 503
COPY
12F C 58 Collect
ALAMEDA CALIF 920A APRIL 8 1927
W. R. HOLMAN
PACIFIC GROVE CALIF

I CONSIDER YOUR PROPOSED NEW CHARTER A GOOD INSTRUMENT STOP
IT HAS MANY EXCELLENT PROVISIONS AND NO FUNDAMENTAL DE-
FECTS STOP IT IS BASED ON THE LATEST AND BEST IDEA OF CITY

GOVERNMENT STOP WHILE MOST SMALL CITIES HAVE A COUNCIL OF
FIVE MEMBERS SOME HAVE MORE STOP PALO ALTO FOR INSTANCE HAS
FIFTEEN MEMBERS ON ITS COUNCIL

RESPECTFULLY

WILLIAM J. LOCKE

The Peninsular Review THURSDAY, APRIL 7, 1927

VOTE YES

WHAT THE CITY MANAGER FORM OF GOVERNMENT HAS DONE FOR
VISALIA, A CITY ABOUT THE SIZE OF PACIFIC GROVE, AND WHAT IT
WILL SAVE FOR YOU "TAXPAYERS" OF PACIFIC GROVE.

The following is taken from a letter received by one of our citizens from Attorney Dixon F. Maddox of Visalia, California, son-in-law of E. Cooke Smith, one of the Pacific Grove Freeholders who framed the charter:

"On July 1, 1927, we will have had here at Visalia four years of city government under a city manager. It has been highly successful here at Visalia, less expensive than the old form of government and above all it has eliminated local, petty politics. During these four years it has been my privilege to serve for two years as president of the Visalia chamber of commerce and I have been in close contact with the administration of city affairs. I do not feel that I could go into details by letter and the newspaper which I am sending you covers the main things accomplished in a general way."

The following is from the *Visalia Daily Times*, April 4, 1927:

Returning, briefly, to consideration of the Visalia city charter, through one of its chief provisions—actual direction of the city's business matters by a city manager—is not inconsistent here to point out some of the civic accomplishments that have been brought about during the past four years of municipal government under the charter, these having to do with the city's finances, physical improvements, economical use of city property, safety from fire, beautification, efficient policing, lighting and other betterments tending to make Visalia a more attractive place in which to reside. Some of these may be pointed out as follows:

Maintaining the city's officiary for $17,000 less per year than before the adoption of the charter.

Change to financial status from a deficit of $14,000 to a reserve of $10,000.

Construction of Imhoff tank and placing of sewer farm in first place condition, changing it from a tangled mass of weeds, sunflowers and willows, with raw sewage ponded all over the acreage, to a use of profit—to produce this year fully $5,000 in tillage.

Installation of sewers in various subdivisions in the south-western part of the city, at less than contract price.

Almost all dirt streets of city widened, oiled twice a year, instead of once: alleys oiled and cleared.

Thirty percent increase in number of street lights.

Fire alarm boxes doubled; many new hydrants installed.

Fire equipment paid for; better protection from fire procured; removal of old wooden buildings and awnings; clean up campaigns reducing fire hazards.

City streets cleaned and placed in better condition or repair; street broom now cleaning paved streets oftener and more efficiently.

Entrance to town bettered; creation of Mayor Park, beautifying a former dumping grounds; Hyde way leased from chamber of commerce and beautified by city.

Old Lincoln school building removed by city; site made into North Park, improved and made attractive.

Tipton Lindsey school grounds square now being parked.

Trees and shrubs grown upon city farm distributed to citizens of Visalia without cost.

It is understood that considerable criticism has been directed at the rumored cost of the police department and its so-called increase. Contrary to such contentions, city hall reports indicate that there are now being employed by the city no more police officers than there were before the charter was placed in effect, with its provision for a city manager. It is also shown in reports that the present force has collected more than ten times as many fines; while there have been no trials conducted to date.

The net saving in expense, through the city's present method of police force management, as compared with the old system, is sufficient to pay the salary of the city manager—$5,000 per year—and no extra sums are paid for such service, as many persons appear to believe.

Policemen and firemen pay for their own uniforms. Because they are in uniform, it may appear to many persons that they are more numerous than heretofore.

A comparison of the city's policing, under the former way of caring for the city's protection with that now employed under the charter, gives the following facts:

Formerly there were one day man; one traffic officer; two night men; one merchants' patrol.

Now there are one day man; one traffic officer; two night men, and one man detailed on merchants' patrol.

Popularity of the Visalia city charter is abundantly endorsed by the fact that various other cities of the county and valley have copied its provisions, almost entirely; and several official delegations from surrounding towns and cities have paid visits to this city, while gathering data regarding the workings of the municipal government here.

John P. Pryor

═══

[Editor's note: Silas W. Mack opposed the charter. Despite their opposing views, W.R. Holman fondly remembered Mack, who was the lawyer during probate hearings for his father's estate.]

The Peninsular Review THURSDAY, APRIL 7, 1927

ATTORNEY SILAS W. MACK GIVES HIS VIEWS ON MUNICIPAL AFFAIRS IN PACIFIC GROVE

As a resident of Pacific Grove for almost a quarter of a century and meeting many in business, people with all kinds of opinions, the writer has formed some very definite views on the issues involved in Saturday's election.

City Manager Not Needed

According to the latest figures available there were in 1926 in the United States 5,039 cities having a population of 1,000 or over and of these only 280, or about 5 per cent, had adopted the city manager form of government and nearly all the latter were much larger than Pacific Grove. Santa Cruz recently turned down the proposition by a two to one vote. Salinas had City Manager Ely, of Berkeley, investigate the advantages which it might reasonably hope to derive through a city manager and he reported that inasmuch as all its income comes from taxes, there would be nothing gained by a change. Monterey not only has two municipal piers the revenue from which last year was $30,033 with an estimate of $40,000 for 1927, but owns its waterfront which it leases to the canneries, besides having many problems arising from its mixed population, crooked streets, etc., which requires constant attention. It is also on the eve of a great commercial development. Therefore the $9,000 to $10,000 which it pays for a city manager, his secretary, and incidental expenses is a justifiable expenditure. Pacific Grove has nothing of the kind, not even so much need of a manager as Salinas or Santa Cruz and the expense, not less than $5,000 per annum, would have to come out of the receipts from taxes. At best he could do nothing more than the force now employed should do to earn their salaries, with such supervision as is given by the trustees. It would be a foolish waste.

Some Other Real Dangers

The proponents of the charter place great emphasis on economy in their arguments but what they would do in practice if given a free rein in government is not at all certain. It was only a short time ago that they urged the establishing of an under-grade crossing just beyond the depot. The engineers of the Southern Pacific Co. made a careful examination and reported the cost at $30,000 and Miss Platt was for putting it through. But Trustee Basham and the others viewed the matter differently. W.R. Holman is a firm supporter of the Municipal Camp Grounds and rumors are that it is planned to turn the rest of that park over for such purposes. This is about the only place where a city manager could function to advantage.

Let Us Boost, Not Knock

From recent articles pro and con I get the idea that the city manager issue is practically dead, the charter affording him no protection in the discharge of his duties, and that the real question is that of street improvements. It is much to be regretted that men in private life enjoying an unblemished reputation and who have given freely of their services for the betterment of the city as it appears to them, are being made the target for accusations of graft. Not only will this injure the hitherto good reputation of Pacific Grove but it will become increasingly difficult to get good men to accept office in our fair city. It is a matter of common knowledge that Trustees Tuttle, Bailey, Cosmey and Basham resigned rather than continue to face unmerited abuse.

Permanent Improvements Overlooked

Yet those same men have to their credit some of the best permanent improvements which Pacific Grove enjoys, such as (1) the acquisition from the Del Monte Properties Co. of a long stretch of land fronting on the beach—this compares very favorably with the proposition of the charter supporters to set apart the old city dump for a park though this may come some day; (2) the paving of the main arteries leading into and through

Pacific Grove as well as the Ocean Boulevard; (3) an efficient and economical management of the city's business. True, this has cost some money and this cost accounts wholly for the raise in taxes, but we are getting value received. In this connection it is not amiss to call the attention of our citizens to the fact that the cooperation of these same trustees, and particularly Mr. Basham, with S. S. Parsons, in the building of the magnificent Forest Hill Hotel and in the improvement of free playgrounds for all of which little or no public recognition has been given, is also to be taken into consideration in weighing the question of efficiency in the discharge of their official duties.

Compensation of Engineer

Much is being said about the cost of paving and the city engineer has been singled out for criticism. Yet what are the simple facts? An architect who draws the plans and specifications for a building and superintends the work of construction receives not less than 5 per cent of the cost. This rule obtains everywhere. For exactly the same reason the engineer who draws the plans and specifications, furnishes the estimates, makes the maps and blue prints and superintends the work, also receives 5 per cent in Monterey (which has a city manager) and in Pacific Grove, which has none. Salinas, I understand, pays from 6 to 7 per cent and Carmel pays the 7 per cent. This may amount to several thousand dollars on a big job like Lighthouse Avenue which was let in three separate contracts and extended over several years. But of the 5 per cent it is estimated that three-fifths represents money actually paid out by the city engineer. Then the compensation to the engineer is much less than to an architect. What W.R. Holman means by saying a competent surveyor ought to do this work in 30 days passes my comprehension. Also why should the engineer be called into question for receiving 7 or 8 cents per front foot for setting grade stakes. $2.10 or $2.40

for a 30 foot lot. Take it year in and year out, averaging the big jobs with the small, and our city engineer is, at the best, only making a comfortable living.

Asphalt vs. Portland Cement

As to the merits of asphalt and Portland cement, for the present the decision rests with the last salesman to be heard. We will all know much more about it if we are alive and still in our right minds ten years hence.

Paving Means Progress

I am constantly approached by people who want to raise money on their property. Do they realize that one of the first questions a finance committee asks is whether or not the proposed security is on a paved street? Purchasers who are looking for the better class of property own an automobile and want to be on an improved street, either paved or having the prospect of being paved in the near future. So far our City Trustees have proceeded systematically and not too rapidly, and the specter of a $3,000,000 program with $150,000 to the City Engineer is a mere figment of the imagination calculated to scare those voters who cannot think or reason for themselves.

What Our Trustees Need

The modern industrial world has learned that to get the most out of labor, the laborer himself must be well treated. The same principle applies to public servants. If we never commend them when they do well but vilify and distrust them when their opinions differ from ours; they will lose interest or resign and the services rendered will become poorer and poorer. It may be that some of the trustees have been seemingly discourteous at times but how would their critics have acted had they been subjected to the same kind of treatment? Answer that.

Charter Elections Every Other Year

I fancy that there are many citizens who are getting tired of all this turmoil and disturbance. And some say: Vote for the charter and we can amend it if it is wrong. Do these people realize that each amendment of the charter will mean another charter election—they are already tired of this one—and after the citizens will have to wait perhaps two years for the state legislature to ratify the charter as amended. Pacific Grove was never more prosperous than now, so why change?

Whether articles are signed or unsigned, matters little. Personality may detract from the weight of an argument of which truth many political speeches are shining illustrations. What the voter needs, but does not always appreciate, are facts. Such I have endeavored to furnish and they lead me to VOTE NO.

Silas W. Mack

[SOURCE AND DATE UNCLEAR]

WHY VOTE YES?

The time for a change in the form of city government is here. The charter gives the most approved form. No one disputes that fact.

It gives the city a city manager.

It gives the man who pays the bill a chance to pay it. It gives him a chance to say what he shall pay for.

The charter makes possible a planning committee to work out a reasonable plan to protect our homes and yet not to impede business development.

The Pacific Grove Retreat Association as a protection to the homes in Pacific Grove as first it was designed, is a TOTAL FAILURE. It is out-grown. It is a miserable misfit. It protects itself only.

The charter gives the opportunity to combine in a city manager the office of city engineer at one salary. Improvements from this time on will demand an intelligent leader in our midst. If we don't pay for a man for that, we will pay for the mistakes made by uninformed men who try and fail to handle the complicated affairs that make up the business of a modern city.

The charter states a minimum salary, a salary that shall be known, for the city manager. The present city engineer has received from Pacific Grove as commission on the road work alone in a little over two years over $16,000.00. Go to city hall, look over the book of contracts and see for yourself—$16,000.00.

If the charter shall not carry, you know what is before you. Mr. Gould has stated in open meeting that every street in the town shall be paved. What will 5 per cent on that amount to? Put that money to work for yourselves. Get your money's worth. Pay some of that for a city manager.

The people who are backing this charter ask only the good of the town. They ask nothing for themselves.

The opponents to the charter include the paving company and back of them the Standard Oil Company of California. They sell the asphaltic concrete. They know that if the charter carries that an era of sane development suited to our town is at hand. There will be open bidding on street work.

AND FINALLY. . .

The charter is not graven in stone. It provides, as all similar documents do, a means to change the parts that prove on trial to be unsuited to our needs. It provides for changes to meet our changing conditions.

All the hot criticism against the charter is dust thrown up to confuse you as to these facts.

VOTE TO PROTECT YOURSELVES.

VOTE FOR THE CHARTER.

B. L. Strong

The Peninsular Review APRIL 8, 1927

VOTE YES FOR THE CHARTER

FREE TAXI TO THE POLLS, CALL 977W

There is apparently some doubt regarding the source of certain provisions of the proposed charter. There have also been misstatements of fact.

Sections 19 and 20 relative to the initiative, referendum and recall, and also section 57 regarding to street improvements, were written by Attorney C. F. Lacey, who neither asked nor received a fee for this service, generously rendered for the City of Pacific Grove.

The provision limiting the date of a special election upon an initiative or referendum petition to not less than 20 nor more than 30 days from the presentation thereof was copied from the Salinas charter.

The paragraph in Section 25 relative to interference with the city manager was taken verbatim from the charter of Sacramento. It was, as I remember, the unanimous opinion of the Freeholders that this paragraph was preferable to the corresponding provision in the Monterey charter which prescribes a penalty. Penalties for violation of a city law may be determined by ordinance, and the Freeholders of Pacific Grove held no brief for Locke or for the framers of Monterey's charter, but were free to act in their discretion.

The statements required of candidates for election to office under Section 8 of the proposed charter were taken from Locke's model charter. I find nothing in these statements indicative of an "undemocratic, pedantic and impractical mind."

At the request of the Freeholder by whom the charter was filed, the pages thereof were at the time of filing securely fastened together by the city clerk.

I have been assured in a letter from Attorney Ar[gyll Campbell] the Grove charter is a very superior one, and that "Insofar as the provision regarding the auditor is concerned, I think your charter is probably in advance of any of the charters which I have seen for cities of the size of Pacific Grove for the reason that an auditor really is not necessary. You have checks and balances without such an officer, and can have your books audited once a year, or at any such time as might be thought proper, without the creation of such an office."

In view of recent statements, this letter signed by Argyll Campbell is of value.

Julia B. Platt

The Peninsular Review APRIL 7, 1927

VOTE YES

ATTORNEY LACEY SAYS:

Board of Freeholders, Pacific Grove, Cal.—In view of the fact that I prepared Section 57 of your proposed charter dealing with street improvements, and that the policy declared by this section has been called in question, I am constrained to send you this communication. In last Monday's issue of the "Review" it is said that this section constitutes a "mutilation of general law."

The first part of the section provides that in the face of a written objection signed by the owners of a majority of the front footage to be assessed, there shall be no further proceedings for a period of twelve months upon the initiative of the Council. That is to say the immediate proceeding will lapse, and the power of the Council to initiate a new proceeding is stayed for twelve months. Of course, meantime, the majority of such owners may initiate and go forward with such improvement.

While I prepared this section it is not by any means new or original. The so-called Vrooman Act of 1885 which was the first comprehensive street improvement law, contained the following provision:

"The owners of a majority of the frontage may make written objection, and such objection shall be a bar for six months to any further proceedings, in relation to the doing of said work or making such improvements, unless the owners of one half or more of the frontage as aforesaid shall meanwhile petition for the same to be done."

It will be observed that other than changing the period from sixth months to twelve months, the proposed section is in substance the same as the law provided forty years ago.

This section of the Vrooman Act contained in force until a few years ago, when doubtless through the effort of persons particularly interested in the matter, the present provisions giving complete power to the council was adopted. Of course this part of Section 57 presents altogether a question of policy, and whether it meets the requirements of a particular city is a question of fact. It is easy to understand that where absent owners and landlords hold extensive areas of urban lands (which owners are usually averse to such improvements), it may be well to give full authority to the Council, while in a city of homes it does not seem reactionary or unreasonable to assert and to claim that where a clear majority of those who are to pay the bill protest against a present improvement, their wishes in the premises should not only be heeded by the Council but should control.

That second part of Section 57 provides that a majority of those who are to foot the bill should have a decisive voice in what is to be bought. It may be that a provision exactly like this is not to be found in any existing charter, but the reason obviously is that such a provision has not been hitherto found to be necessary, for I believe it to be the common practice of City Councils to allow the property owners to select the kind of pavement to be laid. The justification for this practice is found in the fact that if a poor pavement be chosen, the loss will fall on the property owners, for when the poor pavement fails or wears out a new pavement must be laid and at the expense of the same owners.

I have been informed by Mayor Clark of Salinas that it is the common practice of the Council here to abide by the choice of pavement selected by the property owners. I am also advised that concrete pavement is preferred above all others because of the better mending and repair work that can be done with this kind of pavement.

C. F. Lacey

The Peninsular Review APRIL 7, 1927

VOTE NO ON THE PROPOSED CHARTER

What Price Progress?

The proposed charter can be amended if necessary, say its proponents, in which statements they play safe. Amendment will assuredly be necessary, not once but repeatedly, a long and costly process. First an ordinance will have to be passed by the Council calling a special election to vote upon the proposed amendment. Then, if it carries, it will have to be ratified by the state legislature which meets once every two years. Why in the name of civic progress adopt a highly imperfect charter to begin with? Is this progress?

Is it progress to sponsor a civic program that is bound to raise our taxes? How is the city manager to be paid? That question has never yet been answered. Monterey's city management costs over $9000 a year. Can we expect to get a satisfactory manager for $6500 less than Monterey? The idea is ridiculous.

It is said that the manager's salary can be eliminated by dispensing with the city engineer—the manager is to do the engineer's work without additional compensation. Has Monterey dispensed with her city engineer? She has not. She has a city manager and a city engineer both, for she finds the engineer indispensable.

All this talk about the vast sums made by the city engineer of Pacific Grove is the greatest folly. It is not compulsory for our city engineer to set the grade levels of our streets. If property owners can get anyone to do the work more cheaply, they are welcome to do so. Engineer Severance has urged repeatedly that this be done, for he makes nothing on these jobs. Competent civil engineers have frequently expressed a doubt as to how he can break even on this work. If property owners will investigate this detail for themselves, they will find that these statements cannot be contradicted. Is it progress to deliberately spread misleading propaganda about the costs of our survey work?

Another misleading and much stressed bit of propaganda is agitated emphasis on no copy of the surveyor's field notes being filed with the city. Field notes are not in the least essential for our survey records. Grade maps are the important factor in this business, and grade maps we certainly possess. The city of Pacific Grove owns 144 official maps of our streets and sewers. The city of Pacific Grove owns various other profile maps which brings the total number to over 200. All of these maps are kept locked in the vault of the city clerk's office. Does this look like gross negligence in the city survey work? It most certainly does not.

The city engineer's fees are no higher in Pacific Grove than elsewhere.

They are lower than in many other towns—5 per cent on the total cost of street improvement in Pacific Grove and Monterey, 6 per cent to 7 per cent in Salinas and 7 per cent in Carmel. This also is a statement which cannot be contradicted.

Pacific Grove at the present time has 1333 registered automobiles, beside the countless thousands of outside cars that contribute wear and tear on our streets. Can we expect graveled streets to hold up under this terrific strain? It has been proved again and again that surfaced streets are an absolute necessity if a town is to keep in step with the progress of the day. Is it progress for proponents of the charter to argue against paving, in order to win votes for their side?

Is all this innuendo charging reputable citizens with graft being broadcast in the name of progress? It is a strange interpretation of the word. After hearing and reading these ugly rumors, it would be well for the voter to remember the following facts. Indisputable facts are more to be trusted than rumors based on absolute falsehood. Every cent of money that is received by the city treasury and every cent disbursed, is accounted for. The city's books balance to the last cent when experted[42] [sic]. If the average voter would go to the city hall and look at the books, he could quickly see the truth of this incontrovertible statement. But the average voter doesn't do this. A few zealous workers for the charter have tried repeatedly, by every means, to ferret out graft in the city records. They have spared no pains and no energy in their endeavors to discover something wrong. They have failed utterly to unearth even the most trifling discrepancy in the city accounts. All they can do is to fall back on rumors and hints and innuendos which they are unable to back up with a shred of truth. Is this working in the name of progress for Pacific Grove?

---

42 I believe they meant "inspected."

Efficiency, economy and progress are held out by the charter faction as goals to be reached only by the adoption of this charter. We are fortunate in having all three of these desirable civic advantages right here, right now. Pacific Grove is going ahead. She is prosperous. But she cannot continue thus if the charter carries. Not possibly. Efficiency, economy and progress will be forgotten words.

Citizens' Committee

(ADVERTISEMENT)

The Peninsular Review APRIL 8, 1927

VOTE YES

PROGRESS IS DEFINED BY WEBSTER:

"To proceed toward new conditions or results."

TO VOTE FOR THE CHARTER MEANS:

"To proceed toward IMPROVED conditions and BETTER results."

From the "Citizens' Committee" Article of April 5, 1927:

"Incidentally the people will remember that this same W.R. Holman was very instrumental in electing Mr. Basham, Mr. Gould and Mr. Cosmey to our board of trustees and promised the people that they would be able to please 100 per cent of the people 100 per cent of the time in 100 per cent of everything coming before the board. Evidently he is a poor prophet.

"He promises such a fine performance under the new form of City Manager government. Is there any reason to believe that he will be a better prophet this time?"

These men were not endorsed individually by me, but by the Booster's Club in a body. The Booster's Club was made up of business men in Pacific Grove and Mr. Harry Boyd was secretary of that club. No doubt Mr.

Boyd will be glad to show those interested the minutes of the meeting, which cover the nomination, the motions made and carried, also the records showing those in attendance at the time of nomination.

I did work for the men above mentioned, as I personally held the following signed pledge to the taxpayers and voters of Pacific Grove which was published in Pacific Grove as their platform and program which THEY GAVE THEIR WORD OF HONOR THEY WOULD FOLLOW OUT IF ELECTED.

Therefore, those who worked for them and those who voted for them CANNOT BE BLAMED FOR THE VIOLATION OF THEIR PROMISE. The Charter prevents this condition from occurring again.

> We, the undersigned candidates for Trustee, wish to state to the voters of Pacific Grove that we are opposed to the zoning of this City that further improvements such as paving, will only be taken up by us when requested to do so by a large majority of the property owners of said street. That we are against the district assessment of paving streets, and are in favor of a road from Carmel to Pacific Grove, and will use our best efforts to have this road completed. We are for economy and a clean administration.
>
> SIGNED,
> Frank M. Basham
> W. J. Gould
> D. W. Cosmey

I did not make any statement to the effect that if Messrs. Basham, Gould and Cosmey were elected that they would be able to please 100 per cent of the people 100 per cent of the time in 100 per cent of everything coming before the board and the person who wrote the article for the Citizens' Committee KNOWS I DID NOT MAKE ANY SUCH STATEMENT.

I do not claim that the proposed Charter is 100 per cent perfect, OR IS ANY CHARTER 100 PER CENT PERFECT THAT HAS EVER BEEN

DRAWN BUT ALL CHARTERS ARE FLEXIBLE AND CAN BE AMENDED. Even the Constitution of the United States, THE MOST REMARKABLE DOCUMENT EVER DRAWN, has 19 amendments.

City Manager Form of Government Proven Satisfactory

I do not claim to be a prophet and all I desire for the community in which I live is the greatest amount of good for the greatest amount of people and I am willing to fight for the truth as I see it.

364 Cities Now Operate Under City Charter Plan

364 cities have adopted and thrived under this plan with only three having given up this form after adoption. [This] is proof conclusive to me that the City Manager form of government is THE COMING GOVERNMENT FOR ALL CITIES.

YES—HOLMAN'S DEPARTMENT STORE TOOK IN $200,000, MAYBE MORE—EVERY DOLLAR APPRECIATED. Yes, $200,000 was taken in from the citizens of Pacific Grove and we gave them in return DOLLAR FOR DOLLAR VALUE. Out of this amount $125,000 WENT FOR SALARIES FOR THE KEEPING UP OF HOMES AND UPBUILDING OF THIS PENINSULA and every dollar earned by this firm has BEEN PUT BACK INTO CIRCULATION INTO THIS PENINSULA.

And finally, let us remind you that the Two Hundred Thousand Dollars was not taken by a proceeding in invitum, unwillingly as lawyers would say, but it was not taken at all. It was fairly and willingly offered by each customer, after he or she had made selection of what was desired, and its payment, if deferred, was not secured by a lien on the real property of the customer, at a high rate of interest, under the threat of foreclosure.

Check Up On Holman

As to the advice of the "Citizens' Committee" article, "before you swallow all [of] his line take the trouble to check up on him."

I Welcome Your Check-Up

My life, policies, occupation, and business are open for your inspection. The most serious mistake I ever made and the thing I am chiefly ashamed of was the supporting of the present administration when they ran for office.

Monterey County Surveyor Receives $1800 Per Year, Plus Traveling Expenses

This amount is for Monterey County's official engineering work. A number of other competent surveyors working for corporations and subdivision concerns receive under $3600 per year and I am informed by business men who know, also a surveyor, that it is possible to obtain many good surveyors who have handled big work for $200 to $300 per month by the year. According to the writer of the "Citizens' Committee" my knowledge on actual surveying is not sufficient for me to qualify as a witness in court for testimony. Perhaps not. We'll give them the benefit of the doubt.

I haven't anything against our present surveyor and would not blame him if he accepted $100,000 for the surveying of one street in place of about $6777.19, if our present board desired to give it to him. I speak from a business standpoint and that's the subject I am most interested in. No individual, corporation or firm run by competent managers for the purpose of profit or improvement would pay any such fee in the face of the large volume of work which has been going on in our city—even though these fees are not generally exposed to the general public and are paid through contractors.

No Rage Here

No rage here—why should there be—I am quite willing to abide by the wishes of the people on Saturday, April 9th, but until the close of the election I will do everything in my power to bring before the citizens of this community the facts as they exist as per the wishes of those who are for the Charter, and they are legion.

Miss Platt's Charter

That's what the "Citizens' Committee" (whoever they may be) call it, but as 15 Freeholders who you elected by quite a majority, sat into the night for many nights and into the wee hours of the morning going over the many different forms of Charters, which included the Model Charter of the League of California Municipalities, Sacramento Charter, Salinas Charter, Monterey Charter and others—all representative Charters, written and revised and devised by brilliant men such as Wm. Locke who has studied this form of government from every angle. Miss Platt may well be proud in having the Pacific Grove Charter called hers.

Should Be Appreciated—Not Slandered

The Neighbors' Club and Miss Platt, its founder and president, should be appreciated by every citizen in Pacific Grove for their wonderful work. The women of this club have worked unselfishly for the advancement and beautification of this city and have earned—not begged—hundreds of dollars which have been spent on your parks, streets, and boulevards— all without remuneration. These women are property holders, taxpayers, good citizens, and who has a better right to have a voice in our city affairs? I do not wonder that those who speak as they do hide behind the unknown Citizens' Committee.

W. R. Holman

The Peninsular Review APRIL 8, 1927

PACIFIC GROVE WANTS PEACE

More than anything else, we want peace. For over a year this ferment about a charter has been brewing. Never has the town been embroiled in bitter strife as now. We are surfeited with local politics. The charter as it stands is ineffectual and inelastic. If adopted, it can bring only discord. Therefore, let us vote no.

If a charter is so desirable for us, why could it not be kept a clean issue, brought before the people by the usual municipal elections? Why these special elections, this frantic effort to disrupt our municipal fabric? Not a cent of the city's money has been misspent, no abuse of office has occurred. There is no occasion whatever for all this hysteria about graft.

Details of this long quarrel point to the definite conclusion that the whole movement for a change in local government is actuated by proposal rancor, nothing else. Many followers of the movement are sincere, to be sure, as many of the Freeholders undoubtedly were. But personal spite is at the bottom of it all. Can any good come from such sources?

This harmful and untruthful talk of dishonesty is a sword that cuts both ways. Are those who shout the loudest and most earnestly about graft, so upright in their own business methods? That question has caused many a knowing smile. Another query often heard is, why a person so determined to dictate in city policies is so averse to accepting the office of trustee? Why this insistent desire to be, or try to be, the big boss behind the scenes? Does it look like sincere interest for the good of the town to flood the city with vicious propaganda in scare heads, bolstered up with figures purposely made misleading?

We vote tomorrow on the proposed charter, nothing else, no side angles, no personal likes or dislikes. The proposed charter can only bring trouble to Pacific Grove, for which reason it should be rejected, in order that we may return to peace and progress sanely and steadily.

Signed,

Lucia Shepardson

PACIFIC GROVE WANTS PEACE

It has come to our attention that there are rumors and charges that if the proposed charter is defeated the Board of Trustees will immediately inaugurate a campaign to pave every street in Pacific Grove at a cost of $3,000,000. Such a charge is ridiculous and unfounded. The Board has no paving program in view other than as positioned for by a very substantial number of the people who pay the bills. We are not going to cram street paving down anybody's throat as charged.

We are taxpayers and property owners ourselves. We expect to remain so. We want to treat our fellow taxpayers fairly as we would want to be treated.

The opposition to paving our main arteries has caused all this talk. It was in paving these main arteries, which the interest of all demanded, that the only opposition was encountered, and only on Ocean View Avenue (with the aid of the Southern Pacific Company) was there a majority protest.

(Signed)

W. J. Gould

C. M. Bennett

Elgin C. Hurlbert

Paul De Wolf

D. M. Laughery

The Peninsular Review FRIDAY, APRIL 8, 1927

VOTE NO CITY MANAGER NOT THE REAL ISSUE
—HIDDEN MOTIVES

[Editor's note: This entire advertisement is much longer but speaks to points already addressed.]

Star Chamber Proceedings

In the article, "Who said 'Miss Platt's Charter'" the name of B. F. Sowell appears as among the signers of the original document but it is not there. Mr. Sowell was conveniently absent. Several of the leading members were too busy to meet often with the Freeholders on that memorable week. Smith was present four times, but T. A. Work was not present at any times when Mr. Smith was present, neither was W.R. Holman. They were apparently satisfied to let Julia do it. Their sessions were of the star chamber variety. Mrs. Ryan, reporter for the Review, was present the first evening. Miss Platt came to her privately and gave her to understand that her presence was not desired but that the charter would be given to the public when finally approved. No legal adviser was present to answer any question and the enlightenment vouchsafed was Miss Platt's statement that Attorney Lacey said so and so. It is very unlikely that Miss Platt quoted Attorney Campbell yet the dodger, "Who said 'Miss Platt's Charter'" is one of their parting shots. It is truly a dud.

Beware Of Last Minute Arguments For The Charter

This article considers what the supporters of the charter mean either written into or said about it. There has been abundant opportunity for them to bring into the open all of their arguments and if, as will undoubtedly happen, they send out some brand new statements, let the voters beware. They are familiar with all the tricks of the ward politician and do not hesitate to use them. So we are told concerning W.R. Holman's venture, for which he is entitled to commendation, but in the right place that the word was scattered throughout the entire commercial world that this store would not pay and that he maintains offices in San Francisco, New York and Berlin. Unsigned articles need not be given any weight—LOOK ON US; that $150,000 will go to the surveyor; that the trustees are grafters or didn't know what was going on and the course of the Pacific Grove Association is held as a terrifying specter though what it has to do with the charter election is not readily apparent unless it be to confuse people who do not think, the class from which they expect to get the votes they so sorely need.

Snow It Under

The charter will be beaten but it should be snowed under so decisively that it will [not] crop up again. If by any miracle it should carry, and its supporters are continually calling attention to the fact that it can be amended as an inducement to give it a trial, remember that each amendment means another charter election and subsequent ratification by the legislature, a long tedious and costly proceeding.

Citizens' Committee

The Peninsular Review FRIDAY, APRIL 8, 1927

CHARTER MAY POLL RECORD VOTE

INTEREST KEEN AS FATE OF MEASURE HANGS IN BALANCE

Closing two weeks of heated campaigning, proponents and opponents of the proposed Pacific Grove city manager charter will tomorrow file to the polls to cast their ballots and decide the fate of a measure that has created an almost unprecedented awakening of interest in municipal affairs.

With 1829 registered citizens eligible to exercise their right of franchise and to express their views through the medium of the ballot box on one of the most vitally important issues ever served to voters of Pacific Grove, indications pointed to a record vote being polled. While supporters of the measure and anti-charterists have quietly been campaigning over a period of several weeks, the campaigns of the past two weeks have stirred a wave of keen interest which mounted to new heights today as final appeals were made by the opposing actions in preparation for tomorrow's balloting.

Predictions as to the possible outcome of Saturday's election are regarded as purely guesswork, observers believing that the margin either way is too small to permit a definite forecast.

Polls will open at 6 a.m. and close at 7 p.m.

Ballots will be cast at the following precincts:

Chamber of commerce hall, 211 Grand Avenue, [and City Hall].

The Herald APRIL 9, 1927

RECORD VOTE IN CHARTER ELECTION

GROVE VOTERS THRONGING POLLS TODAY–CAMPAIGN WITHOUT PARALLEL HERE

Both Sides Predict Victory As Cohorts Rally Around Respective Standards—More than 40 Per Cent of Registered Voters Polled Before 2 o'Clock

Campaign Unique In Local Annals

Intensity of Zeal On Both Sides Fails To Precipitate Personalities or Recriminations Beyond Margin of Good Taste Throughout Whole Campaign

That a record vote will be cast by Pacific Grove voters today in the balloting on a new charter was indicated at 2 p.m. this afternoon, when 40 per cent of the registered voters had already visited the polls. Probably the final figure will run well above 50 per cent and may exceed 60 per cent of the registration, in the opinion of experienced observers, while some of the more optimistic predict a 75 per cent vote.

The outcome of the election was still in doubt, as both sides were claiming victory on the basis of checking lists kept by partisan workers. Proponents for the city manager form of charter were confident their contentions had been sustained by the action of their fellow townsmen, while their opponents were equally positive the proposed change had been rejected by a decisive majority.

Polling was confined to three places, the city hall, chamber of commerce rooms and 211 Grand avenue. Booths at each place were kept busy during nearly all of the morning, while at noon there were throngs awaiting their turns, with prospects of a still busier afternoon. The inclemency of the weather seemed to matter little, in the heat of election-day enthusiasm, whether for or against the proposition.

Unique Campaign

Today's election marked the culmination of a campaign without parallel in Pacific Grove's political history. Preceded by months of preparation on the part of those dissatisfied with existing conditions and determined to bring about a change, it afforded ample opportunity for the dissemination of information on all phases of the question at issue. This opportunity was fully realized by the proponents of the city manager form of charter, through public meetings, informal discussion and, especially, through the medium of the press.

Although not entirely free from recrimination and personalities, the campaign was remarkable in degree of dignity maintained, by both sides, in view of the intensity with which each side ultimately pressed its claims for consideration by the public, and it is doubtful whether an issue of such fundamental importance and involving such far-reaching implications, could have been fought to a conclusion with a like minimum of rancor and outspoken bitterness anywhere outside of Monterey Peninsula.

The Peninsular Review APRIL 9, 1927

EXTRA!

CHARTER WINS BY VOTE 614 TO 570—RECORD VOTE IS CAST

CITIZENS BRAVE RAINS TO VOICE CHARTER OPINION

At 4:30 this afternoon 833 voters had cast their ballots as follows: City Hall, 341; Chamber of commerce, 256; 211 Grand avenue, 238.

At 2:30 this afternoon nearly half of the registered voters of Pacific Grove had cast their ballots in the election which will result in the establishing of a new form of government or will result in a defeat of the proposed charter. A check-up revealed that 725 electors had visited the polling stations. This is believed to be without precedent here, with every indication that Pacific Grove will have polled one of the largest votes in its history when the voting booths close at 7 o'clock tonight.

At the city hall a total of 290 voters had cast their ballots at 2:30 today; chamber of commerce, 225; Grand avenue, 210.

Election day broke with sunshine this morning but the skies became overcast later in the morning and by noon a drizzling rain was in progress. Unsettled weather, however, failed to keep voters away from the polls. An organized free taxi service was kept busy through the day by supporters and anti-charterists who sought favorable vote.

Predictions were this afternoon significantly few, and as the hour of closing neared there were few who would hazard even a guess as to the outcome. Opponents of the charter declared that a light turn-out at the polls may spell victory for the measure.

The Peninsular Review APRIL 9, 1927

HARMONY URGED AS VOTING ENDS BITTER CAMPAIGN

FINAL RETURNS

Vote Cast for 614; Against 570.

BY PRECINCTS

City Hall

Votes Cast for 184; Against 164.

211 Grand Avenue

Votes Cast for 165; against 181.

Total Vote—1189.

The proposed City manager charter scored a victory at the hands of Pacific Grove voters today, a majority casting their ballots in favor of inaugurating a new form of government in this city. Electors filed to the polling places in a steady stream as Pacific Grove broke all previous records in turning out to express their willingness or unwillingness to adopt a charter providing for a city manager.

Mayor William J. Gould, chairman of the board of trustees, had the following to say regarding the victory of the measure:

"I still will be a citizen of Pacific Grove. The verdict does not alter my loyalty to this community or lessen my desire to work for its welfare. It's my charter, too."

Henry G. Jorgensen, Pacific Grove Attorney, said this evening:

"I trust the people will accept the verdict of the majority and try to work in peace and harmony for the good of the city."

Argyll Campbell, city attorney of Monterey who framed the charter which has functioned with success in the neighboring city, declared that certain provisions of the charter which was adopted today would undoubtedly have to be amended.

W. R. Holman, standard bearer of the charterists who took a leading part in the fight for a new mode of government, was highly elated tonight over the outcome of the election, characterizing the result as "a great victory for every citizen and taxpayer in our city."

"The charter victory," declared Holman, "shows a desire for a better system of government."

Julia B. Platt, head of the Neighbors Club, and one of the firmest advocates of the charter, could not be reached this evening for a statement.

The board of trustees will meet at 7:30 Monday at an adjourned meeting when the votes officially will be canvassed. Work of preparing the charter for presentation to the California state legislature will be rushed, it was stated tonight, in order that the measure may be ratified before the legislature adjourns.

The next step in instituting a new regime in Pacific Grove will be the calling of a municipal election in June for the purpose of selecting seven councilmen and other officers as provided for in the charter adopted today.

Today's election ends several weeks of bitter campaigning by pro and anti-charterists. Under the scrutiny of legal searchlights enlisted by both parties, the charter has been in turn held up as an effective instrument and also as a defective measure. It was conceded that the real issue centered on the matter of street paving and dissatisfaction with the present administration, the merits or defects of the charter being largely a side issue, in the opinion of close observers.

The Peninsular Review APRIL 20, 1927

GROVE CHARTER WINS APPROVAL FROM ASSEMBLY

Ratification by the state assembly was yesterday given the Pacific Grove charter after its introduction to that body by Senator C. S. Baker. The measure, okayed by both the senate and assembly, will be passed on to Governor Young for his signature. The charter will then go to the secretary of state where a copy will be filed. Another copy will be filed in the county recorder's office.

Approval by the assembly marks the end of a period of doubt whether the bill would be action at the present session of the legislature. Its ratification also removed possibility that lobbying would halt its final passage.[43]

A small-scale version of W.R. Holman's opinion piece from April 8, 1927.

---

43 Some handwriting in the original manuscript was indecipherable—this could be W.R. Holman or Ms. Jaques, though it looks like W.R. Holman's handwriting to me. The name "Senator C.S. Baker" is crossed out and "Assemblyman Hodges of this county" is inserted. Some sentences relevant to the Secretary of State and County Recorder's office were lined out in the original. An anonymous scribbler wrote: "As this gov not under the Constitution is relieved from this opportunity, the Concurrent Resolution of Senate and Assembly is thus."

Epilogue

Monterey Peninsula Herald THURSDAY, DECEMBER 31, 1981

W. R. HOLMAN, BUSINESS, CIVIC LEADER, DIES AT 97

Wilford Rensselaer Holman, who headed the family's department store for 75 years and was one of the most influential persons in the history of his hometown of Pacific Grove, died at his residence late Tuesday night following a period of failing health. He was 97.

Services are pending at the Paul Mortuary. W.R. Holman was born August 18, 1884, in Sacramento. When he was 4 the family moved to Pacific Grove, where his father built the residence on Lighthouse Avenue that has been the family's home ever since.

In 1905, W.R. Holman, assisted for a short time by his brother, the late Clarence E., took over operation of the dry goods business which their father, R. L. Holman, had

W.R. Holman in his eighties.

founded in 1891. Before long the store was converted to a department store, one which grew over the years to become known as the largest between Los Angeles and San Francisco.

When his brother dropped out of the business, "W.R." took on full responsibility and served actively as head of the store until 1947. He retained the title of president until his official retirement early last fall. Even during his later years, he maintained a close watch over the store and showed concern for his "family" of longtime employees.

Always an influence in political affairs affecting Pacific Grove, he led a battle with the county Board of Supervisors in the late 1920s to get a road built over the hill to connect his city with the highway linking Monterey to Carmel.

Fearing that Pacific Grove could be cut off from the rest of the Peninsula if the Presidio were closed "in case of trouble," he began his campaign in 1923 for construction of the road.

Told at that time by County Supervisor L.D. Roberts that no highway would be built while he was in office, W.R. Holman set out on a successful drive to block Roberts' re-election. W.R. Holman also threatened to block a county bond issue if funds for the highway were not included.

During the struggle he once led a contingent of Boy Scouts, school marching bands and other concerned citizens to Salinas to lobby for the road before the Board of Supervisors.

The result was the opening of the road over the hill in 1930. It later became part of State Route 68 and in 1972 that section was officially designated by the state as the W. R. Holman Highway.

W.R. Holman served on the Pacific Grove Planning Commission from 1943 until his resignation in 1957.

He actually first became involved in his father's business while still a boy in knee-pants.

Years later he recalled those days: "I can remember each afternoon that as soon as I got out of school, I would get in a little spring wagon behind a gray horse, take a bag with the day's receipts and drive from the Grove down to Monterey," to the bank.

"In the summers then, Alvarado Street was a cloud of dust, and in the winters the wagon axles dragged in the mud."

During his long business career he oversaw the growth of his father's dry goods business and for a time also operated a car dealership and the first automobile service station in Monterey County.

The two automotive enterprises were located at Central Avenue between Fountain and Grand avenues, at the rear of the lot on which the present Holman's Department Store building was opened in 1924.

During the Great Depression of the early 1930s, W.R. Holman defied gloomy predictions for the store's survival, adding the third floor and solarium to the building. This both expressed his confidence in the business and provided needed employment for local workers.

He was known as a fine fisherman and an avid hiker. In his unflagging concern for preservation of natural resources, his daughters recall that he was responsible for the state setting a limited season for harvest of abalone to protect it from extinction by commercial fishermen.

The store was always a family enterprise and W.R. Holman was closely assisted for many years by his wife, Zena, whom he married in 1912 and who for some time was the store's buyer of women's fashions.

Over the years, the couple shared many interests, including the cultivation of a large acreage of English and Dutch holly on a ranch near Watsonville, and the collection of American Indian artifacts. These latter were presented by the Holmans to the state of California and are displayed in the Pacific Building State Historical Monument in Monterey.

A few years ago the Holmans also donated their collection of Eskimo artifacts and 20th century ivory carvings to the Monterey Peninsula Museum of Art.

Mrs. Holman died in 1980. A half-brother of W.R. Holman, Ritter Holman, died in February of this year, and a sister, Mrs. Warren Steven, in 1978.

W.R. Holman is survived by his daughters Mrs. Eugene (Patricia) O'Meara of Watsonville and Harriet Barter-Heebner of Carmel; six grandchildren and eleven great-grandchildren.

Zena and W.R. Holman cut a Happy Birthday Holman's cake.

W.R. and Zena Holman, later years.

Afterword

WHILE ORGANIZING, I HAD ONE BOX WHERE I PUT NEWSPAPER CLIP-
pings, knowing that eventually I would have a breadth of articles to read.
I also knew that I wanted to explain what happened to the once-thriving
Holman's after W.R. Holman's death.

1967 saw the opening of Del Monte Shopping Center, the first large-
scale local competition to Holman's, although Holman's had their own
shop within Del Monte for a number of years. Over time, sales lagged
and the department store did not bring in the kind of money it once had.
Simply put: people had other places to shop, and Holman's was no longer the destination it had been in its heyday.

According to a January 5, 1985 *Monterey Peninsula Herald* article,
by Ken Peterson, Holman's Department Store was sold on January 4,
1985 to Charles E. Ford Co. of Watsonville. As Peterson writes, "The
sale, spurred by flagging business and rumored for days, became official when Holman's president Hugh Steven, grandson of store founder
R.L. Holman, and George Menasco, the president of Ford's, signed
an agreement in a Monterey law office. The decision to sell came at
a 'very emotional meeting' [on] Thursday among family members on

the board of directors, Steven said. 'I can tell you there were tears in my eyes . . . The decision to consider selling was made,' Steven said this week, 'because of declining returns to the 40 family members who own all the stock in the company.' The decline, in turn, was caused by a slump in sales, which he attributed to a too-rapid change in marketing strategy this year."

Ford's was founded in Watsonville in 1852 by Charles E. Ford, and seemed like the perfect fit to buy Holman's—another business started in the 1800s, still going strong 100 years later.

But in 1989, "the Loma Prieta earthquake rocked northern and central California and severely damaged Ford's flagship store in Watsonville. Ford's never recovered financially from the destruction its flagship store suffered from the earthquake and in 1992 Ford's was forced to file for bankruptcy. All eight Ford's Department Stores were closed including the store that occupied the iconic Holman's building, which closed its doors on January 7, 1993." (*The Board and Batten*, Winter 2016/2017).

In 1995, the Holman building at 542 Lighthouse Avenue and surrounding buildings that comprised Holman's were acquired by local developer Nader Agha, who turned the ground floor of the former department store into an antique mall, with assorted retail along the storefront of Lighthouse Avenue. For years, Agha tried, unsuccessfully, to turn the building into a 230-room hotel, a project that continually ran up against a lack of sufficient water (*Carmel Pine Cone*, July 20-26, 2012). In December 2014, the Holman building was put up for auction and soon purchased by Monterey Capital Real Estate Development; founding partner, Dave Nash, began a multi-year project to turn the building into four floors of luxury condos, and a ground floor of mixed-use, commercial retail space, as well as underground parking (*Cedar Street Times*, December 3, 2014, and *Monterey Herald*, September

11, 2018). The luxury condos are nearly all sold, and Holman's is now "The Holman." A new life for a building built in 1918; a landmark for generations of Pagrovians and beyond.

In 2019, when I was serving on the Pacific Grove Library Advisory Board, we were overseeing the library renewal project, a refurbishment years in the making that involved gutting most of the library, adding clerestory windows, upgrading the bathrooms, adding new light fixtures, and reflowing the entryway, among many other improvements. The library needed to relocate temporarily, in order to continue serving the public. Many suggestions were offered. It was a cold and windy evening in December, during our monthly Library Board meeting, when the Holman building was proposed as a temporary site. When then library director Scott Bauer brought up the possibility, the lights flickered in the City Council chambers for a moment. While I believe myself to be practical, I could not help but feel bibliophile Zena Holman in that room right then saying, "Yes, of course the library should come to the Holman building!" There was a unanimous vote from the Library Board, followed by City Council's also-unanimous vote. By August, the library (well, as much as could fit) was moved to the Holman building. Patrons could enter the building, check out books, browse the internet, and view the bay from one of the windows in the back of the building, while finishing touches were being made on the upper condos. By August 2020, amidst the pandemic, interim Library Director Diana Godwin was at the helm and saw the library moved into the gorgeously remodeled building back at 550 Central, the library's location since 1908. Through Diana's generous help I was able to view *The Peninsular Review* from those pivotal days in March and April 1927 regarding the City Charter. During the COVID-related lockdown, Diana obtained the microfilm and reader, and graciously allowed me into the library for research. I am so grateful.

Perhaps you're reading a copy of this book you checked out from the library's shelves!

After W.R. Holman's death, his estate gifted the family home at 769 Lighthouse Avenue to the Monterey Museum of Art. It served as a "space for crafts workshops and meetings for the Museum on Wheels and for storage and work space for the docents' Creative Response program" (*Monterey Peninsula Herald*, November 10, 1982). In 2003, the Museum sold the home and the neighboring lot, which was once the Holman family's sprawling garden, a maze of holly trees, including a pond with a little bridge—my husband's most vivid memory of visiting his great-grandpa. That garden is now 765 Lighthouse Avenue where a condominium complex was built in the early 2000s. The Holman family home was once again occupied by a family, this time Tricia and Tony Perault and their children Daisy, Henry, and Andy. With great care, they improved both the interior and exterior and created a peaceful backyard garden. The home was sold in 2017 to Lawrence and Cassandra Gay and if W.R. could see what Larry has done to the basement, he'd be extremely impressed, while Cassie and Zena would have so many books to discuss.

Mr. and Mrs. Holman left a lasting impression on this community. I hope those who can remember buying a prom dress from the Juniors Department will enjoy reading this history, as well as newcomers, old-comers, naturalists, and tourists. I hope W.R. Holman's *My Life in Pacific Grove* serves as an expansive view of what Pacific Grove once was and the great people who helped make it what is has become. Next time you're downtown, rest on W.R. and Zena Holman's bench in front of their home at 769 Lighthouse Avenue. If they were there, they would have plenty of stories to tell you.

—*Heather Kimberly Spindler Proulx Lazare,*
April 2022

Top: *Holman's stock belonging to Patricia (Holman) O'Meara (front).*
Bottom: *Holman's stock belonging to Patricia (Holman) O'Meara (back).*

W.R. Holman in his twenties.